LePAM

Restorative Justice and Family Violence

D1388303

Restorative Justice and Family Violence addresses one of the most controversial topics in restorative justice: its potential for dealing with conflicts within families. Most restorative justice programs specifically exclude family violence as an appropriate offence to be dealt with this way. This book focuses on the issues in family violence that may warrant special caution about restorative justice, in particular, feminist and Indigenous concerns. At the same time it looks for ways of designing a place for restorative interventions that respond to these concerns. Further, *Restorative Justice and Family Violence* asks whether there are ways that restorative processes can contribute to reducing and preventing family violence, to healing its survivors and to confronting the wellsprings of this violence.

Heather Strang is Director, and **John Braithwaite** a Professor, in the Centre for Restorative Justice, Research School of Social Sciences, Australian National University. They are the co-editors of *Restorative Justice and Civil Society* (Cambridge University Press, 2001).

Restorative Justice
and Family Violence

Edited by
Heather Strang and John Braithwaite
Australian National University

CAMBRIDGE
UNIVERSITY PRESS

CAMBRIDGE UNIVERSITY PRESS
Cambridge, New York, Melbourne, Madrid, Cape Town,
Singapore, São Paulo, Delhi, Tokyo, Mexico City

Cambridge University Press
The Edinburgh Building, Cambridge CB2 8RU, UK

Published in the United States of America by
Cambridge University Press, New York

www.cambridge.org
Information on this title: www.cambridge.org/9780521521659

First published 2002

A catalogue record for this publication is available from the British Library

ISBN 978-0-521-81846-9 Hardback
ISBN 978-0-521-52165-9 Paperback

Contents

Acknowledgements

This collection is the product of a Canberra conference in 2000 sponsored by the Reshaping Australian Institutions Project of the Research School of Social Sciences, Australian National University. We wish to thank all staff of the ANU Centre for Restorative Justice for their hard work in making the conference a success.

Another special element of the success of the conference was the work of Loretta Kelly in organizing a roundtable discussion of Aboriginal restorative justice facilitators to canvass their experience of restorative justice and family violence before the conference proper began. These Aboriginal leaders took part in an informal session of the conference where they acted as a panel and talked about their experiences. Participants saw this as a positive feature of the constructive engagement at the conference. Donna Coker suggested at the end of the conference that this lesson in conference design for bringing communities of thought together with different perspectives on an intransigent problem might have been taken further. Battered women's movement participants, restorative justice advocates and Aboriginal peoples might each have met and planned ways of communicating their experience for the other participants to absorb before the conference proper, and of course before the publication emanating from those exchanges. While our effort to encapsulate all that was learned from the conference in this volume is a flawed one, it is a better book for the exchanges that occurred. On behalf of all the authors, we thank all the other participants for the many ways they enriched our attempts to grapple with the issues, including some moving and powerful personal testimonies.

Heather Strang and John Braithwaite

Figures and tables

Contributors

GORDON BAZEMORE is Professor of Criminology and Criminal Justice and Director of the Community Justice Institute at Florida Atlantic University. His primary research interests include community and restorative justice, juvenile justice, youth policy, victimology, corrections, and community policing. He is currently directing a national study of restorative justice conferencing and a statewide evaluation of restorative juvenile justice programs in Vermont.

LARISSA BEHRENDT is the Professor of Law and Indigenous Studies and the Director of the Jumbunna Indigenous House of Learning at the University of Technology, Sydney. A member of the Eualeyai nation, she writes on Indigenous legal and political issues.

HARRY BLAGG is Research Fellow at the Crime Research Centre, University of Western Australia. He is currently working on Indigenous people and justice, diversion and human rights, restorative processes and community auspiced and delivered forms of policing. He has recently completed projects on prevention, intervention and treatment in Indigenous family violence.

JOHN BRAITHWAITE is Chair of the Regulatory Institutions Network and a Professor in the Law Program of the Research School of Social Sciences, Australian National University. He is working on integrating the theory of restorative justice and the theory of responsive regulation.

GALE BURFORD is Professor and Director of the Social Work Department at the University of Vermont and Director of the Child Welfare Training Partnership between the University and the State of Vermont. He was co-director of the Newfoundland and Labrador Family Group Decision-Making Project.

RUTH BUSCH is an Associate Professor of Law at the University of Waikato, New Zealand. She has published widely on domestic violence-related topics, most recently concerning the effects of witnessing domestic violence on children and judicial approaches to contact decision-making in cases where domestic violence has characterized the spousal relationship

DONNA COKER is a Professor of Law at the University of Miami School of Law, Miami, Florida. The primary focus of her activism, lawyering, and scholarship is the assistance of battered women. She is currently working on developing intervention strategies against domestic violence that are more effective for poor women.

KATHLEEN DALY is an Associate Professor in the School of Criminology and Criminal Justice, Griffith University. She has published widely in the areas of gender, race, crime and justice. During 1998–99, she directed a major research project on restorative justice in South Australia; and during 2001–2003, she is directing a second project on the race and gender politics of new justice practices in Australia, New Zealand, the United States, and Canada.

TWILA HUGLEY EARLE teaches and consults on restorative justice, community-building, and application of chaos theory to human systems. As a counselor she worked with victims of sexual abuse, sex offenders and families of both, and initiated community program development. She has been an adjunct professor at the University of Texas at Austin.

LORETTA KELLY (BA, LLB) is an Aboriginal person from the mid-north coast of New South Wales (she is Gumbaynggirri and Dungutti). She is a lawyer and experienced community and family mediator and lectures on Mediation, Dispute Resolution and Restorative Justice at Southern Cross University School of Law and Justice. She also teaches Dispute Resolution and Aboriginal Communities through the University's College of Indigenous Australian Peoples. She is currently involved in grass-roots community programs for the prevention of family violence and is committed to diverting Indigenous people from the criminal justice system.

ALLISON MORRIS was Professor of Criminology at Victoria University of Wellington, New Zealand until 2001. For 20 years before that she lectured in criminology at the Institute of Criminology, University of Cambridge. She has carried out research on women's prisons, youth justice systems, violence against women and restorative justice and her main teaching and research areas are youth justice, women and crime and victims.

JOAN PENNELL is Professor and Director, Social Work Program, North Carolina State University and Principal Investigator for the North Carolina Family Group Conferencing Project, and served as co-director of the Newfoundland and Labrador Family Group Decision Making Project. She is committed to developing approaches that work to stop family violence by building family–community–agency partnerships.

KAY PRANIS is the Restorative Justice Planner with the Minnesota Department of Corrections and a trainer on peacemaking circles and restorative justice across the United States and Canada. She is working on using peacemaking circles for individual and community healing within the framework of restorative justice.

HEATHER STRANG is Director of the Centre for Restorative Justice, Research School of Social Sciences, Australian National University. She directed the Reintegrative Shaming Experiments in Canberra which examined the effectiveness of a restorative justice alternative to court, and is now directing a series of studies on restorative justice in the United Kingdom.

JULIE STUBBS is Deputy Director of the Institute of Criminology and an Associate Professor in the Faculty of Law at the University of Sydney. She has a particular research interest in violence against women and is currently working on child contact and domestic violence.

1   Restorative Justice and Family Violence

John Braithwaite and Heather Strang

A New and Troubling Political Context

Many of the authors in this collection are both scholars and activists in the social movements that are drawn into conversation here. These are the social movement for restorative justice, the women's movement, more particularly the battered women's movement, and movements for Indigenous self-determination. Some participants, such as Joan Pennell and Kay Pranis, have had significant involvements in all three. Most of our authors are sympathetic to the aspirations of all three social movements, though some are deeply concerned that the social movement for restorative justice is overreaching the limits of the contribution it has to make.

The conversation takes place against a background of considerable growth in popular and political backing for restorative justice, as manifest in the enthusiastic support of many nations, and the lack of opposition from any, to restorative justice in the Declaration of Vienna from the UN Congress on the Prevention of Crime and Treatment of Offenders (April 2000). In few countries, however, has this political support translated into major resource shifts toward restorative justice within criminal justice systems. In no country has there been any such resource shift with respect to the regulation of family violence.

A question we raise is whether the latter fact reflects a lack of courage or an appropriate prudence given the many special hazards we discuss in this book when restorative justice is applied to family violence. It could be a mixture of both. We personally certainly felt influenced by both when the Reintegrative Shaming Experiments (RISE) were set up in Canberra in 1994, the aim of which was to measure the comparative effectiveness of restorative conferencing with normal court processing. Some in the police undertook some preliminary experimentation with restorative justice conferencing for family violence. They viewed it as successful and wanted to push on. The Attorney General opposed this, arguing that domestic violence should be explicitly excluded from

RISE. We supported him in this. Partly it was lack of courage. We did not want this political fight; we wanted local women's groups to be sympathetic to what we were attempting, which basically they came to be. Secondly, we felt that while it was quite possible that conferencing could be redesigned to cope with the special dangers of family violence, we and our colleagues in the police did not have the competence to accomplish the redesign. In retrospect, we were right here; we clearly did not have the competence that Joan Pennell, Gale Burford and the local communities where they worked subsequently mobilized to develop their successful Canadian conferencing programs. Thirdly, we felt there was much validity in the feminist critiques of mediation and Alternative Dispute Resolution (ADR) as they had been practised until that time. So we saw disturbing potential to do harm rather than good.

In the year the papers in this essay were first written (2000), we learnt that it was in the RISE violence experiment that Lawrence Sherman, Heather Strang and their team found conferencing to have the biggest effect in reducing criminal reoffending (a net reduction of 38 percent compared to cases randomly assigned to the Canberra courts). These were violence cases that explicitly excluded domestic violence. So for us as editors this collection is a labour of conscience. We have to ask ourselves the question whether in the name of women's rights we actually did a disservice to women in excluding violence against them from the Canberra experiment. We still feel quite unsure about the answer to that question. But we are sure there is a moral imperative to keep asking the question. The qualitative experience from South Australia that Kathleen Daly is marshalling through the South Australian Juvenile Justice project (Daly, this volume), where at least with juvenile conferencing, a decision was made not to exclude family violence and rape, is yet to reveal that this was a terrible mistake. One of us was consulted on that decision as well. This was an easier policy judgement – whether the South Australian conferencing legislation should be drafted to explicitly exclude family violence or rape. It still seems that it was right to say that legislatively to exclude conferencing for all time from what Daly describes in her essay as gendered violence would have been premature. Indeed it would have precluded the very policy prescription about judging cases concretely rather than abstractly that Daly develops in her chapter here. No such legislative exclusion had been included in the prior New Zealand law (see the chapters by Morris and Busch).

A Changing Evidentiary Context

The new openness to thinking about the applicability of restorative justice to family violence also occurs in the context of increasing though still cautious optimism that restorative justice may have promise for reducing crime and quite convincing evidence that citizens who experience restorative justice as victims, offenders and participants perceive it to be fairer and more satisfying than courtroom justice (Braithwaite, 2001). In 1999 one of us published a review of the evidence that reached encouraging, though hedged, conclusions about the efficacy of restorative justice (Braithwaite, 1999a). Only one of more than 30 studies could be interpreted as showing an increase in reoffending for any type of offender put into restorative justice programs and many showed reduced offending, though mostly not very convincingly, given the quality of the studies.

Just one year on, this optimism was increased somewhat by new evidence that only became available during 2000. We have mentioned the RISE results, which, while mixed, are especially encouraging on violence. First results of a replication of RISE, or rather certain aspects of it, on only minor juvenile offenders in Indianapolis by McGarrell et al (2000) reveal a reoffending rate for cases randomly assigned to a restorative justice conference 40 percent lower than in the control group after six months, declining to 25 percent lower after 12 months. Another set of results of great importance, even though not based on random assignment, is that from the John Howard Society's Restorative Resolutions project in Winnipeg. The reoffending rate of the Restorative Resolutions group was one-third of that in a matched control group. The importance of this result is that it comes from a sample of serious adult offenders referred by prosecutors, Aboriginal legal aid and other organizations at the deep end of the system. Cases were not supposed to go into the restorative diversion unless they were headed for a prosecutorial recommendation of at least six months of prison time, an objective achieved in 90 percent of the cases. Allison Morris in her essay also discusses a new evaluation of two adult (mostly) restorative justice programs in New Zealand (that included some family violence cases) where significant reductions in reoffending occurred compared to a control group, though there are not enough family violence cases to analyse these separately (Maxwell, Morris & Anderson, 1999).

The most important recent empirical evidence for our concerns in this volume is the results of Gale Burford and Joan Pennell's (1998a) study of a restorative conference-based approach to family violence in Newfoundland. It found a marked reduction in both child abuse/neglect and abuse of mothers/partners after the intervention. A halving of abuse/neglect incidents was found for 32 families in the year after the conference compared to the year before, while incidents increased markedly for 31 control families. Pennell and Burford's (1997) research is also a model of sophisticated process development and process evaluation and of methodological triangulation. While 63 families might seem modest for quantitative purposes, it is actually a statistically persuasive study in demonstrating that this was an intervention that reduced family violence. There were actually 472 participants in the conferences for the 32 families and 115 of these were interviewed to estimate levels of violence affecting different participants (Pennell and Burford, 2000a). Moreover, within each case a before-and-after pattern was tested against 31 different types of events (e.g. abuse of child, child abuses mother, attempted suicide, father keeps income from mother) where events can be relevant to more than one member of the family. Given this pattern matching of families × events × individual family members, it understates the statistical power of the design to say it is based on only 63 cases. Burford and Pennell (1998a: 253) also report reduced drinking problems after conferences.

We take the empirical evidence as tentative yet sufficient to impose an obligation on criminologists to be open to the possibility that restorative justice has something to offer in the domain of family violence that courts do not have to offer. We take feminist theory on ADR as instructive about the heavy obligations we bear to be cautious about rushing at innovation and to be mindful of the limits of our competence where lives are so precariously at risk. At a personal level we feel it is a test of our professional courage, our prudence, our openness to new evidence that might prove us misguided or naïve.

The Concepts

In light of all this uncertainty we have not been prescriptive on what either restorative justice or family violence should be seen to mean. Some contributors prefer domestic violence as a feminist concept (e.g. Stubbs), others follow the preference of many Indigenous women to use family violence (e.g. Kelly), while Daly makes a case for 'gendered harms'. As Wittgenstein might say, there is enough family resemblance among these concepts for us to have conversations across them. Nevertheless, it is clear that family violence is not a unitary phenomenon: it involves varying levels of violence, varying frequency and persistence and varied interpersonal and structural dynamics.

Similarly we wanted to set up the meaning of restorative justice as a matter to be contested rather than as a matter of prescription. The most general meaning of restorative justice is a process where stakeholders affected by an injustice have an opportunity to communicate about the consequences of the injustice and what is to be done to right the wrong.

Most of the contributors to this volume believe that face-to-face processes are important to realize the potential of restorative justice. However, there is no consensus on how to craft the relationship between separate face to face processes where victims draw support from loved ones and other victims and where offenders meet with other offenders, or reformed offenders and supporters. With family violence there is a lot of support, drawing on experiences such as Hollow Water (Lajeunesse, 1993; Ross, 1996; Bushie, 1999), for victim circles and offender circles to be separate in the first instance, with these circles only being brought together if cycles of denial and intimidation are broken. With sexual offences, Howard Zehr (1990: 206) has counseled against face-to-face meeting unless non-domination can be secured, though he does find virtue in such circumstances in certain restorative programs where offenders meet victims other than their own. In other cases there may be merit in a degree of shuttle diplomacy where a go-between gathers information from both sides instead of from just one side and where certain limited communication is agreed to, such as a letter of apology or a victim impact letter.

The Issues in the Essays

Hope

A particular challenge with restorative justice for family violence is how to make the personal political. Kay Pranis (Chapter 2) advocates 'regular self reflection by the larger community on the issue of family violence included as part of [restorative] process design'. The recent beginnings of restorative justice in Northern Ireland provide some clues as to how this might be transacted. There the ideal being discussed is of local restorative justice initiatives reflecting on the standards and rights in the law and developing their own local principles of restorative justice. Then it is suggested there should follow processes for gathering together the experiences of groups of people who have experimented with restorative justice for healing their conflicts to revise the principles and standards with which they regulate their practice. Ultimately, one would hope that such institutionalization of making the personal political would bubble up into the law (Braithwaite & Parker, 1999). In this way the challenge can be conceived as one of the prudence of the law and the politics of the people each mutually influencing the other: community problem solving constrained by law and law reconstructed through community deliberation and participatory practice.

The chapter by Kay Pranis is in a different style from the others. Kay wanted to tell her story at the conference and in the book as a woman who is not an academic. We have not compromised that style. Perhaps no person has a stronger claim to represent the heart of the social movement for restorative justice than Kay Pranis, though this does seem an invidious thing to say of a social movement with an ideology that values collective accomplishment. Certainly there are few who enjoy the respect within that movement that she does.

Kay Pranis speaks in the voice of a grass-roots activist who has experienced the power of a passionate vision and whose method is storytelling in a personal voice. For her there is integrity of connection between this method and the restorative justice theory of empowerment. She argues that you can tell how powerful a person is by how many people listen to their stories. It follows that a way to empower disempowered people is to institutionalize active listening to their stories, to create spaces of dialogue where consequences will also flow from the listening. The evidence is that women's voices are as often (sometimes more often) heard in restorative justice conferences as men's voices (Braithwaite, 1999a: 93–94). The fact that this is not true of courtroom justice is part of the feminist analysis which, through the work of Kay Harris, brought Kay Pranis to restorative justice. Yet Kay, like so many of the writers in this collection, does not seek to reject statist justice for women. She wants a new synthesis of state and restorative justice. In particular, with family violence she wants legal system participation in restorative justice 'to ensure that the community is accountable to the values encoded in the laws against family violence'.

A crucial insight in Pranis's paper is that community control of family violence fails because while concerned individuals know what is going on, they are afraid to reach out to help or to confront behaviour 'because they fear they will be overwhelmed by the needs of the family' or that they will be punished in some other way for the intervention. An appeal of restorative justice for Pranis is that it provides social support for the needed community intervention. Crucial in this is the creation of a space where active responsibility can be shared so that no one individual need fear being lumped with the whole burden of solving the problem. Obversely, the critique of courtroom process is that it limits both the kinds of stories that can be told (only to stories that are legally relevant) and the kind of shared support that can be mobilized. While courtroom justice may be information-poor and support-poor compared with the 'potential' of restorative justice, it might be that a creative synergy between formal law and restorative justice may mobilize the most potent combination of information and support.

Pranis captures the hope of those of us who have experienced restorative justice in positive ways: 'Over and over again in restorative processes, participants report behaving in a way – a good way – which they had not expected to behave'. Through this optimistic lens, people are seen as having multiply selves, dominating and empowering, cruel and kind, retributive and forgiving, stubborn and responsive. Restorative justice can be conceived as a democratic ritual designed to give people the chance to put their best self forward.

Critics of restorative justice with some truth point to the nostalgic attachment of restorative justice advocates to the politics of hope for a communitarian past where it may have made more sense to expect the best. In return, the charge is made against legalists that they are locked into an early modern Hobbesian analysis which has it that institutions should be designed for knaves. The restorativist says that if you design institutions on the assumption that people will be knaves, they are more likely to become knaves. The right balance seems to us to see both hope and prudence as ancient virtues that are relevant to the twenty-first century. Yet both are inadequately enacted into our practice for dealing with domestic violence.

Prudence

Julie Stubbs' thoughtful essay (Chapter 3) is more dedicated to the dangers of imprudence, to the risks of restorative justice, a theme rejoined in Ruth Busch's final essay. Stubbs makes some quite original points about commonly touted virtues of restorative justice that cannot conceivably be virtues for the specific problem of domestic violence. For example, with restorative justice for young offenders, one of the benefits frightened victims frequently report is relief that an offender whom they had built up in their mind as a terrifying spectre is in fact a person weak and racked with palpable inadequacies and fears of his or her own. The victims also typically learn that they were not specifically targeted but were chosen more randomly. This is one reason why the evidence is that victims exit from conferences with young offenders much less afraid on average than when they went in (Strang, forthcoming). Julie Stubbs fairly points the finger at writers such as ourselves who have made this victimological claim for restorative justice. We have failed to think about the contextual specificity of domestic violence. Domestic violence victims are not chosen at random, are likely to be re-victimized, in most cases are objectively in fear of someone with the physical and other resources to dominate them. If they learn otherwise from the experience of restorative justice, they learn something false.

Another acute analysis in Stubbs' paper is that restorative justice has failed to come to terms with what she calls 'the relational agency of women with children'. We cannot empower women to make their own undominated choices through an institution like restorative justice when the contextual fact of the matter is that they will refuse to make choices other than in the interests of their children, children perhaps who love a father who batters their mother. While this critique is right, it throws down a challenge in terms which restorative justice, as a relational theory of justice, must meet. Pennell and Burford's chapter is in part a beginning to rising to this challenge. Harry Blagg makes a different point about choice in Aboriginal communities with similar implications: 'The capacity to exit family relationships (indeed, the very concept of 'choice' in such matters) – to repackage and reconstitute one's identity as an autonomous individual in some new location, is a profoundly eurocentric construction.'

A related challenge is to a restorative justice theorized as a response to a discrete past event, as opposed to an ongoing pathology, a critique with application beyond domestic violence (see also Blagg's chapter). A concomitant defect of restorative justice theory is the inadequate account of the discrete apology in a context characterized by cycles of manipulative contrition and violence. These features of restorative justice manifest its development in the terrain of juvenile justice where the focus on the discrete past incident and it alone was part of a strategy for averting the pathologizing of young people, and averting net-widening. Yet the implication of the Stubbs analysis is that nets of social control need to be widened with domestic violence (see also the Daly and Busch chapters). Indeed, perhaps domestic violence is one of those problems where both nets of formal legal regulation and nets of community control need to be strengthened. Corporate crime is another such arena. In these arenas conflicts have not so much been stolen, to use Nils Christie's (1977) formulation, but suppressed, denied, downgraded as something less than a crime problem. The privatization of such problems as sub-criminal means that they are not shameful for large sections of the population and therefore, according to Braithwaite's (1995) analysis, they become our biggest crime problems.

Where this leads is that domestic violence (like corporate crime) is not just another crime problem with specificities that make a history of overwhelmingly privatized regulation and cover-up at risk of being reinscribed by restorative justice. These are our biggest, most destructive, crime problems; the ones that hurt the largest numbers of people in the biggest ways precisely because of this history of privatization (Braithwaite, 1995). With domestic violence, the women's movement has made some limited but very significant gains in transforming domestic violence from a private trouble to a public concern, from 'just another domestic' to a crime (see Busch's chapter). Ideologies of victim–offender mediation that are morally neutral about violence, that domesticate it as a dispute rather than an injustice (Cobb, 1997), that 'silence narratives that suggest the directionality of violence' (Presser and Gaarder, 2000: 180), really are a threat to those hard-won gains of the women's movement.

Stubbs is also right that 'community-based initiatives often have placed the development and delivery of programs into the hands of men, some of whom are themselves abusers who have continued their physical and sexual abuse'. Behrendt's discussion of the importance of female Elders, Blagg's on crafting a regulatory role for 'women's business' and Stubbs' own discussion of the role of women's advocacy groups open up some of the possibilities for countering this concern. Ultimately, none of these options gives enough assurance and they must be complemented by the further assurance enabled by resort to formal law.

One of the Stubbs critiques we are not so sure about is that the reactive nature of restorative justice, reacting to specific injustices, limits its potential as a transformative ideology. This tension is one of the things that motivates Donna Coker in this volume and David Moore and John McDonald (2000), who presented a paper at the conference, to plump for transformative justice in preference to restorative justice. At the same time, these thinkers make the point that reacting to the truth of the concrete story is often necessary for transformation because human beings are storytelling animals. They react to a story more than they do to a political abstraction. The history of social movement politics seems to confirm the transformative power of reactions to the single story. If an environmental group wants to put in place a new regulatory order for oil pollution at sea, it sometimes must wait for the oil tanker that causes the massive spill. The campaigners against mandatory sentencing laws (see Larissa Behrendt's chapter) make little progress with an abstract campaign until an Aboriginal youth sentenced to jail under that law for stealing crayons hangs himself in his cell. The problem, the risk, with restorative justice is that it has not worked through a philosophy and practice of how the injustices it confronts in the private sphere of families and friendship networks get translated into the public sphere. Similarly, as Stubbs points out, it has not worked through the means to give women external validation when they have endured injustice, 'a public record of the abuse'. The corner of the restorative justice debate where some progress has been made on this question is the debate around the appropriateness of the highly public yet largely non-criminal truth-telling of Truth and Reconciliation Commissions. We have not yet come to terms with how to craft a satisfactory truth-telling institutional response to family violence. However, we believe a number of the essays in this collection take some important preliminary steps down this path.

Vindication

Kathleen Daly (Chapter 4) attempts to tackle what Stubbs conceives as the problem of the public record of the abuse. For Daly the central difficulty is how to (a) show respect to victims by treating harms as serious, without making the mistakes of over-reliance on harsh forms of punishment; and how to (b) '"do justice" in an unequal society'. Daly argues that while restorative justice is developing some alternatives to a structurally inegalitarian reliance on prison as a solution, restorative justice must be reconciled with retributivism if harm vindication is to be accomplished. Secondly, substantive criminal law must be reformed along the lines suggested by Nicola Lacey (1998) if it is to adequately enable vindication of the affective and corporeal dimensions of the harms at issue. Thirdly, there is a need to be aware of the different meanings and contexts of sexual violence, domestic violence and family violence. Hence, gendered harms must be considered concretely, not abstractly, in deciding how to take them seriously, to denounce them (rather than excuse them) in a way that vindicates the suffering and dignity of victims and that keeps open the possibility of healing. Daly shows she is serious about revealing the follies of abstraction by confronting us with some troubling concrete cases of gendered harm and restorative justice from South Australia. They are troubling cases in that most of them do not fit neatly into our stereotypes of what family violence or domestic violence is about. More generally, we need to come to terms with the fact that for many of the more mundane forms of gendered violence between brothers and sisters, patriarchy is not the main explanation for what is going on, and when it is violence between sisters, patriarchy may not be an explanation at all.

Power imbalance

Allison Morris (Chapter 5) further enhances the empirical base for making more nuanced policy judgements through a number of New Zealand case studies of family violence that have been dealt with in a restorative way. New Zealand has the longest history of evaluated empirical experience, having had in place a system of restorative justice that deals with some forms of family violence for more than a decade. We have already mentioned the adult panels evaluated by Maxwell et al (1999). The important contribution Morris makes in her chapter of this book is in analysing the work of care and protection family group conferences in a restorative justice framework. Such conferences would seem to have dealt with thousands of cases of physical and sexual abuse of children over the past decade. Morris concludes that the evaluations of these conferences have been mostly favourable about the safety of children, the holding of abusers accountable and the empowerment of families and whanau (Maori extended families). Indeed, we might add that this literature has been influential in persuading many other nations to follow the New Zealand family group conference approach to care and protection (as opposed to juvenile justice).

Morris uses this empirical experience to test her own feminist concerns about imbalance of power. She concludes that if the huge imbalance of power between an abusing father and an abused little girl can be better managed through care and protection conferences than through court, there is hope that the imbalance of power between a battered adult woman and her abuser can be better bridged through restorative justice. Foreshadowing Pennell and Burford's findings in the next chapter, she draws from the New Zealand experience the lesson that even seemingly highly dysfunctional families have strengths. An empowerment approach that builds out from those strengths will offer better practical protection than the police, professionals and courts.

Finally, picking up the concern in the chapters by Stubbs, Busch and Daly about impunity and the need to vindicate victims, Morris argues:

> The use of restorative processes for men's violence against their partners would not signify its decriminalization. The criminal law remains a signifier and denouncer, but it is my belief that the abuser's family and friends are by far the more potent agents to achieve this objective of denunciation.

Nathan Harris's (2001) analyses of the RISE results for court and conference cases indeed suggest that it is *only* disapproval by family and friends whom one holds in the highest regard that has the capacity to leave offenders feeling ashamed of what they have done. Disapproval by remote agents of the state or even family and friends for whom one has only moderate respect did nothing to induce remorse. It may follow if this is true that victims will gain more meaningful vindication that their suffering is serious from the denunciation of family and friends that hits home with the offender. This will be especially true if these are the family and friends whose regard is also most important to them as victims.

Feminist conferencing praxis

Joan Pennell and Gale Burford (Chapter 6) show how in Newfoundland and Labrador (and now in North Carolina) they developed a feminist praxis of family group conferencing to confront family violence and sexual abuse of adults and children. Their approach is one of critically reflective action that *interrupts* assumptions, notably about gender identity, while still fostering the *links* necessary for working together (particularly among women) to oppose injustices. The feminist praxis of 'links, interruptions' fosters a partnership-building strategy for advancing safety and empowerment. It built out from cultural respect and family strengths, particularly the strengths of the women, as opposed to targeting family deficits. An important part of cultural respect was to trust extended families to meet alone without state professionals – private family time. At first the professionals were afraid to risk this lest violence or other dominations might spin out of control. These were families with quite endemic problems of violence that were connected to a multitude of other problems. Feedback from the families was overwhelmingly positive, as were the outcomes for both safety and empowerment.

Through a case study approach, Pennell and Burford show how the conference provided an opportunity for various women to band together across family and professional lines to take leadership in undermining the influence of a dominating male. The data show that these were not encapsulated meetings of nuclear families – rather nuclear families were linked to extended families, community Elders and state professionals. While the model is about empowering families, particularly by giving them private time, there is a crucial role of state authorities, particularly in supporting these links across the women and in supplying legal leverage over perpetrators. The profound meta-lesson seems to be that making the personal political requires both private space for personal troubles to be spoken and public engagement to do the linking that transforms private troubles into public issues. As Presser and Gaarder (2000: 188) put it, through seeing crime as neither 'just personal' nor 'just political', a restorative feminist praxis may 'reconcile the private-public distinction that underpins the battering problem'.

An interesting feature of the interruptions–links approach was problematizing who was victim and who was offender, a concern well articulated in Julie Stubbs' essay. Instead of the normal conferencing practice of organizing supporters around just known offenders and victims, all family members likely to feel at risk during the conference were 'encouraged to choose a support person who would stay by them emotionally and help to prepare in advance a statement of what they wished to say'.

Transformation, anti-subordination

Donna Coker (Chapter 7) makes the case for reframing restorative justice as transformative justice. She identifies a number of theoretical weaknesses of restorative justice. A central concern is that restorative justice seeks to ignore the state or bypass it, when it must engage the state, transform it and engage with political action directed at state inequalities. Some feminist discourse is seen as making the obverse mistake of allowing domestic violence to be positioned as a public issue 'subject to co-optation in ways that increase state control of poor women and women of colour' (see also Daly, this volume). 'The critical dilemma for feminists who seek to empower battered women is to develop strategies for controlling the criminal justice system without increasing state control *of women* [and one might add of children]'. An interesting question is to what extent the Bazemore and Earle model of 'balance' (Chapter 8) can rise to the challenge of averting both errors. But Coker prefers the transformative theoretical move rather than the 'balanced restorative' move.

   Coker advocates a struggle for justice via anti-subordination practices that seek to transform both the public and the private. Anti-subordination practices must be crafted to transform multiply oppressive systems. Coker asks us to consider the following weakness of restorative justice theory: 'it offers no clear principles for dealing with crimes, such as domestic violence, where majoritarian opposition to the crime is weak or compromised' (see also the Busch chapter). What is needed is a process that mobilizes families and communities to intervene against domestic violence in a way that 'seeks to transform the norms of family and community members, rather than rely on existing anti-battering norms that may not exist.' On the crucial issue of race and class subordination being used to excuse domestic violence, Coker concludes that discussion of such subordination can be productive so long as 'battering men are encouraged to connect their own experiences of subordination with their subordination of women'.

   Coker invokes her study of Navajo peacemaking in which traditional Navajo stories that contain gender egalitarian themes are a resource for women and a resource for men in creating a masculine identity that supports gender egalitarianism. She conceives of such identity transformation not as 'treatment' but as 'justice-*making* processes'. States, families and communities are thus conceived as projects of political will and imagination, where the guiding normative ideal is to steer them away from subordination. When part of such a transformative project, 'violence is not privatized when a man reads an apology to his wife and daughter in the presence of others, particularly when those others are in a position to monitor his future behaviour'. At the conference Donna Coker spoke of the need for restorative justice practitioners to borrow from domestic violence activists tools such as assistance for women with safety planning and engaging in lethality assessments of the batterer. Other participants spoke of options that included plans for checking victims at high risk times, personal alarms for women, teaching third parties intervention scripts so that they might move from being bystanders to being change agents, and reparation with resources that increase women's autonomy. Donna Coker complemented these ideas with the perspective that there were limits to a state law that focuses on acts of physical violence; that fails to reach the variegated controlling behaviours of a battering system in a way that community controls might be more able to accomplish.

When we asked Donna Coker at the conference how one should struggle for transformative justice in a more patriarchal culture that lacks the anti-subordination narratives she found in Navajo culture, she said she suspected that in most cultures anti-subordination narratives could be retrieved with greater or lesser difficulty. The crucial point is that restorative/transformative justice must not allow fairness to mean neutrality, must not domesticate violence as conflict (Coker, 1999). It will falter without an ideal of justice as requiring anti-subordination practices.

Balanced restorative justice

Gordon Bazemore and Twila Earle conceive the evidence on family violence as revealing an increasingly complex picture of multidimensional factors contributing to the problem. This implies a need for balanced and nuanced deliberation of cross-cutting concerns in context. It argues against 'cookie cutter' approaches that involve training in standard scripts. It argues in favour of a principle-based approach to restorative justice that is creatively attuned to the complexity of different crimes. Bazemore and Earle structure their argument around a consideration of three kinds of balance: *principle balance*, where the key principles are repairing harm, maximizing stakeholder involvement in decision-making and restructuring/transformation of state and community roles in a way that empowers communities as the primary drivers of justice solutions; *stakeholder balance* between victims, offenders and communities; and *goal balance* between public safety, accountability and reintegration.

Bazemore and Earle show how a principle-driven pursuit of balanced restorative justice can lead, for example, to a contextual judgement that it is necessary to amplify the voice of victim concerns by urging a victim supporter in a pre-conference meeting 'to express issues of harm and need for reparation when the victim herself seems reluctant to do so'.

In an argument that bears similarities to those of Pennell and Burford and Morris on building from strength, Bazemore and Earle suggest building out from the common ground where stakeholder interests intersect. This, they suggest, is where the 'fertile soil' for repair and prevention will be found. Restorative justice is conceived as institutionally attuned to the pursuit of this common ground, while the current criminal justice process conduces to separating interests. This may be the key to understanding how restorative justice may enable healing to lead to justice (Drummond, 1999), as opposed to the retributive notion of healing only being possible after justice. Strang's (forthcoming) RISE data are consistent with this aspect of the Bazemore and Earle analysis. They show that win–win is much more likely in restorative justice than in courtroom justice. The sample size is insufficient to test this adequately, but across a range of victim and offender needs the pattern of the RISE data also suggests that in conferences a win for victims in meeting their needs, especially their desire for emotional restoration, increases the prospects of offenders meeting theirs, and vice versa. There is no evidence of this dynamic in the cases that go to court.

Indigenous empowerment

Larissa Behrendt (Chapter 9) uses the case of Australian Indigenous peoples to show how both the formal legal system and diversionary alternatives disempower Indigenous people. While one might hope that restorative justice would create a space for the 'speaking from the heart' that is fundamental in Indigenous disputing, in practice professionalized Western mediation has been the norm. Behrendt sees mediation as more an extension of the Western legal system than an alternative to it. There is little improvement over a formal justice system where 'the Indigenous focus on feelings, hurt and perspective when speaking also runs into conflict with the formal rules of evidence ...'.

The efficiency emphasis with case flow management in Western mediation and speedy trial imperatives in criminal law both undermine the imperative of Indigenous justice to allow time for feelings to be resolved (see also Blagg's chapter). Introducing strangers in a privileged role, whether as judges or mediators, counters Indigenous philosophies about who has a right to speak. When mediators or judges are required to have special training this undercuts traditions grounded in experience as training. Behrendt argues for a ground-up approach where instead of adapting a Western mediation model to an Indigenous community, the starting point is a local community developing the process. When Indigenous communities face continually the challenge of healing the wounds of colonization, restorative justice must not open up another wound by being 'more interested in the method and models' than with results that will heal in a post-colonial context.

Harry Blagg (Chapter 10) echoes the two latter conclusions from Behrendt's work and takes them into the context of regulating family violence. Blagg finds that Aboriginal women seek an holistic process of community healing for dealing with family violence. This violence is largely perpetrated by Aboriginal men destructively searching to reinstate a masculine role stripped of dignity by colonialism. This may be a reason why Aboriginal violence in Australia is much more directed at intimates than white violence. Locking up their men has little appeal to most Aboriginal women as a solution, Blagg finds. Instead they prefer 'forms of intervention that stop abuse, cool out situations, and open pathways to healing, with minimum intervention by the criminal justice system'.

One interesting aspect of Blagg's paper is the examples he gives of culturally specific preventive ideas:

Women on small isolated communities find it difficult to escape violent men. One answer has been to construct shelters on women's 'law grounds' (barred to men) and placing sacred objects in shelters as a deterrent to violent men. These solutions directly empower Indigenous women both at the point of crisis and within their communities by reinstating the power of traditional 'women's business'...

Loretta Kelly's analysis (Chapter 11) gives a more specific focus to the fears Aboriginal women have about sending their men to prison for family violence, the fear of death or injury in custody. Kelly finds the unwillingness in Aboriginal women to grant legitimacy to the colonizing criminal justice system as limiting its effectiveness in providing safety. Where legitimacy is granted to Aboriginal Elders, their regulation for safety can be more effective. Kelly makes a special plea with family violence for empowering women Aboriginal Elders. What they can make a special contribution toward, on Kelly's analysis, is an holistic approach to safety and restorative justice. One of the things she finds it best to empower Elders to decide is how to integrate Western state justice into Aboriginal justice, if at all: 'in some communities, Elders may wish the magistrate to sit with them and convey their decision to the offender. The purpose of this may be to prevent the offender taking revenge on any individual Elder'. Kelly finds much in common between restorative justice values and traditional Aboriginal customary values. However, poor practice in the experience of Aboriginal people makes restorative justice schemes culturally inappropriate in practice. She points out that while shame might be an important concept in helping the scholar understand what is happening in criminal justice processes in the Aboriginal community, contemporary distinctively Aboriginal ways of using the concept make shame an unhelpful usage for discussing restorative justice within Aboriginal communities.

Kelly, Coker, Behrendt, Busch and Blagg are all concerned about what Blagg describes as forms of 'consultation' that 'aim simply to appropriate aspects of Indigenous governance when it suits the agendas of non-Indigenous agencies'. Coker's anti-subordination principle appealed to us at the conference as a way of thinking clearly about the cultural appropriation problem which has been so central to Blagg's scholarly contribution. The normative theory would be that it is acceptable to appropriate aspects of Indigenous governance when doing so would reduce subordination. Obversely, it would be acceptable to import certain Western notions of, say, human rights into Indigenous governance when that would reduce subordination. Otherwise, these cultural imports and exports would be questionable and subject to Blagg's (1997) Orientalism critique.

Integrated strategies for safety and autonomy

In the final essay (Chapter 12) Ruth Busch argues against the use of restorative justice in the vast majority of domestic violence cases, even though she concludes that 'mandatory arrest policies and no-drop prosecutions result in outcomes which can be destructive to victims' autonomy'. Busch argues persuasively that better choices can be made on how to make state intervention against domestic violence work and that progressively better choices have been made in New Zealand over the past 15 years. Among these are police policies that make for prosecutions that stick without relying upon victims as witnesses at trial. This can protect victims afraid of retribution and grant offenders less control; their intimidatory tactics then do not work as well in deterring arrest/prosecution. Effective enforcement against breaches of protection orders has been another step forward. Most tellingly Busch argues that restorative justice advocates caricature state law enforcement as punitive and stigmatizing of offenders when the New Zealand reality is that rehabilitation of domestic violence offenders is a much more predominant response than punishment. Finally, contemporary responses of the New Zealand state include assistance with developing culturally appropriate coordinated community interventions to challenge the power disparities within which domestic violence occurs. Busch rightly suggests that it would be a terrible mistake to throw all of this away in favour of just restorative justice conferences.

Like Stubbs, Busch reveals a number of assumptions about the supposed superiority of restorative justice that do not apply with domestic violence. The theory of restorative justice assumes that prior relationships assist healing. Yet we know that spousal relationships that disintegrate often leave relational residues that are more of a hindrance than a help to healing. While the empirical experience of restorative justice with juveniles is that the voices of women, especially mothers, are extremely influential, we are also cautioned that with domestic violence there is evidence that abused women report greater fear of being 'out-talked' by their partners and a greater fear of retaliation from them. Ruth Busch also challenges an assumption which we think is generally right – that there are many lay people with the interpersonal skills to be good restorative justice facilitators after a few days training (even if the majority of lay people do not have these skills). She makes the point that with domestic violence highly developed skills in a number of areas are imperative – understanding of the power control dynamics of domestic violence, knowledge of risk-assessment issues, among others.

On the positive side, Busch does see Pennell and Burford's approach (Chapter 6) as having promise because it involves a thoughtful hybrid of formal legal enforcement options and restorative justice. The facilitators were highly trained on domestic violence power dynamics and risk assessment in the terms suggested in the last paragraph. Safety mechanisms that could be enforced by court sanctions were put in place first. The preparation for these conferences was considerable and extended to concern for the safety and emotional well-being of all conference participants, not just a victim and an offender. The follow-up was also more rigorous than with standard restorative justice conferences. For Busch, the crucial feature in the apparent success of the Pennell and Burford program is that it was strategically integrated with the formal system of state enforcement rather than an alternative to it. As we will see below, in important ways this is also true of the other influential Canadian program at Hollow Water.

We actually think this integration has been a failure of restorative justice on a much wider front beyond domestic violence. Restorative justice should be a superior vehicle for getting extended families or networks of friends to commit to provide social support for offenders in rehabilitation. Its empowerment philosophy of deliberative democracy should deliver more richly considered (and therefore more apposite) and more volunteered choices for rehabilitative options. In practice, this does not happen – partly because restorative justice has been sold as an alternative to the therapeutic state rather than as a vehicle for making rehabilitation more decent and effective. Equally, it has been often over-sold as an alternative to the punitive state when in reality, especially with intransigent problems like the worst domestic violence, it can only be effective in the shadow of the punitive state.

On this integration theme, there is much to be learned from the Busch critique by those of us who think there is wider potential for restorative justice to deal with family violence. Beyond family violence, there are some rather constructive suggestions in Ruth Busch's paper about how restorative justice preparation might increase prospects of success – for example, encouraging offenders before the meeting to accept responsibility without blaming someone or something else can 'elicit a more empathetic response from victims who tend then to talk about times that they themselves have made mistakes'.

Above all, we must take in Ruth Busch's admonition that 'safety and autonomy' must be prioritized over other outcomes, including reconcil-iation. Reconciliation might be the highest priority with a child who is being stigmatized by his family for a minor act of shoplifting. It even might be the highest priority in the aftermath of Apartheid or a civil war that has ended. But in the context of domestic violence that is ongoing, safety should absolutely be a priority that trumps reconciliation. A com-mitment to universal values to guide criminal justice, like Braithwaite and Pettit's (1990) republican value of freedom as non-domination (dominion), is still bound to require contextual judgements on how the empirical complexities of domination differ for different kinds of crime. Even if it is empirically true that in a wide range of contexts, from shoplifting to war crimes, apology–forgiveness–reconciliation can increase safety and autonomy, Busch shows us that in many domestic violence situations it can have the opposite effect. On the other hand, as Loretta Kelly's chapter suggests, there may be contexts where Indigenous families have been so disrupted by colonialism, where fears of harm in custody are sufficiently real, as to justify a prioritizing of fam-ily reconciliation and reconciliation with Elders over threats to victim safety that are not extreme. The path to wisdom and prudence may lie in the capacity to look at a problem like domestic violence through the lens of the kind of feminist analysis advanced by Ruth Busch at the same time as we look at it through the lens of restorative justice theories, theories of Indigenous justice and other theoretical frameworks as well. Indeed perhaps this is the wisdom Joan Pennell and Gale Burford have shown in crafting with their local stakeholders a program that seems to have worked.

Restorative justice and responsive state regulation

A common feature of all the essays in this collection is that they see both the state and civil society as having important roles in the regulation of family violence. While Julie Stubbs has a measured pessimism about the capacity of resource-poor advocacy groups to monitor the abuses of restorative justice, all authors agree that women's groups and Indigenous groups have important roles both in regulating violence and in regulating flawed official efforts at regulating violence. This is more than agreement that we need to strengthen the regulatory capabilities of families, communities, non-government organizations and the state with respect to family violence. All the authors in this collection also see critical synergies between public and private regulation. It is common in restorative justice collections for it to be argued that backing restorative justice with coercive threats by the state irreparably corrupts the ideals of restorative justice. In wider arenas this seems as naïve as it does here. Do we seriously believe youth offenders would regularly turn up to restorative justice conferences were the coercion of the state not lurking in the background?

In our romantic moments, those of us attracted to restorative justice like to laud the accomplishments of the Hollow Water healing circles:

When and where has the traditional criminal process succeeded in uncovering anything approaching 48 admissions of criminal responsibility for sexual abuse of children in a community of just six hundred? (Braithwaite, 1999a: 16)

However, Berma Bushie (1999: 59) from the Anishnaabe clan at Hollow Water is clear that 'When abusers agree to take the healing option, they usually do so out of fear of going to jail.' Two abusers who opted out of the healing circles did go to jail. It seems to us that there is a startling reality of the accomplishment of Hollow Water. It is not an accomplishment of restorative justice; it is not an accomplishment of state enforcement. It is an accomplishment of a new kind of creative synergy between state power and the power of restorative justice. We hope the contest of perspectives in this book casts some new light on how to understand the transformative possibilities of such synergy.

Transforming contexts of choice

In forthcoming work from the Centre for Restorative Justice at ANU we hope to show that it need not be utopian to struggle for a world where subordinated people have a genuine choice of whether to opt for restorative justice or court. This means a world where restorative justice is always available as an option in a serious legal dispute and legal aid to go to court is always available to a person of modest means. Whether restorative justice or court is better for a subordinated person is a profoundly contextual and personal judgement. We see little merit in deciding which is better in general or on average. Even the project of attempting to sort out which are the contexts where court is best and where restorative justice is best seems a second-best project. The best project is to conceive how to totally transform the regulatory order so that both options are always available.

So much of the public debate is between those who rightly point to why the haves come out on top in court and those who rightly point out why the haves come out on top in Alternative Dispute Resolution. We need to consider instead how the have nots can be guaranteed both better practical access to court and better access to restorative justice under terms they are empowered to choose. This is most simply illustrated by family law disputes. A wife batterer who controls the family bank account can afford an excellent lawyer should a family law matter go to court. This is another whip he holds during family law mediation beyond the fear of his violence. He can dominate in court because he can pay for the lawyer and he can dominate in mediation partly because he can credibly threaten to exit the mediation in favour of court and she cannot. The most crucial feature of the gendered power imbalance is not about whether the power imbalance is worse in court than in mediation. It is about the fact that he can make a contextual judgement on when court suits him best and when mediation suits him best, whereas she cannot. An anti-subordination alternative integration is needed: one that absolutely guarantees the woman a right to a contest in court with well-funded legal aid and one that guarantees her a restorative justice alternative where she does not confront her partner alone, but with the advocacy of as many lay and professional supporters as she chooses to have present, including publicly funded domestic violence advocates if fear of battering is an issue for her. Violence against women and children will remain endemic until societies get serious about gendered social justice and about meeting the needs of those affected by power-based injustices (Sullivan & Tifft, 2001).

We believe that in a world where women are given that choice they will opt for (balanced) restorative justice in droves. But that is not our parting point. Our point is that the anti-subordination challenge is transforming the legal system so that a genuine non-dominated choice of that sort is available to women. Building on the work of Christine Parker (1999), John Braithwaite (2001) is now seeking to show that such a transformation need not be impossibly expensive. Whether or not it is utopian to struggle for a world where both restorative justice and litigation are always affordable to the subordinated is the stuff of another book. Where we believe this book has taken us is to is this: that such a world would be a better one than a world where litigation is always available, or restorative justice is always available, or our existing world where neither is effectively available to the poor. The feasibility of radical transformation aside, it might be a better world if we could have enough impact on the conditions of domination to make both the healing of the circle and the justice of the courthouse choices family violence victims are realistically able to make more often than now.

2   Restorative Values and Confronting Family Violence

Kay Pranis

Personal Introduction

I wish to begin by sharing key pieces of my history regarding both family violence and restorative justice so that you may have a sense of my context and my potential biases and limitations. I was involved with domestic violence as a community volunteer before I ever dreamed that I would work in the criminal justice system and before I had ever heard of restorative justice. In the mid-80s, looking for an additional way to serve the community I lived in, I responded to an appeal for volunteers to serve on the Board of Directors of a local battered women's agency. Shortly after joining the Board, the executive director asked me to be chair of the Board. The agency was young and struggling for survival. I served as Chair of the Board for three years – during that time we navigated some very rough waters but came through with a solid, stable agency. I learned a great deal about domestic violence and even more about the power of a passionate vision. The woman who was the executive director when I was on the Board died in the early 90s of cancer. She continues to be an inspiration in my life – a reminder that the impossible can be made possible if you believe in it.

I came to my current work by a very untraditional route. I have no formal training in any related field – not law, not criminology, not social science, not psychology. I have not done direct service as a professional in any related field and I am not an academic scholar. I was a full-time parent and community volunteer for 16 years. I went to work for a criminal justice agency in 1988 because no one else would hire me.

Within the field of criminal justice my first exposure to the core values I see embodied in restorative justice was in an article by Kay Harris (1987), which was not about restorative justice, but about a vision of justice based on feminist principles. Kay identified the following as key tenets of feminism and discussed their importance to issues of justice:
- All human beings have dignity and value.
- Relationships are more important than power.
- The personal is political.

Later, when I stumbled across writings about restorative justice, I found those principles articulated by Kay Harris to be at the centre of what I understood restorative justice to represent. The lens through which I viewed restorative justice was a lens influenced by Kay Harris's writing and my own experience as a community activist and a parent. The importance placed on relationships within a restorative framework has always for me meant more than the single relationship between a victim and an offender – it includes as well the larger web of relationships in which we live. And the harms considered in a restorative approach for me have always included larger social harms as well as individual harms. Crime seems to me to always be embedded in a community context both in terms of harms and responsibilities. So I am always looking at the relatedness of things and the way that outcomes may be influenced by that relatedness in a deliberate way.

The following discussion reflects my understanding of the values and principles of restorative justice. I cannot claim to speak for the movement as a whole.

Overview

Family violence is often thought incompatible with restorative justice because of the emphasis on face-to-face processes and reconciliation between parties which in its most familiar form may not be suitable to the power imbalance present in family violence cases. However, the underlying aims of restorative justice are broader than the particular face-to-face meetings associated with restorative justice. Face-to-face meetings of victim and offender are a strategy for achieving certain goals. Those goals are suitable to family violence crimes but may require different strategies with family violence or a different emphasis in using particular strategies (Bazemore and Earle, this volume).

There is significant common ground between the efforts to reduce family violence and the restorative justice movement. Both are greatly concerned with clear acknowledgement of the wrongness of the behaviour, with messages to the victims that they are not responsible or do not deserve what happened (Achilles & Zehr, 2001), with a recognition that the community bears some responsibility for the broader social climate related to the behaviour and with making both individual and social changes which will end the behaviour (Pranis, 2001).

That desire to both influence community norms and to use community norms to shape new behaviours is the focus of this paper. Community-based processes that have emerged in the restorative justice movement offer hope that in the response to family violence a larger group of parties can be engaged to influence the offender, to create safety nets for victims and to stimulate a larger community discussion about the origin of such behaviour.

In the restorative justice framework the community is responsible for rallying around victims, facilitating responsible resolutions to harmful behaviour, supporting offenders in making amends, establishing appropriate norms of behaviour for all members and addressing underlying causes of harmful behaviour (Pranis, 1997). Each of these community responsibilities is important in resolving family violence.

The processes of group conferencing and peacemaking circles provide opportunities to engage more people in taking responsibility for the safety of victims, responsibility for the future behaviour of the offender and responsibility for the norms of the community. Without that kind of community engagement our responses to family violence will remain inadequate.

Mutual Responsibility

Restorative justice has at its core the concept of mutual responsibility and interdependence. Individuals are responsible for their impact on others and on the larger whole of which they are a part. Communities are responsible for the good of the whole, which includes the well-being of each member. Because all parts of the community are interdependent, harm to one is harm to all; good for one is good for all. This is an ancient understanding of Indigenous peoples around the world which Western science has recently 'discovered' (Melton, 1995). Modern physics and biology suggest that nothing exists except in relation to something else, that the content of matter is not as important as the relationships between things – the between-ness of existence. The importance of relationships is at the centre of restorative approaches – not just the relationship between a victim and an offender, but all the relationships connected to the victim and offender in the web of life (Pranis, 1997; 2001).

The well-being of the collective is the responsibility of each individual and the well-being of each individual is the responsibility of the collective. The interaction of any individual with any other individual affects those individuals and affects the collective because actions affecting any one member of the collective impact the overall well-being of the collective. So our actions must be assessed for their impact on the group as well as their impact on specific individuals.

Mutual responsibility between the individual and the community is not just a passive responsibility to do no harm but is an active responsibility to support and nurture the well-being of the other in his/her unique individual needs (Braithwaite & Roche, 2001). Consequently, the mutual responsibility between individual and community at the core of restorative justice does not entail the suppression of individuality to serve the group, but entails attending to individual needs in a way which takes into account the impact on the collective and seeks to meet needs in a way that serves both, or at least balances the needs of both the individual and the group.

It is quite clear that family violence affects the health of the larger community. Through research our heads tell us:

- Children raised in violent homes are more likely to become involved in violent behaviour toward others in the community (National Research Council, 1998).
- Victims of family violence are less able to contribute to the community.
- The costs of social services and medical care resulting from family violence are often borne by the larger community (National Research Council, 1998).

But even more importantly our hearts and souls tell us that because we are all connected in the web of life, a wound to any part of the community is a wound to the whole community.

The restorative justice principle of mutual responsibility suggests that:

- Individual perpetrators of family violence must answer to the larger community for the impact of their behaviour on the community.
- The community bears responsibility for the well-being of the victims of family violence.
- The community bears responsibility for the well-being of the offender.

From its inception the domestic violence movement has held that family violence is not a private matter and that change in individual offenders is not sufficient to address the problem of family violence, that we must also change the social context in which family violence occurs (Cameron, 1991; Tifft, 1993). For example, in Minnesota grass-roots agencies funded by state victim funds were required to demonstrate that they were involved in activities directed at social change in addition to whatever direct services they provided to victims. There has been tremendous effort in the domestic violence movement to raise the larger questions of gender roles, socialization of males and females, power differences in social and economic structures, and issues of oppression as relevant to domestic violence (Cameron, 1991). Unfortunately, the traditional criminal justice system treats each domestic violent incident as unconnected to other incidents and provides no effective forum for challenging and encouraging change in community social structures. Emphasis on accountability through individual punishment has left most communities still in denial about their role in the problem of domestic violence.

Because restorative justice assumes some level of community responsibility for the behaviour of its members, a framework is provided for public discussion of larger social issues contributing to the violence. Two processes promoted under restorative justice values, group conferencing and peacemaking circles, by involving a larger community than the nuclear family often produce discussion of the larger social climate (Bazemore, 2000a; Pranis, 2001). In a peacemaking circle for a domestic violence case where several women described their own experience of victimization, circle members began to ask themselves what was wrong with their community. Community members see the connections. When they have the opportunity to participate in a reflective process, community members do not typically see behaviour in isolation. They look for underlying causes and examine the complexity of connections to other issues. In an organic way the larger social issues related to family violence become part of the discussion of what needs to be done as the result of an individual case. By participating in a discussion of what happened in a particular family, the community begins to examine itself (Stuart, 1996; 2001; Pranis, 2001).

Legal Authority and Moral Authority

Social behaviour is often not responsive to change based on the legal status of the behaviour, if that legal status is not consonant with the moral status of the behaviour. Illegal behaviour is likely to continue if there is not general social disapproval of the behaviour. Moral authority is ultimately more powerful than legal authority in shaping behaviour. Moral authority is a product of relationships. It must be grounded in some form of connection, of shared beliefs and common ground. For most offenders the legal system does not embody that sense of mutuality that is essential for moral standing. Relationships in community are the source of mutuality that results in moral authority.

Because the community is the source of moral authority and because long-term behaviour change is more responsive to moral suasion than legal force, the desired change in family behaviour necessary to reduce oppression of women and children cannot occur without engaging the community in:

* establishing expectations about family behaviour;
* communicating those expectations in myriad ways on a daily basis;
* challenging transgressions of the expectations.

Restorative processes provide a forum for engaging the conscience of the community and its moral responsibility. The values of restorative justice require that dialogue be respectful, inclusive and reflective. Restorative dialogue processes do more than address the offender's behaviour. They establish expectations for all the other participants as well. When we articulate an expectation for others in a public process, we are in effect also committing ourselves to that standard. Discussion of an offender's behaviour in a circle sets the standard, not only for the offender but for everyone sitting in the circle.

We have few places in our current social structure for community dialogue about expected standards of behaviour – few places for making the case for behaviour based not on legal constraint but moral imperative. In the past those standards were passed down without discussion. Major social change in the 1960s and 70s dismantled many of those standards because some were racist, sexist and intolerant of differences. We now have an urgent need for forums in which we can explore our shared values, the implications of those values for behaviour and ways to be accountable to one another for our behaviour.

The nature of the forums for this dialogue is critical. Those forums must be deeply respectful of all individuals, must allow for reflection, must create space for every story to be heard and must include all voices in decision-making about community norms and expectations. These characteristics are true of restorative processes.

Restorative processes seek to engage the moral authority of the community toward serving the best interests of all those affected by crime. However, legal authority remains an important partner to the moral authority of the community and should be used when a community does not exercise its moral authority for the best interests of all members. There is fear among family violence advocates that the community might set a standard that condones the use of violence within a family. I believe that the apparent support in some communities for violence is based on denial of the actual impacts of violent behaviour. In a reflective dialogue in which all the harms are spoken and the focus is not on blame but problem solving, I believe most people will acknowledge the wrongness of family violence (see Pennell & Burford, 2000a; Pennell, this volume). Participation by the legal system in community-based processes is an essential safeguard to uphold the values of non-violence. In family violence cases it is especially important that the legal system participate to ensure that the community is accountable to the values encoded in the laws against family violence (Van Ness & Strong, 1997; Bazemore & Earle, this volume; Coker, this volume).

Most communities to date have not exercised their moral responsibility around issues of family violence regarding both domestic violence and child abuse. It is difficult to engage communities in an abstract way to become more active on these issues. However, restorative processes provide a way to engage community members in individual cases in a way that leads to recognition of a broader community responsibility and provides spaces for designing actions toward that responsibility.

Increasing Agency Through Collective Action and Shared Responsibility

I believe that many people – neighbours, relatives, work colleagues, friends – would like to help those they know are struggling with family problems which may be manifested in child abuse or neglect or partner abuse. But often individuals are afraid to reach out to help or to confront behaviour because they fear they will be overwhelmed by the needs of the family or that the family may react in a negative way. So, potential supporters remain inactive – not sure how to offer their help or how to become involved in a safe way. They may also feel that the little bit they can do will not make much difference, because the problems are too large. They often stand by feeling helpless and inadequate and may gradually withdraw because it is so uncomfortable. The sense of helplessness leads to denial or hopelessness among those around families in trouble.

Restorative processes, especially group conferencing and peacemaking circles, create a space in which the responsibility for assisting the family can be shared among numerous supporters so that any one individual does not feel the whole burden of solving the problem. The small contributions of several different people become significant when combined. By creating a collective process of problem solving and action, restorative processes empower supporters of the family to become agents of change in the lives of the struggling family. Acting as a group, supporters can find the strength and courage to take action to protect women and children and to intervene with perpetrators when there are signals of trouble (Pennell & Burford, 2000a).

A sense of efficacy, a belief that individuals can take actions that make a difference, changes the climate of a neighbourhood or community

(Sampson et al, 1997). It builds a sense of hope. Restorative processes create opportunities for effective actions by ordinary citizens. People find they do not need an advanced degree to be able to help their friends and family.

Problem Solving

Restorative justice is a values-based approach to responding to crime. The emphasis on acting on values is at the same time very pragmatic. Acting on values should produce results that serve the well-being of others. Values should guide us in very concrete ways to better relationships. The application of our values should help produce solutions to difficult problems. Restorative justice is thus a values-based approach to problem solving regarding crime.

Because restorative justice emphasizes problem solving, the underlying problem is probed at greater depth and a much broader understanding of the problem is achieved. Especially in processes like conferencing or circles, where multiple perspectives are heard, the problem is explored in many dimensions producing a much more detailed and rich picture of the issue and consequently informing a much more detailed and rich approach to solving the problem. Court processes constrain the type and sources of information to be used in decision-making, resulting in decisions based on limited information. The problem solving of restorative processes also relies less on professional expertise and assumes that those closest to the problem have the greatest insight about the problem and its possible resolutions.

Storytelling

A very important value in restorative justice is that of empowering unheard voices. That is most often and most powerfully accomplished through personal narratives. Listening respectfully to someone's story is a way of giving them power – a positive kind of power. Both victims and offenders most often come from disempowered populations. Listening respectfully to a person's story gives that person dignity and worth. For victims it is an important part of the healing process. Telling the story is a part of taking back personal power.

Often the harmful behaviour of family violence is an attempt to gain power. Providing an experience of empowerment that is not gained by harming others, but being heard respectfully is a powerful way to teach a new form of personal empowerment to offenders. Telling the story can be a way of taking responsibility as well (Toews-Shenk & Zehr, 2001).

Personal narratives are the primary source of information and wisdom in restorative justice approaches. Those narratives may be told in face-to-face processes or in separate processes for victims and offenders or a combination of both. The critical element is the use of personal narratives to understand the harms, the needs, the pains and the capacities of all participants so that an appropriate new story can be constructed. Personal stories allow people to engage emotional and spiritual components of their being as well as the physical and mental. In restorative approaches storytelling is often an iterative process – the story is told many different times as understandings are increased and greater and greater depths of communication become possible.

The Personal is the Political

One of the most important insights of the feminist movement is the idea that there is no separation between an ethical personal life and an ethical public life. We cannot have one set of rules for our personal lives and a different set of rules for our public lives. What happens in our private life affects our public life and what happens in our public life affects our private life. At some level each is accountable for its impact on the other.

Interestingly, restorative justice is pushing the same frontier, in very concrete ways. Those involved in the most intense restorative practices find themselves doing as much internal work as external work – as much healing on themselves as healing for others. In walking a path of healing with victims and offenders practitioners find they must walk their own healing path. Because restorative justice is a set of values, not a set of techniques, values must be at the forefront of practice. They can only remain so through articulation and dialogue – by conscious use of the values.

In encouraging respect, listening, accountability, self-forgiveness, etc. for others, practitioners are constantly confronted with their own levels of respect, accountability and self-forgiveness in their lives. The internal work is often more difficult than the external work. Circles, with their emphasis on equality and their assumption that every participant has a gift to offer, blur the lines between those being helped and those helping, those being judged and those judging (Stuart, 2001; Hudson et al, 1996b).

Guidelines for Restorative Justice Practices in Family Violence Cases

Family violence situations present complexities and potential risks not present in other types of crimes. Long-established power imbalances, secrecy, ongoing relationships, economic dependencies, family pressures are factors that may be significant in family violence. Effective restorative practices must address those issues.

Involvement of family violence experts in the design of the restorative process: Good intentions are not sufficient. Processes must be built on information and experience of those closest to the issue including advocates, former victims and former offenders.

Involvement of larger community in design and oversight of the process: Communities must take responsibility for the larger social climate in which family violence occurs. Community involvement in program design is essential to ensure that the patterns of family violence that transcend individual responsibility are acknowledged and addressed. The community perspective will naturally move to broader questions of underlying causes beyond individuals that can inform prevention strategies.

Involvement of the formal justice system in design and oversight of process to ensure that the harmful nature of family violence is addressed: Communities have more power than the justice system to influence behaviour, but must be accountable to the laws of our society both in the standards they uphold and the manner in which they uphold those standards. Additionally, the formal justice system has a role in backing up the community in its process (see Van Ness & Strong, 1997).

Presence in each case of persons knowledgeable about family violence: Family members and community members may not be attuned to the subtle dynamics of power or the issues of safety. Every case should have someone involved in decision-making who is alert for danger signs and can raise key issues for participants to address.

Involvement of persons outside the nuclear family who have close ties to the family and who disapprove of the violence: Breaking the secrecy around family violence is a critical element of accountability. Involving extended family or other supporters who disapprove of the behaviour engages the power of relationships to influence the offender and monitor the safety of the victim.

Continual feedback loop for information from victims about the impact of the restorative justice process: Because each situation will be unique, results will never be predictable. The process must include safe avenues for feedback from victims so that the process can be modified or halted if necessary.

Regular self-reflection on the use of restorative values in their own lives by practitioners: Restorative justice moves from the old paradigm of 'client/service provider' in which there is a clear giver and a taker, to a model in which every participant is presumed to be learning from every other participant – everyone has a gift to offer for the good of the whole. That orientation requires practitioners to recognize their own needs for healing and ways of receiving help from others.

Regular self-reflection by the larger community on the issue of family violence included as part of process design: Family violence is not simply a matter of individuals making bad choices. Family violence is a product of many forces, some of which function at the community level. The aggregate experience of numerous family violence cases provides a community with an opportunity to learn about itself, to identify underlying causes and to begin planning for long-term prevention.

Breathing Life Into the Theory – A Story of Engaging Community Dialogue to Create New Community Norms

I will now seek to illustrate the potential of restorative processes to begin bridging inequalities to change community norms. St. Paul, Minnesota now has one of the largest Hmong communities outside of Laos. There may be as many as 50,000 Hmong people in St. Paul. This community faces very difficult struggles in its transition from life in the mountains of Laos to that in America. In an effort to assist the community we have been working with Hmong leaders to explore the potential of the peace-making circle process for dealing with community problems. In a circle held to inform the community about the process a woman spoke about her deep pain and humiliation at becoming a 'first wife'. Her husband had taken another wife and she was devastated. When the talking piece came around to the judge he spoke sternly about the illegality of having more than one wife in the US, invoking the legal authority of the justice system. After the circle was over several community members explained to the judge that the second marriage was a cultural marriage, not a legal marriage, and so there was no action that could be taken by the courts to assist this woman. It occurred to me in thinking about this dilemma that if the Hmong clan leaders collectively proclaimed polygamy as unacceptable in the community, it would probably disappear. Without force of law the clan leaders can establish standards which carry enormous authority. Where individuals may be able to get around a legal standard, a moral standard is much more difficult to circumvent.

This story demonstrates both the potential and the risks inherent in community-based moral forces. In the example above the moral authority of the leaders could serve the interests of women in the community. But huge questions arise. Who is deciding the moral standards? Are the interests of women and children present in the development of those standards?

The fact is that these standards already exist and already exert considerable influence in the Hmong community. And it is true that traditionally they are dominated by male Elders and often do not serve the interests of women and children. The Hmong community in Minnesota faces very severe problems with domestic violence and child abuse. Women and children have no forum in traditional Hmong culture to have their voices heard directly. They can take their problems to their own family but the story will then be taken by a brother or father to the clan leaders.

Guided by the values and framework of restorative justice we are working with the Hmong community using the peacemaking circle process to create respectful, reflective dialogue between men and women, young and old and various political factions of the community. The old men of the community are being heard in their pain at the loss of status and fear of losing their culture. The young people in the community are being heard in their frustration at the failure of their Elders to recognize that they live in a different world now – and that the old ways will not work. The women in the community are being heard in their desire for equal voice. Extensive community dialogue using restorative processes to share pain and express feelings is necessary for community members to learn how to listen to and hear one another before these processes are used for specific crimes.

Concerns of Family Violence Scholars and Advocates

From the earliest days in my position with the Minnesota Department of Corrections domestic violence and sexual assault advocates have raised difficult and important questions about the philosophy and implementation of restorative justice. Those concerns helped me understand ways that the good intentions of restorative justice could go seriously awry. They taught me to pay closer attention to language and they raised my awareness of the complexity of the issues and variations in meaning associated with certain terms. Those were often difficult conversations, but I am grateful for them. Likewise, I am grateful to the contributors to this volume who raise very difficult questions. Restorative justice is not fully formed. It is still in a process of exploration and development, and perhaps it always will be because it places high value on acknowledging and learning from mistakes. I share many of the concerns raised, though in some cases I do not share the conclusions drawn from those concerns.

There is great concern expressed that the conceptual framework of conflict resolution associated with restorative justice is inappropriate for family violence. I agree and, in fact, believe that the conflict resolution framework is not the core foundation of a restorative response to crime. There is some common ground with conflict resolution theory, but not full alignment. The early writing and thinking on restorative justice grew out of face-to-face meetings for non-violent offences, generally in situations where the parties did not know each other. It was a very individualistic approach to working through a singular incident, usually involving strangers, which drew heavily on contemporary Western thought around dispute resolution. Those early writings did not include considerations of community, the impact of both the event and the resolution on others, did not link individual events to larger social issues and typically envisioned a short-term intervention. The conceptualisation of restorative justice has gone through significant evolution from those original attempts to develop theory from actual experience. Kay Harris (1989) prompted a rethinking about community context and social justice issues when she challenged the focus on individual responsibility that ignored the structural harms of social and economic inequality. The influence of processes from non-Western cultures, particularly family group conferencing and circles, further reshaped the thinking about the deeper concepts reflected in the practices. The framework of healing, taught by First Nations people of Canada as the basis of the circle process, provides a conceptualisation that seems to more thoroughly reflect the aims and experiences of restorative justice processes.

In this framework a restorative response is one that seeks to promote healing of all harms associated with a particular situation. The healing framework immediately raises safety as the first concern. Victims cannot heal without safety. Nor can the community or the offender heal without safety. Consequently, safety becomes the highest priority and includes emotional safety as well as physical safety. The very first responsibility of a restorative response is to attend to the wounds of the victim and address safety issues. Addressing safety can include using the tools of the court such as protection orders. In some cases the safety required for victim and community healing may require secure custody for the offender. From a restorative justice perspective secure custody is not used to inflict pain on the offender, but to create a space for healing and requires respectful treatment of the offender and an ongoing relationship with the community.

Healing for those harmed also requires vindication, as discussed by Daly in this volume. Vindication requires acknowledgement to the victim that what happened was wrong and was not deserved. Vindication is not necessarily linked to what happens to the offender and does not require inflicting pain to prove that the behaviour was wrong. The story of a hate crime in Billings, Montana, provides a clear example of the community vindicating a victim family in a way that has nothing to do directly with the offender. When the home of a Jewish family in Billings was vandalized by rocks thrown through the window and swastikas painted on the house, a next door neighbour hung a Star of David in the window to express support for the family. Subsequently, the Billings newspaper printed a half-page Star of David and residents across the city hung the newspaper Star of David in their windows. These residents of Billings communicated to the victim and to the entire community that the hate crime was wrong and the family did not deserve such treatment. The offender was never caught, but the vandalism stopped. Vindication for victims does not depend on what we do to offenders and is not incompatible with compassion for offenders as suggested in Daly's chapter. We can and do in our daily lives practise both vindication for those hurt and compassion for those who caused harm. Good parenting requires that combination of skills. We have not given much attention to how to vindicate victims in ways that are not related to deliberate infliction of pain on offenders, but that does not mean that we cannot develop that capacity. Vindication for victims of family violence may take a different form than it does for victims of other crimes because of the ongoing nature of the harm and power differences present in family violence. Victims themselves are likely the best source of insight into ways to provide vindication that do not depend on what happens to offenders.

The healing framework does not suggest shared responsibility for the harm. Responsibility is clearly placed with offenders, but the healing framework directs the energy of next steps toward healing, assessing the wounds and addressing them, rather than putting energy into inflicting an equal amount of pain on the offender.

Causing harm to others is assumed to cause harm to the self as well, at a deep level of the spirit or integrity of self. As a result, the healing framework suggests a need for healing for those who cause harm as well as for victims and communities. Healing is neither easy, nor painless, but the pain involved in healing is constructive rather than destructive. In order to heal perpetrators must take responsibility for the harm they caused, which includes acknowledging the harm and recognizing that causing the harm was a choice. That is generally a painful process. Healing for perpetrators also requires making changes so that the harm will not be repeated. The pain and hard work inherent in taking responsibility and making internal changes is very difficult to undertake without strong support from others. Restorative practices emphasize the importance of supporters throughout the healing process.

The healing framework also recognizes that healing is not instantaneous. The healing path often is a long, difficult path. The doubts expressed by domestic violence advocates about changing behaviour through a short-term intervention are well grounded in experience. Restorative processes for domestic violence cannot simply replicate processes that work with other kinds of offences. They must be designed to address the specific healing needs related to the nature of domestic violence, which is generally chronic, deeply entrenched behaviour with many possible manifestations. In Minnesota a pilot project using peacemaking circles with domestic violence cases works with the participants for over a year on average and the work with victims and offenders is done separately for the most part. Domestic violence advocates participate in the circles for offenders and the facilitator of the circles is someone with personal experience as a victim of domestic violence. The project was initiated and designed by the local domestic violence agency. The peacemaking circle process does not replace other kinds of therapy such as batterers' programs or chemical dependency treatment but integrates the other interventions into an holistic approach to taking responsibility and making change.

The healing framework helps us to deal with the problem of apology raised by family violence experts. The term has a completely different connotation to people knowledgeable about the cycle of domestic violence than it has for other audiences. Apology may make sense as an important element of healing in other kinds of crimes. If we understand apology as a specific strategy sometimes appropriate for the purpose of healing, not as an end in itself, we can begin to differentiate the situations in which an apology might contribute to healing and the situations in which it might be an ongoing part of the harm. The purpose of apology is to demonstrate remorse and acceptance of responsibility. In cases of family violence demonstration of remorse and acceptance of responsibility remain important, but different strategies are needed to achieve that end in a meaningful way.

Early work on restorative justice emphasized reconciliation between parties involved in a crime, but reconciliation is not a presumed outcome of a healing framework. Healing does not require reconciliation in a particular relationship. Healing may involve some sort of closure and it requires regaining a sense of lost personal power, but not necessarily an ongoing friendly connection.

In an excellent and extensive discussion of mediation in this volume,

Ruth Busch identifies the risks of that model for victims of family violence both in civil settings and in the criminal justice setting. Her discussion makes it clear that mediation is unlikely to promote healing and carries risk of further harm, and thus would not be an appropriate intervention. Although victim–offender one on one meetings were the most common restorative practice ten years ago, that is no longer the case. Not only have other forms of face-to-face dialogue emerged, but from the healing perspective, many interventions can be used which are specific to the victim or offender but do not involve both. Victim services can support victim healing, but do not involve the offender. Healing circles are held in a domestic violence shelter in Minnesota for women living in the shelter, whether or not their case is even in the criminal justice system. Restorative community service can support offender healing but may not involve the victim. No particular restorative practice is appropriate for all cases, but the goal of healing is appropriate for all kinds of harms. The goal of healing does not assume an absolute state of being healed is possible, but defines the direction of efforts.

Fears are expressed that restorative approaches will delegate decisions to communities with no oversight. I believe that restorative justice requires a partnership of government systems and citizens or community organizations. Communities have some tools and resources not available to government systems that need to be brought to bear on family violence. For instance, neighbours can support a victim of domestic violence on a daily basis and can monitor safety plans in ways that the system cannot. Close associates of a perpetrator may influence his behaviour with disapproval more effectively than a judge. Government systems have different resources that must be engaged as well, including the capacity to require compliance with treatment plans or the payment of restitution if voluntary compliance is not forthcoming. It is the responsibility of government to ensure that the community process and norms honour the laws that embody the larger values of the society, such as fairness or non-violence. Restorative justice sets value limits around community processes. In a restorative framework communities are not free to do whatever the majority wants, but are expected to take into account the interests of all members, are expected to allow all voices to participate in decision-making and are to respect the dignity of all persons. Where communities are not able to act within those parameters the responsibility lies with government to protect those vulnerable to mistreatment by the community.

For the past five years restorative justice has grown rapidly in acceptance. Because of opposition by victims groups and the complexity of issues related to family violence, the application of restorative justice to family violence has been largely avoided. There are exceptions, but for the most part practitioners have kept family violence issues at arms' length. A period of learning with less complex cases has been useful and appropriate, but ultimately, failing to explore the possible applications to family violence is a disservice to victims of family violence whose options are limited and needs are not being met in the current system. The most recent developments intertwining domestic violence and child abuse make it urgent to find less adversarial approaches. Victims of domestic violence may find themselves charged with child abuse for failing to protect their children from exposure to domestic violence. Courage is required by both advocates for restorative justice and critics of restorative justice to search for responses to family violence that draw on what is being learned in the restorative justice movement, but do not oversimplify the issues or rush forward without the involvement of experienced family violence advocates.

Importance of Engaging Spiritual and Emotional Dimensions

This is a scholarly collection. The academic endeavour is led by analysis and debate, by mental effort and mental engagement. The criminal justice process is a process of mental and physical engagement. But creation of a non-violent world – a world in which we understand that harm to another is harm to ourselves, a wound to another is a wound to ourselves – is an effort of heart and spirit as much as an effort of mind. For me, in the end, the most compelling reasons for following a restorative vision are because it calls the heart and spirit to a higher level of performance. Over and over again in restorative processes, participants report behaving in a way – a good way – in which they had not expected to behave. Participants transcend their own sense of themselves and their capabilities, and in so doing create a new sense of how they can be in the world and how they can relate to one another differently.

Restorative justice is spiritual in the sense defined by the Dalai Lama (1999) in his book, *Ethics for the New Millennium*. He defines spirituality as, 'concerned with those qualities of the human spirit – such as love and compassion, patience, tolerance, forgiveness, contentment, a sense of responsibility, a sense of harmony – which bring happiness to both self and others.' (Dalai Lama, 1999: 22). He suggests that, 'spiritual practice according to this description involves, on the one hand, acting out of concern for others' well-being. On the other, it entails transforming ourselves so that we become more readily disposed to do so' (Dalai Lama, 1999: 23).

Those qualities the Dalai Lama ascribes to spirituality (love, compassion, patience, tolerance, forgiveness) are the qualities we want in families and other relationships. Restorative justice promotes, elicits and models those qualities.

The Dalai Lama goes on to discuss the importance of empathy in determining whether our actions enhance the well-being of others. He writes, 'if we are not able to connect with others to some extent, if we cannot at least imagine the potential impact of our actions on others, then we have no means to discriminate between right and wrong, between what is appropriate and what is not, between harming and non-harming' (Dalai Lama, 1999: 72–73). He also notes that if we enhance our capacity to feel the suffering of others then our tolerance for other people's pain will be reduced. Restorative justice places a similar emphasis on the importance of empathy and on strategies to increase empathy for the pain of victims, for community harms and for the struggles of offenders. Creating spaces that encourage empathy is a primary goal of restorative justice. Empathy is an essential characteristic of a healthy family.

Restorative justice asserts we cannot solve problems of violence and coercive force through greater use of coercive force (Pranis, 2001). We cannot solve problems of misuse of power primarily through the use of a different power. If we want families to operate on values of respect and genuine attention to the well-being of every family member, then we must model respect and genuine attention to the well-being of everyone even in the face of wrongdoing. We have to live the values we want others to honour.

Conclusion

The family violence movement has made enormous progress using the adversarial criminal justice system to raise awareness, clearly define family violence as wrong and unacceptable and to create a response to individual cases of violence. However, the limitations of the adversarial approach for making fundamental social change have become increasingly evident.

The vision of the family violence movement has always been a radical vision about restructuring the use of power in our society. I believe the challenge now faced by the family violence movement is whether it can move beyond using the tools of the patriarchy. Restorative justice provides a vision of a way to challenge the patriarchy without relying on the tools of the patriarchy itself. The vision of restorative justice is paradoxical to our usual sense of making social change. Restorative justice calls for radical change done in a loving way.

What is our vision of how family members should function with one another – especially when a family member is hurt or makes a mistake? Should not that same vision guide us in how we as a community function with one another when someone is hurt or makes a mistake? I do not believe that the practices of restorative justice yet have all the tools necessary to turn this vision into immediate reality, but I believe that the direction is good and powerful and that by using our hearts, spirits and minds we have the capacity to create the tools to achieve this vision.

3   Domestic Violence and Women's Safety: Feminist Challenges to Restorative Justice

Julie Stubbs

This chapter deals with domestic violence rather than other possible forms of family violence. It also proceeds from the position that domestic violence is different in many ways from other forms of crime. It takes as fundamental the need to provide safety to those who experience domestic violence, most commonly women and their children. An appeal to victim safety need not imply a punitive or exclusionary logic (see the debate between Scheingold, Olson and Pershing, Braithwaite and Pettit, and Daly in *Law and Society Review*, 1994). Restorative justice has made strong claims about providing better outcomes for victims than conventional criminal justice system practices and these claims are analysed with reference to empirical data concerning domestic violence. The chapter also examines the extent to which restorative justice practices mobilize resources for the protection of women and children – this is especially crucial at a time when resources are being withdrawn from the formal legal system and from the community.

The term restorative justice *practices* is used in this chapter to high-light the diversity among initiatives undertaken in the name of restorative justice. While some proponents of restorative justice prefer to locate their analyses at the more general level of the allegedly shared values that denote restorative justice, I argue for greater specificity in the analysis. Attention to the effects of specific practices offers the opportunity to contrast different models of restorative justice and to benefit from the findings of important empirical work undertaken in related domains such as mediation (Pavlich, 1996; Cobb, 1997) and peacemaking (Coker, this volume and 1999).

Part 1 raises questions about the competing conceptions that seem to underpin the debate about alternative forms of justice for domestic violence. Part 2 considers diversity among women with reference to their different experiences of violence, their different pathways to the legal system, and their particular subject positions. Part 3 examines the claims made about what restorative justice is said to offer victims. Are these so-called benefits likely to offer victims of domestic violence meaningful resources – economic, symbolic or otherwise – with which to secure their safety?

Part 1 Theorizing Domestic Violence

In analysing alternative models of intervention for domestic violence it is apparent that three key dimensions on which the literature concerning restorative justice, victimology and domestic violence differ are: the theoretical underpinnings of domestic violence; conceptions of agency; and the relationship of alternative interventions to the formal legal system.

Incident-based or control-based?

Much of the literature on restorative justice seems to assume a discrete incident between a victim(s) and offender(s) who are unknown to each other, or are not well known to each other. This is evident in claims that restorative justice offers benefits such as: to allow the victim to meet the offender and to learn that they were not specifically targeted but were chosen more randomly; that the consequences of the violence were unintended or not fully appreciated by the offender; that the offence is not likely to repeated (Hudson & Galaway, 1996). Such assumptions typically are not valid in domestic violence cases and may need to be challenged for other forms of victimization (Crawford, 2000b: 286–87). Incident-based theoretical approaches to domestic violence which focus narrowly on physical harm and on discrete episodes of violence foster an individualistic analysis of violence (see Pavlich, 1996 on individualizing discourses), may ignore the social context of domestic violence and may exacerbate the social entrapment of women (Ptacek 1999; Richie, 1996).

Domestic violence is typically not an isolated event but arises through strategies that attempt to implement gender ideologies (Ptacek, 1999). Thus, a control-based theoretical analysis of domestic violence is preferable because it has the capacity to recognize a number of features of domestic violence such as that: domestic violence includes a range of behaviours and coercive tactics not all of which are immediately discernible to others; it is often repetitive, meaningful and strategic, reflecting deeply held attitudes and beliefs rather than an isolated incident; and there are social and cultural dimensions that give meaning to the violence, that may authorize or sustain gender-based violence, and may constrain women's options in dealing with violence (Ptacek, 1999: 9; Dobash & Dobash, 1979, 1992).

Victim versus agent: a false dichotomy

Literature concerning domestic violence and criminal victimization more generally commonly portrays a dichotomous construction of victim and agency. Within this literature women are constructed as either on the one hand too victimized to exercise choices or on the other hand as active agents who are empowered through choice. There has been relatively little attention to this issue in the restorative justice literature, much of which simply assumes that victims are well able to assert their own interests in restorative processes. Moreover some authors have made claims about the allegedly positive value of restorative justice in overcoming power differentials between the parties in contradistinction to mediation practices[1] which are seen as more susceptible to inequitable outcomes (Braithwaite & Pettit, 1994). These claims warrant much greater scrutiny.

The dichotomous construction of victim and agent is conceptually limited and at odds with empirical research. There are numerous studies that demonstrate women's resilience, courage and recourse to multiple strategies to deal with domestic violence (Bowker, 1983; Schneider, 1992; Mahoney, 1994; Young et al, 2000; Gondolf & Fisher, 1988; Keys Young, 1998). Dobash and Dobash discuss 'the effects of men's violence on women's negotiations of everyday life', a useful phrase that transcends the victim/agent dichotomy and recognizes women's active role in resisting violence but nonetheless emphasizes that men's violence can effectively limit women's choices in crucial ways (as cited by Ptacek, 1999: x). Women may face choices between negative alternatives (Davies et al, 1998). For some, remaining silent about abuse and/or accommodation to their abusers may be important survival strategies.

A second limited conception of women's agency is evident in the construction of women as 'atomistic, mobile individual[s]' rather than as highly interconnected to others, particularly to children (Mahoney, 1994: 74; Maguigan, 1991; Coker, 1999). Women who seek legal assistance to deal with domestic violence are commonly mothers (Ptacek, 1999; see also Davies et al, 1998) and often do so when the children become targets of violence or the mothers fear the effects of the violence upon the children. Batterers may use children as a means to manipulate or intimidate their partners or former partners: '[o]ne of the most common threats made by batterers is to take the children away from their mother, whether physically by snatching the children or by winning a custody fight' (Davies et al, 1998: 33). Women's strategies to deal with domestic violence frequently are constrained by concerns about their children (Lewis et al, 2000) and where women's interests do not coincide with those of their children they face difficult choices.

A more complex conception of agency, together with an understanding of the control-based nature of domestic violence, should caution against easy assumptions that women's capacity to exercise choice is unconstrained. This more complex view of women's agency has important implications for the development of domestic violence programs. Whether in the formal justice system, or in informal processes, women who have been the target of domestic violence need information, services and support to ensure that their decisions are as freely chosen as possible within the available constraints. Restorative justice scholars are yet to consider how to accommodate the relational agency of women with children.

Engagement with the formal legal system

The literature debating the role of the legal system in response to domestic violence ranges the full gamut from the uncritical appeal to more law and more enforcement whatever the consequences, to the absolute rejection of criminal justice intervention on the basis that it empowers the state but not women (Snider, 1998; 1994; see also Mills, 1999). Proponents of restorative justice also differ in how they would see restorative justice deployed vis-à-vis the formal legal system (Hudson & Galaway, 1996).

Much of the restorative justice literature offers a damning critique of the formal legal system and promotes restorative justice as an alternative (Walgrave, 2000a). By contrast Braithwaite and Daly (1994) have proposed that restorative justice, in the form of community conferencing, should be offered at an intermediate stage in a hierarchy of responses with other criminal justice processes and sanctions being invoked where conferencing fails. Others promote restorative justice as a tool through which to transform the criminal justice system (Hudson & Galaway, 1996). Joan Pennell and Gale Burford's model (this volume) suggests a process intersecting with formal legal intervention.

Some restorative justice scholars assume that the victim's involvement in a restorative justice process is a singular event, capable of being conducted independently of the formal legal system. However, domestic

violence victims are often enmeshed in a complex range of legal interventions, especially where child contact and residence, divorce and/or
the division of property are in dispute. Rather than offering an alternative to the formal legal system as some restorative justice scholars
suggest, a restorative justice intervention may add an additional layer to
this complex picture.

Advocates of alternative legal interventions that privilege informal
over formal responses to violence, or the converse, sometimes suffer
from singular constructions of 'the state' or 'the criminal justice system',
an idealized notion of restorative justice or a too rigid acceptance of a
formal/informal dichotomy. Yet there are a number of domestic violence
models in practice that deploy community-based programs in conjunction with the criminal justice system in interesting and innovative ways
that challenge such depictions and transcend dichotomous constructs
(for instance see Busch & Robertson, 1994). Such initiatives are deserving of more serious consideration, and demonstrate the need for careful
evaluation of specific initiatives and a nuanced approach to conceptualization beyond the formal/informal dichotomy.

Crawford has argued that 'much of the restorative justice literature
and current policy ... tend to obfuscate the role of the state and third
parties, replacing these with a particularly ambiguous appeal to "community" ordering and individual choice' (2000a: 17; see also Walgrave,
2000a). The capacity of informal or community based processes may
often be determined by resources provided by government and the
back-up and authority of criminal justice agencies (O'Malley, 1997; see
Braithwaite & Daly's pyramid of enforcement, 1994). Herman, a
victims advocate, has argued that only the state has the authority and
the capacity to marshal the necessary resources to repair the harm done
to victims: 'in a commendable effort to humanize the justice system and
keep the state in the background, [we] will create another system
without adequate resources for victims' (Herman, 1999: 10). The need
to mobilize resources to provide safety for victims is crucial and is
discussed further below.

There is good reason to be critical of criminal justice practices especially because of their impact on the most marginalized groups in our
societies (Ruttenberg, 1994; Snider, 1994, 1998; Fedders, 1997;
Hudson, 1998). However, the wholesale rejection of the criminal justice
system also may limit women's options and their safety. In contrast to
over-generalized claims made about the failures of the formal legal system, others have documented how victims, especially in cases involving
interpersonal violence, may deploy various combinations of recourse to
criminal justice and/or bargaining with the offender 'in accordance with
their personal strategy independent of any logic of punishment'

(Zauberman, 2000: 45; see also Lewis et al, 2000; Ford, 1991). Legal interventions may offer (some) women resources to deal with the violence (see Stubbs & Powell, 1989; Trimboli & Bonney, 1997; Young et al, 2000; Chaudhuri & Daly, 1992):

By creating a legal crisis, these women challenged the coercive control that men were exercising over them. Most women felt supported by the process and left the court with new resources that placed them in a better negotiating position with their partners or former partners. (Ptacek, 1999: 166)

Ptacek also found that '... the leverage they were able to gain through the threat of criminal sanctions was seen as beneficial; for many women standing up for their own rights offered its own rewards' (1999: 167; see also Merry, 1995).

Part 2 – Women's Diverse Experiences

It is trite to say that women's experiences of violence vary and that different women have different needs and expectations of the legal process. Yet policy-makers face the dilemma of how to develop policies and programs that are responsive to difference. Victims of domestic violence come to be enmeshed in the criminal justice system in different ways, willingly or otherwise. Some are marked as offenders, perhaps because they have fought back against a violent partner, or too often due to the excesses of mandatory arrest policies that may result in action against both parties. For many women involvement with the criminal justice system commences at a time of crisis. They may seek immediate police protection from injury but have little or no conception about any consequent legal proceedings. Others may make strategic choices about seeking longer-term protection through intervention orders or other legal interventions. Women also may need or want different forms of intervention at different points in time as their circumstances change. As Lewis et al argue, it may be futile to consider interventions in isolation from the context in which women find themselves (2000: 202).

Domestic violence, race, ethnicity and racism

The damaging impact of the criminal justice system on minorities offers a significant challenge to the development of domestic violence policy (Fedders, 1997; Blagg, this volume). Racist criminal justice practices have been expressed in various forms including the over-policing of minority men but also through the failure to protect minority women and children (Aboriginal and Torres Strait Islander Women's Task Force on Violence, 2000; McGillivray & Comaskey, 1999). Evidence indicates that Black women in the US are more likely to report domestic violence to the police than are other groups (Bachman & Coker, 1995; Hutchinson & Hirschel, 1998). We cannot conclude that this reflects a positive choice for criminal justice intervention rather than a lack of other alternatives. However, we need to be cautious in assuming that minority groups do not wish to use the criminal justice system in domestic violence matters.

As in other areas of feminist scholarship, research and practice concerning violence against women have been subject to criticism for failing to attend to differences among and between women (Crenshaw, 1991). Racism constitutes a significant obstacle for women seeking to deal with domestic violence and has shaped our capacity to talk about the issue (Ptacek, 1999: 19). A gendered analysis of violence which is inattentive to diversity can obscure important differences in the vulnerability of different social groups to domestic violence and in their recourse to deal with or escape violence (Ptacek, 1999; Stubbs & Tolmie, 1995). Suggesting that different social groups may experience differential levels of vulnerability to domestic violence too easily can be put to racist uses (Fontes, 1997; see also Daly & Stephens, 1995). As Sherene Razack has written:

Culture talk is clearly a double-edged sword. It packages difference as inferiority and obscures gender-based domination within communities, yet cultural considerations are important for contextualizing oppressed groups' claims for justice, for improving their access to services, and for requiring dominant groups to examine the invisible cultural advantages they enjoy. (1994: 896)

We have a responsibility to ensure that law and policy recognize and respond to the different needs and interests of women in different social locations. Sadly, in Australia the level of domestic violence experienced by Aboriginal women is extremely high (Greer, 1994; Bolger, 1991; Strang, 1992; Aboriginal and Torres Strait Islander Women's Task Force on Violence, 2000). Here I make no claims to speak on behalf of Indigenous women – I have no such authority. However, there is an urgent need to acknowledge such issues and to listen to Indigenous women in order to craft responses that are culturally appropriate and effective in offering Indigenous women, children and men safety, security and autonomy (see Behrendt; Blagg, Kelly; this volume).

Restorative justice programs have been promoted as being especially responsive to Indigenous communities, although Blagg (1997), Tauri

(1999) and Cunneen (1997) have demonstrated the problems of approaches that have used singular notions of indigeneity, and have failed to genuinely consult Indigenous peoples. Restorative or community based practices used in response to violence against women in Indigenous communities have produced mixed outcomes. Strong claims have been made about sentencing circles, healing initiatives or conferencing offering benefits to Indigenous communities but these accounts also have been challenged for relying on limited sources, and especially the interpretations offered by white, male commentators. For instance, Razack (1994, 1998) has argued that high rates of violence have meant that Indigenous communities in Canada have not been safe places for women and children but outside those communities women also face the violence of racism. Moreover, community-based initiatives often have placed the development and delivery of programs into the hands of men, some of whom are themselves abusers who have continued their physical and sexual abuse (see also Griffiths & Hamilton, 1996; Nahanee 1992; McGillivray & Comaskey 1999; Nightingale, 1994; Brooks, no date).

Here an intersectional framework which acknowledges the multiple and indivisible operation of race, class and gender may assist (Crenshaw, 1991; Daly & Stephens, 1995; Daly & Maher, 1998). In the absence of such an analysis, an appeal to community-based practices may fail to examine how cultural practices work to sustain the power differences between groups. They may privilege culture over gender (Razack, 1994, 1998). Without recognition of the intersection of race, class and gender too often Indigenous women have been left with the invidious choice between politics and practices which represent their race but ignore their gender or the converse. A number of Aboriginal and Inuit women's organizations throughout Canada have questioned the capacity of local or community-based initiatives to protect their physical integrity and have lobbied to retain the external criminal justice system to respond to physical and sexual abuse (Griffiths & Hamilton, 1996; McGillivray & Comaskey, 1999).[2]

Hollow Water and Canim Lake are two Canadian Indigenous communities said to have had success in challenging sexual and physical violence against women and children through restorative practices. However, in other Canadian communities victims' safety has been compromised. Griffiths and Hamilton note the failure of a program on South Island as arising, in part, from the following weaknesses: insufficient community consultation; lack of credibility of key participants; failure to address specific needs of the communities; political unrest in the communities; family feuds within communities; failure to meet the specific needs of victims and offenders; and, an inability to consider that not all community residents shared the same cultural values (1996: 186). Even in those models lauded as most successful, a role has been maintained for outside criminal justice agencies to deal with serious offenders (Griffiths & Hamilton, 1996; Warhaft et al, 1999). Restorative justice processes might offer great promise, but they do not in them-selves guarantee victim safety or just outcomes. The successful models suggest that the inherent qualities of the communities are fundamental to positive outcomes. Dealing with physical and sexual violence may challenge community solidarity and risk further racism. Just as in the non-Indigenous community, not all communities have the interest, the skills or the resources to take on such matters. Poorly funded initiatives based on volunteer work by community members are unlikely to be effective or sustainable over time (The Aboriginal and Torres Strait Islander Women's Task Force on Violence, 2000). In the absence of infrastructure and resources to secure the safety of women and children, well-intentioned programs that impose restorative justice on Indigenous communities may be counter-productive and may undermine the capacity for self-governance by communities.

Part 3 – Empirical Findings Concerning Domestic Violence and Challenges to Restorative Justice

Women who seek legal intervention following domestic violence fre-quently do so after long periods of abuse, when the abuse is becoming more serious and affecting the children, or as a last resort when other efforts to stop the abuse have failed, saying 'enough is enough' (Harrell & Smith, 1996; Keilitz et al, 1998: 47). Australian studies of domestic violence have found that women who sought legal protection generally had experienced more severe violence than women who did not seek such intervention. For instance, Young, Byles and Dobson (2000) found that as compared to other women victims of domestic violence, women who sought legal protection were more likely to: have experienced more serious levels of violence; be injured; have children; be in a de facto relationship; and, have a partner who had been in trouble with the police before and/or had been violent in other contexts (see also Coumarelos & Allen, 1998, 1999).

What are the alleged benefits of restorative justice for victims?

Within the restorative justice literature there is a strong emphasis on the alleged benefits for victims of having the opportunity to participate in an informal process that gives them the chance to speak, to receive an apology and to gain reparation (Hudson & Galaway, 1996; Strang, 1999). Hudson (1998) has emphasized the capacity of restorative justice to deliver both expressive and instrumental functions of punishment (see also Daly, this volume). To what extent are domestic violence victims' concerns and interests coincident with the claims made about the benefits of restorative justice for victims of crime?

Given the characteristics of domestic violence noted above it is not surprising that research findings indicate that women's primary concerns in pursuing legal intervention are protection for themselves and their children, and deterrence of and/or rehabilitation for their (ex)partners. Punishment is typically a lesser concern (Lewis et al, 2000). Several studies also have found that some women express 'a desire for external validation, a mechanism to communicate loudly and clearly that they were serious, and a public record of the abuse and their effort to stop it. All these goals contribute to their feeling of power in the relationship' (Davies et al (1998: 77) citing Fisher & Rose, 1995; see also Erez & Belknap, 1998; Ptacek, 1999). The desire for external validation[3] has been found to be linked to women's sense of justice (Ptacek, 1999: 157) and thus, for some women, restorative justice may be seen to be offering a form of second class justice, particularly if gendered violence is seen as being re-privatized and/or treated differently from other offences (Coker, 1999; Hudson, 1998).

Thus, while the restorative justice literature emphasizes participation, apology and reparation, victims of domestic violence have emphasized safety and external validation of their attempts to stop the abuse, together with deterrence and rehabilitation, over other possible outcomes. These apparent differences are worthy of much more research. However, they may suggest differing underlying understandings of domestic violence. For instance, an incident-based analysis of victimization may be implicit in the focus of restorative justice on apology and reparation. Arguably such a focus implies a *discrete, past* event. However, for victims of domestic violence who have experienced repeated violence, their interests lie in securing their safety against the threat of *ongoing* violence.

Perhaps the weakest part of the restorative justice literature concerns outcomes.[4] This may be because restorative justice has developed mainly in the juvenile justice domain where the young offender typically agrees to undertake a discrete task(s) and compliance with the task(s) results in the closure of the case file at the earliest possible time. Such an approach will be inappropriate in many cases of domestic violence and in any event may do little to enhance the safety of the victim. Outcome plans for domestic violence may require a significant commitment of resources over time in order to respond to a victim's concerns. For instance, Hudson (1998) has argued that for community disapproval to be effective and to provide protection, it needs to be backed by extensive resources including programs for offenders, holding facilities and recourse to injunctions, curfews, and strong sanctions. Can the 'community of care' assembled for the restorative process sustain such demands? Who will monitor the outcome? Over what period?

Restorative justice processes are said to engage the community in responding to the offending behaviour (Presser & Gaarder, 2000). However, this appeal to community offers little real guidance as to mechanisms for accountability. As Crawford has argued:

> ... joint and negotiated decisions, as the outcomes of restorative processes, tie the parties into 'corporate' decisions, but often fail to identify lines of responsibility thereafter and how these should be monitored, such that it becomes difficult to know who is accountable to whom, and for what. (Crawford, 2000a: 17)

The rhetoric of the state stealing crime from the parties/community

While this often-repeated claim, typically attributed to Nils Christie, has been an important rhetorical device for the victims movement and for informal justice more generally, it is inaccurate in its account of domestic violence. It denies the history of feminist activism that challenged the failure of the criminal justice system to respond to women's calls for assistance in domestic violence matters. Rather than stealing the conflict, the criminal justice system had long ignored women's calls for protection. While we have good reason to be concerned about criminal justice practices, and especially mandatory arrest policies, we should not overlook the fact that many women actively seek legal intervention.

Communities typically know about domestic violence long before a matter is reported to authorities. Some domestic violence matters are successfully resolved within the informal domain (Bowker, 1983) but other cases are brought to the criminal justice system precisely because personal or community-based strategies have failed (Lewis et al, 2000). In their study of 6,000 women who entered shelters, Gondolf and Fisher (1988) found that on average the women had tried five different types of help seeking (cited by Davies et al, 1998: 75). Many women seek legal intervention as a means of mobilizing additional resources. These resources may be symbolic, such as in denunciation of violence and the legitimation of victim claims to non-violence by judicial authority, or they might be material. For instance, evidence indicates that police are more likely to act to protect women from violence where a court order is already in place.

Liz Kelly found that the support offered to victims of domestic violence by informal networks was important but typically provided temporary respite only, seldom brought a resolution to the problem of violence and where the women's supporters also became targets of violence, the problems were often compounded (1996: 77). The community is not necessarily well educated about domestic abuse (Kelly, 1996: 80). Family and friends may lack the capacity to offer assistance, or at times may collude with the violence (Keys Young, 1998). Denial, family solidarity and/or divided loyalties also may intrude (Coker, 1999). In some communities, such as those that place great emphasis on the privacy of the family, there may be powerful disincentives for community members to be seen to assist women and children who experience domestic violence.

The community – both source of the problem and the solution?

Commentators have noted confusion in the appeal to community within some of the restorative justice literature. Pavlich (1998) has argued with respect to mediation, that a 'dubious formulation of community' is often deployed which is conflict-free, spontaneous and informal, and tapped for various and often contradictory political purposes (see also Cohen, 1985; Hudson, 1998). As Crawford argues 'if "community" is a free-floating social identity, internally ascribed and easily escaped ... it fails to accord to "community" any significant structural or institutional characteristics around which the suasive capacity of communities is constructed and maintained' (2000b: 301). In addition, 'community' is represented in a contradictory light as having the capacity to offer a solution to crime in the present, but yet also a future outcome to be achieved through restorative justice practices (Crawford, 2000a: 6). Further, the restorative justice literature fails to give due regard to the community as having a role in the creation of crime (Coker, 1999; Crawford, 1997, 2000b).

As noted above, an adequate theorization of domestic violence must recognize the social origins of gender and race based domination. In addition, Liz Kelly (1996) cautions against a conceptualization of community that appeals to an ideal type that stresses consensus, shared history and values and fails to see the power relations, tensions, contradictions, conflicts and alliances. As she argues '[r]elationships of dominance and subordination are present in families and kinship networks, in localities and institutions, making the achievement of community much more complex than previously envisaged' (Kelly, 1996: 72).

This is important for a number of reasons. First, the appeal to the involvement of the community in restorative justice processes offers no certainty concerning the values that will prevail in any particular restorative practice. This may be so particularly in models where no clear guiding theoretical commitments are evident (by contrast see republican criminology with its guiding principle of dominion, Braithwaite & Pettit, 1994). The requirement of a plea of guilty, a non-neutral facilitator,[5] and the inclusion of victim supporters as utilized in *some* conferencing models offer the potential to support victim's interests, but the outcome cannot be pre-determined. We cannot assume that the group assembled for the conference has shared values or are knowledgeable about domestic violence (Hooper & Busch, 1996). The tensions, contradictions, conflicts and alliances identified by Kelly may be played out in any number of ways. As Kelly (1996) also notes, within the broader community the perpetrator often enjoys higher status than the victim, and this may have an impact on her credibility, the legitimacy accorded her claims and her capacity to access community resources. Finally, it has been recognized that:

Making amends and restoring troubled relations in an unequal society may mean restoring unequal relations and hence reaffirming inequality. If restorative justice is to be an element within a much wider policy concerned with constructing the conditions under which civility and mutuality breed, then it is limited by its reactive nature ... its reactive essence, in responding to acts of victimization, confines its potential as a transformative ideology. (Crawford, 2000a: 16; see also Dobash & Dobash, 1992)

What resources can the community generate?

Concerns have been raised that a call for more involvement of the community is likely to rely on informal support from other women. Bea Campbell (1993) has documented the manner in which the withdrawal of social capital from the former industrial cities of northern England has resulted in women in those communities carrying huge burdens in trying to maintain community networks through their volunteer labour. In Australian Aboriginal communities, it is common for women Elders to 'work relentlessly' to sustain their communities in a volunteer capacity with little support. In the absence of their services the prospects for some communities are grim (Aboriginal and Torres Strait Islander Task Force on Violence, 2000). Thus, sheeting responsibility back to communities could be a gendered form of privatization (Kelly, 1996). Community involvement must be more than a euphemism for the unpaid work of women.

According to Crawford '[t]he weakness of community action is that it lacks authoritative means to mobilize resources above and beyond that which can be procured on a voluntary basis' (1997: 200). Communities are likely to differ in their capacities to offer resources to victims and offenders. The handing of crime control to communities at the same time as the withdrawal of state resources (Crawford, 1997: 275–76), or the absence of significant resources to begin with, is likely to exacerbate social disadvantage. As Garland (1996) argues, '[a]ctivating communities, families and individuals, is made much less likely if these have been economically undermined and socially excluded' (1996: 463). This issue has general relevance but also may be especially significant in many Indigenous communities with inadequate resourcing to allow genuine community control. LaPrairie has labelled this 'responsibilisation without resources' (1999: 150). As Herman has warned, 'if victims' needs are addressed only with the inherently limited resources of offenders and communities, restorative justice will ultimately be unsatisfying for victims' (1999: 7–8).

One model of restorative justice that may answer these criticisms is Joan Pennell's feminist praxis (this volume), which uses conferencing explicitly to mobilize resources. This model has a strong commitment to investing resources at the outset, careful planning, consultation and selection of conference participants. It is likely to be very resource intensive and contrasts sharply with the much leaner and more standardized approaches that have been adopted in many of the juvenile justice conferencing models. The fact that Pennell's model is exceptional reinforces the need for careful scrutiny of the various practices that appear under the umbrella of restorative justice.

What are the victim's legitimate expectations and responsibilities in restorative justice?

Evaluation studies of restorative justice commonly include a measure of victim satisfaction with process. However, little attention has been given to questions about the responsibilities of victims and their legitimate expectations in restorative justice. Might victims feel pressured or obliged to participate in restorative justice? Are they given adequate information on which to base informed consent to participate? What legitimate expectations might they have about the process and its aftermath? The salience of such factors is likely to be magnified in domestic violence matters. For domestic violence victims these issues need to be examined from a perspective that privileges victim safety.

Shapland (2000) has argued that victims are likely to face additional responsibilities in restorative justice as compared with the criminal justice process. The chance to actively participate in the process is often promoted as a benefit of restorative justice. Yet being required to face the offender in an informal setting and participate in determining the outcome of his case may offer little appeal to a domestic violence victim and may entail real risks. Domestic violence advocates have long recognized the potential burdens and risks for victims of being held responsible for decisions to prosecute. Some restorative justice scholars are beginning to recognize potential risks to victims in restorative practices (Bazemore & Umbreit, 2001). The related question of victim responsibility to accept an apology or offer forgiveness is examined further below.

Moralizing discourses and the meanings of victim and offender

The content of the terms 'victim' and 'offender' is not morally neutral – both are imbued with meanings drawn from the wider culture and may reflect incomplete knowledge, stereotypes or prejudice. Victims of crime are often judged to be deserving or undeserving, appropriate or inappropriate, innocent or complicit (Bumiller, 1990; Stanko, 1999; Madriz, 1997). Victims of domestic violence or sexual abuse are commonly subjected to moralizing judgements based in competing conceptions of gender appropriate behaviour. Feminist critical race scholars remind us too that such judgements are often racialized such that while White, middle-class women are frequently presumed to be 'good women' provided they don't depart from their prescribed role, 'black women have never had the benefit of that presumption' (Ammons, 1995: 1041–42; see also Crenshaw, 1991). As noted above, in the absence of an analysis of the social bases of gender and race based hierarchies, women who depart from idealized notions of victim status (and/or female gender roles) may be at risk in restorative justice processes of being denied legitimacy or judged as complicit in their own victimization. This risk is likely to be greatest where the prevailing understanding of domestic violence is incident-based.

Might restorative justice compromise victim safety?

Work on safety planning for battered women has identified a range of risks that battered women face generated by the batterer and through

life circumstances. Leaving the relationship does not necessarily alleviate these risks (Davies et al, 1998). We need to ask whether restorative
justice practices offer protections from partner and life generated risks
and secondly, whether they may generate additional risks for battered
women.

Presser and Lowenkamp argue that victim–offender dialogue 'entails
a kind of risk for victims that routine criminal proceedings do not'
(1999: 336). A close encounter with the offender and the offender's supporters may hold little appeal for victims of domestic violence and may
signal an opportunity for further abuse, especially emotional abuse. The
risk of trauma may be compounded when victims participate from a
sense of obligation or guilt. Offenders may exercise considerable control
over victims who are intimates and victims often have learned to accommodate to the interests of the offender as a survival strategy, or through
fear of further violence (Hooper & Busch, 1996). The exchanges that
occur between victim and offender in restorative justice take place
under real constraints and may derive their meaning, which may not be
obvious to others, from past events. Other risks of restorative processes
include: a focus on consensus decision-making may dilute concerns
about victim interest; the absence of a genuine capacity for ongoing
community support of the victim and for effective surveillance and
social control of the offender; unwarranted assumptions that the process
is likely to induce behaviour change in the offender; the potential for
popular misconceptions of domestic violence to prevail, for instance the
resort to family dysfunction models, or individualizing discourses; and
the focus on restoration may offer pressure for the couple to reconcile
(Hooper & Busch, 1996).

In recognition of such risks, guidelines precluding direct victim–
offender dialogue have been introduced in mediation, family therapy
and counseling because of the fear of further abuse and victim blaming.
For instance, in 20 US states, standards and guidelines for batterer
intervention expressly prohibit joint couple counselling (Healey &
Smith, 1998). Tolman (1996) warns that if restorative justice were to be
pursued numerous safeguards for battered women would be necessary
and he cautions that 'face-to-face contact must not be required' and
'[s]uch proceedings must not be used to exchange dropping charges or
orders of protection in return for restitution'(1996: 182).

Offender screening to exclude those who are dangerous has been
advocated as one means of reducing the risk of direct exchanges
between victim and offender. While many restorative justice programs
include offender screening, usually this does not focus on victim safety
but on offence seriousness and willingness of the offender to participate.
Presser and Lowenkamp (1999) have characterized offender-screening

criteria used in restorative justice encounters as 'neither victim-oriented, research-driven, nor consistently applied' (1999: 335; see also Brown, 1999 and Umbreit, 1996: 7 as cited by Presser & Lowenkamp). Moreover, effective screening may be difficult to achieve since clinical assessments and statistical predictions of violence are not very accurate (Saunders, 1995) and the prediction of intimate homicide is even more imprecise (Campbell, 1995).

These concerns raise important practical and ethical questions for restorative justice practitioners. What mechanisms can be used to offer safety to victims before, during and after the restorative process? What are their ethical obligations with respect to the victim? Do they have an obligation to warn victims of potential risks and is a warning sufficient (Saunders, 1995; see also Hart, 1988)? This issue of ethics is returned to below.

Several researchers have highlighted indirect risks in restorative justice practices that use victims in the service of other ends. For instance, there has been criticism of UK mediation reparation schemes being in the service of offenders not victims (Crawford, 2000a) and Moore and McDonald have acknowledged that in conferencing many victims have been 'used' in seeking a better outcome for young offenders (1995: 149).

The appeal to apology (and forgiveness)

The restorative justice literature invests great significance in an apology. Some restorative justice scholars see the giving and accepting of an apology as the hallmarks of restorative justice (Moore, 1995; see also Braithwaite & Daly, 1994: 205). While Pavlich has noted with concern that the regulatory environment of mediation exercises subtle pressure to forgive (Pavlich, 1996), some scholars argue that within restorative justice victims have a *responsibility* 'to accept the expressions of remorse made by the offender and to express a willingness to forgive' (Hudson & Galaway 1996: 2). This assumes a certain level of trust between the parties and that an apology will be offered genuinely and accepted in good faith. Yet often there is little basis for trust since domestic violence is commonly characterized by repeated offending and apology. Domestic violence perpetrators often are adept at using apology to manipulate their partners and others (Stubbs, 1995, 1997; Coker 1999: 86). This over-emphasis on the value of the offender apology has been labelled 'the cheap justice problem' (Coker, 1999: 15).

The focus on apology and its acceptance implies a validity and veracity in the speech acts of, and a shared meaning between, the participants. Yet research indicates that men and women talk about violence very differently. For instance Dobash et al (1998)[6] found significant discordance between men's and women's reports of domestic violence. Men tended to minimize the violence, blame the victim, and under-reported the following: serious violence; the number of violent acts; sexual violence; the infliction of injuries on their partner; and of controlling behaviour generally. The authors were careful not to assume simply that the women's accounts were accurate, but pointed to the importance of examining the idea that 'men and women are likely to interpret their victimization and perpetration of violence against intimates in very different ways' (p. 407). The authors challenged the notion that men's accounts of their own violence can be used uncritically.

The tendency for men to rationalize and trivialize their own violence has been found in a number of studies. According to Dobash and Dobash, the dominant view from those working with perpetrators of domestic violence is that 'offenders are deemed to be highly self-oriented, lack empathy and frequently deny responsibility, minimize the harm done and deflect blame onto others, particularly women' (Dobash & Dobash 1999a: 4). Based on his own experience working with male batterers, Ptacek has reached a similar conclusion: '[men tend to] minimize or deny the intentionality of their violence ... individuals often shift back and forth between denying responsibility for their violent assaults and arguing that women deserved it' (1999: 71).

Some proponents of restorative justice have placed great faith in social movement politics to ensure progressive outcomes in restorative processes (Braithwaite & Daly, 1994; Hudson, 1998). It has been suggested that pro-feminist and anti-racist groups should be participants in restorative processes in order to bolster victim narratives and to challenge those who do not take responsibility for their offending. However, in many locations such social movements are under threat through conservative government policy and funding cuts. In Australia we are currently witnessing the ascendancy of 'fathers' rights' groups in shaping law, policy and funding decisions and women's organizations are becoming increasingly marginal. Massive cuts to legal aid have pushed many women into informal processes and some women into making poorly framed and unworkable agreements around domestic violence and children, which are often breached (Rhoades et al, 1999). The capacity for progressive social movements to act as guarantors of safe outcomes in restorative justice processes is limited both by their diminishing resources and by the threats to their legitimacy offered through conservative government rhetoric.

Those engaged in restorative justice practices face an ethical dilemma. Does encouraging a battered woman to accept an apology and any reassurances about her future safety offer false hopes and act to compromise future safety? As Tolman has argued false hopes for victims fostered by apology may actually hamper victims' attempts to leave or take other action to deal with the violence (1996: 183). A number of studies have demonstrated the impact of apology on battered women's decision-making. For instance, Pagelow (1981) found that 73 percent of a shelter sample returned to their partner because he had apologized and they hoped he would change (see also Barnett & LaViolette, 1993; Okun, 1986; Gondolf & Fisher, 1988, as cited by Davies et al (1998: 76). Welfare and Miller caution that from a therapeutic perspective there are risks for abuse survivors in privileging an apology: 'An ill-timed, perpetrator-led apology or "face-up" session is yet another insulting and potentially damaging process for the survivor, where yet again she is asked to put his demands first and to deny the complexity of her own experience' (1999: 6).

Conclusion

Scepticism about the alleged benefits of restorative justice for domestic (or family) violence victims should not be dismissed as arising from a feminist 'myopia of police-courts-corrections' (Braithwaite, 2000b). For the most part the restorative justice literature has failed to engage meaningfully with the issue of domestic violence. Critical scrutiny of the claims made on behalf of restorative justice suggests that they rely, at least in part, on assumptions about victimization that are at odds with empirical findings concerning domestic violence, and perhaps other forms of victimization. Participation, apology and reparation have been promoted as benefits of restorative justice practices for victims, without due regard for the potential risks of participation and the knowledge that apology is a common tactic in abusive relationships. Without clear norms to guide restorative justice practices there is a real risk that common misconceptions about domestic violence will prevail. Individualistic conceptions of domestic violence or constructions of such violence as 'relationship problems' may compromise victim safety.

The interests of victims of domestic violence will be served best by finding mechanisms that offer enhanced safety and security. However, serious questions remain about accountability for the decisions reached in restorative justice practices and about the capacity for such practices to generate resources to assist victims of domestic violence. It should not be assumed that 'communities' have the capacity or the collective will to offer tangible support to victims or to exercise surveillance and control over offenders. Communities, however defined, will differ in their capacity to respond to the demands of restorative justice. For many victims of domestic violence having responsibility for their welfare sheeted back to the community may be hollow and unsatisfying.

I would like to acknowledge the research assistance of Sarah Ellison. The research on which this chapter is based was supported by a grant from the Legal Scholarship Support Fund, Faculty of Law, University of Sydney.

Notes

1   There is a certain ambivalence, however, about mediation in the restorative justice literature. Some authors embrace it as restorative justice whereas others seek to differentiate restorative justice from mediation.

2   McGillivray and Comaskey (1999) undertook research with Aboriginal women in Manitoba to examine their views toward alternative processes for dealing with intimate violence. 'Respondents viewed community-based dispute resolution as partisan and subject to political manipulation' (p. 143). Other concerns expressed included: that offenders might stack the process with their supporters and avoid responsibility for their actions; that given the intimacy of reserve living the process might further shame women and children rather than the offender; the need to respect disclosures of abuse; and, that diversion may meet offenders' needs but not victims' needs for safety. The respondents did not reject the Anglo-Canadian criminal justice system on cultural grounds (pp. 142–43).

3   External validation seems to imply more than the 'expressive function' emphasised by Hudson which suggests a focus on community disapproval of the offending behaviour. By contrast, external validation seems to imply a further step, that is the affirmation of the woman's entitlement to live without violence and perhaps also of her right to seek legal redress (see also McGillivray & Comaskey, 1999 on the benefits of rights-based discourse, especially for Indigenous women).

4   Here I acknowledge the debates about consistency and proportionality. My concern in this chapter is the question of what might be appropriate (effective?) restorative outcomes for domestic violence.

5   Whether or not restorative justice is committed to a non-neutral facilitator who promotes certain normative values is contested within the literature.

6   Using in-depth interviews and three quantitative scales to measure violence they studied 122 men who had perpetrated violence against women, and 144 women who had been the victims of such violence, including 95 couples.

4   Sexual Assault and Restorative Justice

Kathleen Daly

An Unsolvable Justice Problem

What is the problem we are trying to address when we ask, is restorative justice appropriate in cases of sexualized violence?[1] We are trying to solve a justice problem that cannot ultimately be solved. The problem is encapsulated well by Barbara Hudson and Jean Hampton. Hudson (1998: 245) asks:

> How does one move away from punitive reactions which – even when enforced – further brutalize perpetrators, without, by leniency of reaction, giving the impression that sexualized ... violence is acceptable behaviour?

Hampton (1998: 35) asks:

> How do you combine the respect for criminals' personal responsibility and agency to which conservatives are committed, with the compassion that leftist analysis would have us show these criminals, especially given the variety of ways that the legacy of various forms of oppression will be implicated in the criminal acts of some of them?

What interests Hudson, Hampton, and me is a problem with two components: How do we treat harms[2] as 'serious' without engaging in harsh forms of punishment or hyper-criminalization? How do we 'do justice' in an unequal society?

Harm vindication and the limits of criminalization

The symbolic and instrumental purpose of criminal law is the state's vindication of harms, and ideally, an affirmation of behaviours considered right and wrong in a society. Focusing for the moment on the sexual assault of adults ('rape') rather than minors ('child sexual abuse'), recent feminist scholarship has shown conclusively that the harm of rape is not recognized or understood within the terms of criminal law.

Some feminists suggest that because women's experiences of sexual violence are ultimately 'disqualified' by criminal law and justice system processes (Smart, 1989), efforts to reform criminal law to recognize the harm of rape will be frustrated. Despite the known limits of the rape law reform (Spohn & Horney, 1992) and the many studies of rape victims' re-victimization in the criminal process (Bumiller, 1990; New South Wales Department for Women, 1996), from a symbolic point of view alone, feminists cannot cede the ground that has been won in demonstrating that the harm of rape is far wider than the law's 'real rape' scenario. Susan Estrich (1986) coined the term 'real rape' to refer to stranger rapes, where a woman appears totally blameless for the act. Embedded in the real rape classification are elements such as clear marks of injury to the body that demonstrate a lack of consent, a victim's reporting the rape right away to the police and not drinking or using drugs at the time of the incident (see also Frohmann, 1991). A woman's biography, along with incident elements, must show conclusively that, from a male-centred viewpoint, she could not have 'provoked' the attack in any way. Therefore, for feminist and victim advocacy groups, the vindication of the harm of rape is today as much a political as a legal act.

Yet, we know that the law's vindication, especially its more harsh manifestations such as prison, is visited on the more marginal members of society and especially on its male marginal members. A growing number of feminist scholars and activists now recognize that increasing the penalties for crime and jailing more violent men may not create safer societies.

Dianne Martin (1998) and Laureen Snider (1998) analyse what goes wrong when feminists attempt to vindicate gendered harms through recourse to criminal law.[3] Dianne Martin suggests we should not view 'recent innovations in criminal law [as] a triumph for feminism, despite appearances' (p. 157). There is no victory for feminists, she would say, in 'measur[ing] the judicial "recognition of harm" against the length of the prison sentence imposed' (p. 169). Snider points out, as others have, that the vindication of gendered harms via harsh penal sanctions has the potential to incarcerate more minority group men.[4]

Doing justice in an unequal society

The idea of doing justice means different things to people. For some, it means identifying the 'right punishment' for a wrong, often calculated based on its seriousness and the offender's blameworthiness in proportion to other harms (von Hirsch, 1985). For others, it means identifying the 'right response' to a person and the harm, with attention to the wider problem of social justice (Hudson, 1993). For those in the former position, it is possible to 'do justice' in an unequal society, even if only in the restricted sense of having uniform and consistent decisions. For those in the latter position, it is not possible to 'do justice' legitimately in an unequal society because social and economic inequalities structure what is considered criminal and non-criminal harms, and these inequalities are reproduced in the justice process. While each position has a different view on the meaning of doing justice, they may work with presumptively similar understandings of the problem of inequality, what I shall call the *familiar analysis of inequality*.

The familiar analysis addresses the impact of class relations, of race–ethnic relations, and of colonialism and cultural differences on crime and justice system responses. It demonstrates that society's more marginal members, that is, those with fewer economic resources and who are marked as racially, ethnically, or culturally 'other', are, relative to their numbers in the general population, disproportionately more likely caught up in the justice system and disproportionately present in arrest, court, and prison populations. We know this analysis very well; it structures all sociological theories of crime, and for critical criminologists, in particular, it grounds an analysis of the immorality and injustice of criminal law and its application, past and present.

The familiar analysis is missing a key social relation, however, and that is sex/gender,[5] which challenges it in two ways. First, when sex/gender is brought into view, we notice that the heavily criminalized population is composed of marginalized *men*, not simply marginalized *persons*. Thus, social and economic disadvantage does not have similar 'effects' on people; women tend to be more law-abiding and conventional than men.[6] Second, while we might wish to blame the wider society for the inequalities that produce the crime problem (at least in part), that indictment does not go far enough in explaining a universal and ubiquitous phenomenon: men's physical and sexual abuse of women and children they know.[7] There are different logics, competing loyalties, and competing justice claims when we consider the relationship of sex/gender to class, race–ethnicity, culture, and colonialism in responding to gendered harms, including sexual assault. For example, McGillivray and Comaskey's (1999) research on Canadian Indigenous women who had been abused by their partners for many years finds that when the women sought redress in the justice system, they believed their partners had 'more rights' than they did (p. 149) and that the system often treated their men too leniently (p. 118). Their experiences and justice claims reveal an apparent no-win situation for Indigenous women (or other racialized women) seeking redress for harms via the traditional (White and Western) justice systems. 'Invoking either [the traditional criminal or child protection systems] may be seen not only as rejecting one's partner and extended family, but also as denying one's culture and going against the politics of one's people' (McGillivray & Comaskey, 1999: 156). Doing justice in an unequal society is thus a more complex exercise than critical criminologists have imagined. Relations of sex/gender and the harms associated with them pose fundamental challenges to how we think about the nature of crime and a just response.

This then is the unsolvable justice problem, and it surfaces in our discussions of the impact of inequalities on traditional and alternative justice system practices. For the traditional system,[8] we focus on how inequalities are reproduced and amplified through the system, observing that the symbolic bark of criminal law has its greatest bite on society's more marginal members, even as these offenders may be 'more powerful than their victims in the individual crime relationship' (Hudson, 1998: 255; see also Daly, 1989). For alternative practices, we focus on how inequalities are expressed in an informal process. When one attempts to bring into conversation parties who are unequal, it is likely that the more powerful person will have his or her way. For cases of sexualized violence, a male offender will be in a position to deny the offence, and perhaps to intimidate the victim, and a female victim will be less able to tell her story, less able to be heard. Therefore, it may be impossible to achieve just outcomes with gender power imbalances in a room of people discussing gendered harms (in addition to Stubbs, Coker & Busch, this volume, see also Astor, 1991; Hooper & Busch, 1996; Stubbs, 1995).

A Way Forward?

Is there any way around this unsolvable justice problem? My answer is yes; there may be a way forward if we do three things:
1. We must rehabilitate 'retribution' and make it part of a restorative justice process. Relatedly, we must cease seeing restorative justice as the opposite of retributive justice. I shall draw on Hampton (1998), Hudson (1998), and my own work (Daly, 2000a, 2000b, 2002), which utilizes arguments by Duff (1992, 1996).[9]
2. We must redefine the harm of rape, other forms of gendered harms, and perhaps violence more generally. I shall draw on Nicola Lacey's (1998) arguments about how both criminal law and the criminal process need to be reconstructed so that the affective and corporeal dimensions of these harms are discussed in the criminal process.

3. We must be cognizant of the variety of meanings and contexts of sexual violence, domestic violence, and family violence. These terms are associated with particular scenarios in people's heads, of cases they are familiar with, of situations they have experienced. Because of this variety, we may find ourselves disagreeing with each other because we are imagining different scenes of gendered harms.

Consider, for example, what we learn from Australia in the *Aboriginal and Torres Strait Islander Women's Task Force on Violence Report* (Robertson, 2000) and from Canada in McGillivray and Comaskey (1999). Women who live in more remote areas and who are beaten or raped have no place to run to, no refuge, perhaps no place of real safety. Compare that to women living in urban areas, where there may be programs, refuges, and the like, and where there is some place of separation and sanctuary. Consider also the term 'sexual assault'. So much has been written about rape and sexualized violence, but the variety of offence scenarios people have in mind centre on *adults* as victims and offenders *or* children abused by adults. Throughout this paper, I move between feminist analyses of the sexual assault of adult women ('rape') and actual cases of sexual assault of *child victims* ('child sexual abuse') by *juvenile offenders*. While this movement can be justified by analysing sexual violence as a continuum (Kelly, 1988), it is not a graceful movement. We attach different meanings to the seriousness of violence, depending on the character of victim–offender relations and an offender's maturity.[10]

In South Australia, young people charged with sexual assault (and related) offences, who have admitted to what they've done, may be diverted from court prosecution by the police, and instead participate in a restorative justice process called conferencing. Throughout eight states and territories in Australia and the country of New Zealand, there exists extraordinary variation in the form, purpose, and organizational location of conferencing (for overviews see Bargen, 1996, 1998; Hudson, Morris, Maxwell, & Galaway, 1996; Daly & Hayes, 2001, 2002). However, the general idea is that an admitted offender and their supporters, a victim and their supporters, and other relevant parties meet to discuss the offence and its impact. Conference participants discuss the sanction, with at least one legal actor (a police officer) present. In Australia and New Zealand, there are typically two professionals present: a coordinator or facilitator who runs the conference, along with a police officer. New Zealand police data for 1991–93 show that 17 to 20 percent of youth cases were dealt with by conference alone or by referral to conference by the court for pre-sentencing advice; the rest were handled by the police (Maxwell & Morris, 1996: 91–92; since that publication and a review of New Zealand's statistical data, Gabrielle

Maxwell says that the percent of cases handled by conference is likely higher, about 20 to 30 percent). In South Australia, from 1995 to 1998, of the total referrals of cases to formal caution, conference, and court, 18 percent were referred to conference.

Many people object to using conferences in sexual assault cases; they believe it lets offenders off too easily or puts victims in an untenable position. Plainly this is the dominant worldview. As far as I know, conferencing is used routinely in sexual assault cases in only two jurisdictions in the world: New Zealand and the Australian state of South Australia. In this paper, I describe a sample of sexual assault cases that were referred to a conference in South Australia during 1998. My aim is to show the varied harms that fall within the sexual assault offence category and the implications of this variation for imagining what would be just responses.

Caveats

Before launching into the three points, I have several caveats.
1. *Distinctions among gendered harms.* My essay centres on one kind of gendered harm, sexual assault, and whether a restorative justice process would be appropriate for it. Gendered harms take many forms, including domestic violence (which refers to a male abusing a female partner) or family violence (the preferred term for many Indigenous women, which refers to a wider set of violent behaviours in family groups, including sexual abuse of children by family members). An important distinction between gendered harms and other offences is that they are not incident-based, but repeated and ongoing, often for many years (see Stubbs, this volume). Sexual assault can be both ongoing and incident-based behaviour, the former more likely in the abuse of children and partners, and the latter in the context of acquaintances or those unknown to each other. The distinctions between sexual assault, domestic violence, and family violence can sometimes be important, but depending on the contexts of the abuse, at other times, these distinctions are artificial for those victimized.
2. *Defining gendered harms.* I have been searching for a concept that is inclusive of sexualized violence, domestic violence, family violence, and violence against children, even as I recognize this is a heterogeneous category. *Gendered harms* is my umbrella concept. They are gendered in that they are indicative of sex/gender power relations. However, they may not always involve male offenders or female victims; they can include violence in same and heterosexual relationships; and they can include violence of boys and girls against their

parents (typically mothers). I am less certain where to place assaults between boys or men, which may reflect homophobic violence, or where to place assaults between girls and women, which may have been provoked by sexual jealousies over 'their' men. There are many causes of gendered harms, that is, they reach into histories of colonial, cultural, race, and class oppression, and consequently, they embed these histories and particularities.

3. *Gendered harms as one site for feminist analysis.* Many assume, wrongly, that sex/gender is mainly or exclusively present in gendered harms but not in other offences. Furthermore, as Lacey (1998: 48) suggests, there is a 'feminine intellectual ghetto' (albeit also a feminist one) in criminal law, where in an otherwise male-dominated preserve, it is women who analyse and teach on 'sexual offences in general, and rape, in particular'. Like Lacey, I have refrained for some time from conducting research on rape because like her 'I was damned if I was going to occupy the pigeonhole which both feminist and other scholars seemed to have created' (p. 48).

However, gendered harms do offer a litmus test for a feminist evaluation of any new justice practice. As Hudson (1998: 245) reminds us, 'these crimes have been over-tolerated, whereas burglary, car theft, street robbery, and the like have been over-penalized ... The symbolic force of criminal law has only recently ... been deployed to demonstrate that society ... disapproves of these forms of behaviour.' Having said that, I would also say that gendered harms need not be the sole focus of feminist inquiry because sex/gender relations are in *every social encounter*, in *every crime encounter*, and in *every justice encounter*. Studies must consider these other offences. For example, I am finding from my research in South Australia that women may experience some forms of property victimization as a potential violation of their bodies and spirit, and that the physical and emotional effects of offences may linger longer for some female victims. Thus, while it is crucial that feminist attention be given to the applicability of restorative justice in responding to gendered harms, other harms must be considered as well. We do not want restorative justice to establish a feminist (and Indigenous) ghetto by permitting our voices and intellects to be present solely in discussions of particular offences.

Point 1: Rehabilitate retribution and cease the retributive–restorative justice contrast.

For several years I have argued against the oppositional contrast of retributive–restorative justice (Daly & Immarigeon, 1998; Daly, 2000a,

2000b, 2002). I initially found that the contrast was not accurate in describing the conference process. And in time, I have come to see that the contrast is not desirable in a normative sense. That is to say, not only is retribution part of a restorative justice process, it *should be* part of it.

Part of the difficulty in communicating this position is that people have strong images in their heads about a system of justice they don't like and a new system of justice they find more appealing. They call the system they *don't like* the 'retributive' justice system, with all of its problems. And they call the system they *do like* 'restorative justice'. I can agree that we may wish to refer to an old and new justice system, and I would like to call it just that, the old and the new justice.

In the old justice (or established, traditional courthouse justice), court processes leave little room for communication between the parties in a crime, they stigmatize and demonize offenders, and shut out victims. But it is patently inaccurate to call the old justice 'retributive justice' because a variety of theories of punishment have always been present, and over time, we find different ideological emphases in the state's response to crime (that is, treatment and punishment). Retribution means many things to people. Most analysts (with the possible exception of philosophers and some legal analysts) tend to use the term loosely – far too loosely in my view – to refer to responses that are harsh, vengeful, punitive, degrading, among others. They tend to assume that a retributive response is one involving incarceration. None of these assumptions or loose definitions needs to be part of retribution, but until we have a frank discussion of the many meanings of retribution, we shall forever be talking past each other. Calling the old justice 'retributive' and the new justice 'restorative' invites trouble and confusion. We can avoid some of that confusion by referring more simply to 'old' and 'new' justice practices. My argument is that new justice practices must have elements of retribution in them, but those elements may not have the same meaning or be present in the same way.

What, then, do I have in mind when I say we need to rehabilitate retribution? Empirically, when you observe family conferences, you see that people are moving flexibly across three major justice domains: first, retribution; then, restoration (or reparation); and finally, to rehabilitation (or reintegration). That is, the group moves from 'holding offenders accountable', registering a form of retributive censure that says 'what you did was wrong', to ideas of restoration, saying to the offender, 'in order for you to make up for what you've done, then you need to do these kinds of things'. Or, 'show by your amends to the victim that you've done wrong and we want to believe in your capacity to do that, to repair the harm'. And third, the group wants to say, 'Once you've shown you're sorry and that you'll make amends, we will welcome you back to the society.' The group may also identify programs or interventions that may assist the offender in staying out of trouble. Ideally, the conference setting is a dialogic encounter, that is, it is not just a group holding an offender accountable or proposing remedies for reparation; the offender (and supporters) should be actively engaged and participating in the process as well.

Empirically, then, I found that what people did in conferences was a flexible blend of retributive and restorative practices, but the next step was to consider, can these practices be defended normatively? In Daly (2000b), I worked through philosophical arguments by Duff (1992, 1996) on retributive censure and punishment and how these related to restorative justice. And in this paper, I utilize Jean Hampton's (1998) arguments on retribution because she addresses directly the unsolvable justice problem in responding to rape.

During 1995, Jean Hampton was asked to testify as an expert witness in a Canadian case concerning the constitutionality of a law prohibiting those prisoners, who had been federally sentenced to serve two years or more, from voting.[11] According to Hampton, the plaintiffs, who were arguing that prisoners *did* have the right to vote, believed that the current law effectively disenfranchised the poor and more marginal members of society, and especially minority group members. The government's (that is, the respondent's) case was that Canadian citizens not only had 'rights, but also responsibilit[ies], so that people who violated the rights of their fellow citizens should be expected to bear responsibility for doing so' (Hampton, 1998: 26–27), which included a suspension of voting rights while imprisoned.

Hampton (1998) suggests that what was missing in the arguments and in the courtroom were 'women' and 'minority groups' in a literal and analytical sense.

... Apart from the court reporter, the court clerk and a wife of one of the lawyers, I was the only woman in the courtroom. There were no women lawyers involved in the case and no other expert witnesses on either side that were women. ... Although none of the prisoners who brought the litigation was a Native [American], there were no members of any minority community in the courtroom and in particular, none involved as lawyers, court personnel or expert witnesses. This was almost entirely a white male trial. (p. 29)

What concerned Hampton about this case and what she saw as its feminist aspect was the expressive significance of law. She frames the problem this way: 'Does a law depriving prisoners of the right to vote in any way compromise a democracy's commitment to political equality, a principle which universal suffrage realizes' (p. 30)? The question raises two concerns: one is systemic discrimination against Native peoples, and the second is what democratic governments must always repudiate: 'the idea of "natural subordination", that is, that people are "by nature" the superiors of others because of race, class, religion, gender' (p. 29). Hampton assumes that universal suffrage (at least for adults) reflects a government's commitment to 'the political equality of all their citizenry' (p. 29).

Although Hampton ended up siding with the government, her reasoning did not fit either the government's or the plaintiff's cases, which she equates, respectively, with traditional 'right-wing' and 'left-wing' arguments. Although she considered herself a left-wing thinker, she couldn't accept the plaintiff's argument. Her reasoning is that women cannot easily adopt a 'sympathetic attitude toward violent men of the sort urged by the plaintiff's left-wing expert witnesses' (p. 31). A sole focus on the injustices arising from an over-criminalization of the poor is not sufficient because, Hampton argues, that position is 'blind to the way these offenders are actually encouraging and helping to enforce a form of oppression in our society' (p. 32).

She argues against two courses of action, finding both unacceptable:

- Disenfranchising prisoners to denounce not only their conduct but also them. This she believes is 'abusive, degrading, and unjust' (p. 36).
- Not disenfranchising prisoners as a form of rehabilitation 'designed to return the offender to the community as a reformed person' to signal that he/she is one of us. This she sees as wrong because the victims of the offenders' actions 'are given nothing' (p. 36). In her view, permitting prisoners a right to vote fails to express condemnation for their acts.

She imagines how rape victims would feel if prisoners were given the right to vote:

If a policy [of enfranchising prisoners] were enacted, women who were raped and other women whose lives were threatened because of rape, would have to watch while their rapists were systematically embraced by the community and given the political levers of power, without any denunciatory message. (p. 37)

In Hampton's view, both disenfranchising prisoners and not disenfranchising them are unjust courses of action because

each ... is too skewed in the direction of one of the parties involved in the dilemma: the denunciatory policy is unacceptably indifferent to the .. offender; the rehabilitative policy is unacceptably indifferent to ... victims. The right policy must involve an acknowledgment of both parties ... [but] this can be only imperfectly done. No matter how hard we try, it is unlikely that we will be able to construct a policy that will give both parties their due. (p. 37)

Is there any way around this justice deadlock? Hampton suggests a 'more sophisticated way of thinking about the nature and goals of a punitive response – one that incorporates both compassion and condemnation, both healing and justice' (p. 37). She argues that crime creates or instantiates an inequality: the offender has said 'I am up here, and you are down there, so I can use you for my purposes' (pp. 38–39). Punishment should redress that inequality by expressing the 'victims' equal value'. But this infliction of suffering on the offender 'cannot be accomplished in a way aimed at degrading the criminal's value or that has the effect of denying or lowering his worth'.

Hampton is a retributivist, but she wants to distinguish retribution from a revenge response. The avenger 'wishes to degrade and destroy the wrongdoer, the retributive punisher wishes to vindicate the value of the victim, not denigrate or destroy the wrongdoer' (p. 39). She argues for a retributive response that includes moral education to the offender and the wider society.

Retribution requires that offenders be treated with dignity insofar as the point of retribution is, among other things, to vindicate the equality of victim and offender. But you don't secure that vindication by refusing, in the name of being 'nice' to him, to take a punitive stand against his offence. (p. 41)

She admits that

To disenfranchise prisoners whose offence is causally connected to ... oppressive forces fails to respond to the injustice of those forces, and ... is a serious cost of the policy I am advocating ... [but] if, say, poverty and a history of discrimination played a part in a young man turning to violence, our failing to punish him, or our punishing him lightly, ends up further hurting the people who were already hurt by his violence. (p. 42)

In a comment that reinforces what Canadian Indigenous women said to McGillivray and Comaskey (1999) in explaining why they were against diversion from court for the men who abused them, Hampton says: 'It has been insufficiently appreciated that well-meaning compassion toward offenders can, in and of itself, do damage. Kindness toward the criminal can be an act of cruelty toward his victims, and the larger community' (p. 43).

'Once we acknowledge that we can't have clean hands, we have to choose' (p. 43, emphasis added). Hampton chooses to vindicate victims: 'For

the sake of victims and our communities, we can't pull back on or mitigate the appropriate retributive response to criminal conduct; hence, we have to choose a criminal code that is committed to retribution' (p. 43). She is concerned, however, with leaving it there. She asks whether it is possible to 'add something to this retributive response in order to express a kind of compassion for the criminal himself, in ways that might do him some good and, if he has been the victim of injustice, acknowledge and address that injustice' (p. 43).

She suggests two additions to a retributive response. One lies within the justice system, that of a 'reformative aim' that has both rehabilitation and moral education as goals. A second lies outside the justice system, that of retributive responses to those 'who are players in systemic forces that encourage impoverishment and discrimination against some [groups] in society' (p. 44). She sees such retributive responses taking place via tort law, legislation, and public opinion. Like retributive responses operating within the criminal justice system, she calls for policies 'to be fair, yet not hateful, healing yet not complicit in the harm' (p. 44). The aim of the second addition is to engage wider debates about domination in society and about social justice, although Hampton doesn't use these terms.

Hampton helps to clarify many things for me, but she leaves other things unanswered. She clarifies a meaning for retribution and a retributive response to crime that is morally defensible and sensible. It strikes the right tone in taking gendered harms seriously and in not excusing them. Her analysis reveals the limits of a restorative process that does not directly confront the problem of retribution, or that does not explicitly vindicate victims. It is not a 'benefits and burdens' justification for punishment (or for retributivism) but rather one about how criminal acts themselves create inequality which must be redressed in some way, even as we may recognize that those criminal acts may have come about because of, or be linked to, relations of inequality and oppression in the larger society. She suggests, further, that the state has a duty beyond retributivism to assist in the reformation and moral education of wrongdoers. Like other legal philosophers (such as Antony Duff), she anticipates that a 'well-crafted' retributive response should be cognitive, to 'provok[e] thought' in the mind of the wrongdoer (p. 43). Duff (1992, 1996) conceives of this cognitive dimension being provoked (at least ideally) in the communication between a person (or group) denouncing the offence and the wrongdoer's acceptance of his/her responsibility for it.

Hampton leaves unanswered a key problem: what form and amount of retributive punishment are appropriate or necessary to vindicate harms suffered by victims? Should imprisonment continue to be used as the measure by which certain offences, such as sexual assault, are taken seriously? Barbara Hudson (1998: 253) discusses these questions, proposing that 'restorative responses' to particular offences or offenders need to be 'introduced in a general framework of restorative justice'. That is, there should be an overall 'penal deflation' (such as Braithwaite has consistently argued for), and restorative justice should be used in all offences, not just a small number of less serious ones. Hudson proposes a radical idea for those interested in restorative justice:

> to serve the expressive functions of punishment, restorative processes will have to devise ways of *clearly separating condemnation* of the act from the *negotiation of measures* appropriate to the relationships between the particular victim, offender, and community. (Hudson, 1998, p. 253 [my emphasis]).

Hudson proposes that we separate the quantum of punishment (or perhaps the quantum of reparation) from the condemnation of the act. It means that censure should be decoupled from a sanction, but censure must occur nonetheless. The challenge for restorative justice is to consider how censure and retribution can explicitly feature in the process.

Hampton makes a compelling case for how victims are harmed when it appears that offenders are treated too leniently or their acts are not condemned in an appropriate manner. She also acknowledges the difficulties of doing justice in an unjust society, that is, whether we choose to be compassionate to offenders (many of whom are socially marginalized) or to vindicate victims' suffering. Hampton's and Hudson's analyses reveal the limits of restorative justice when applied to serious harms. Concretely, for sexualized violence, doing justice in an unjust society translates to whether one should be compassionate to marginalized men who harm women and children they know *or* whether one should vindicate the women's and children's suffering. When stated this way, perhaps the choice is not that difficult.

Point 2: Reconstruct criminal law and criminal process to include emotions and bodies.

Lacey (1998) argues that criminal law has not satisfactorily addressed the actual harm of rape. The idea of harm communicated by the legal definition of rape is 'a peculiarly mentalist, incorporeal one. Its essence lies in the violation of sexual autonomy understood as the right to determine sexual access to one's body ... Rape thus amounts to something between expropriation of a commodity and a violation of will' (p. 59). What is missing, she suggests, is what is valuable about sexuality itself –

self-expression, connection, intimacy, relationship – and what risks are associated with it: 'violation of trust, infliction of shame and humiliation, objectification and exploitation' (p. 54).

Why, Lacey asks, does criminal law have such an 'oblique relationship' to these values and risks? Her answer (briefly) is that criminal law generally views legal subjects as 'rational and disembodied individuals' and the law of rape conceptualizes the harm of rape in terms of the 'taking' of sexual autonomy. Both are related to the mind over body dualism at the heart of Western liberal law.

Lacey wants to bring 'the sexed body' to law and legal argument, but not in a way that ends up 'reaffirming an untenable mind–body dualism, as well as [a form] of essentialism' (p. 57). She wants to make it possible for rape victims to describe the harm of rape with reference to 'affective experience' and 'embodied existence' (p. 62). At present, however, rape victims giving evidence in court are 'effectively silenced, caught between ... the discourses of the body as property ... and the feminine identity as body, which pre-judges ... experience by equating it with stereotyped and denigrating views of female sexuality ...' (p. 62). Such silencing 'denies rape victims both the status of personhood and the chance to approach the court as an audience capable of acknowledging their trauma'. She suggests that the acknowledging of the trauma is 'among the most important things which a public rape trial should achieve' (p. 62), and while she does not propose that victims' accounts 'have the unassailable status of truth' (drawing from Wendy Brown's (1991), arguments), she wishes to 'reconstruct the trial process as a political space in which precisely the contestation of meanings ... might take place' (p. 62, note 48).

Lacey argues for two major reconstructions to criminal law and process:

1. The inclusion of the affective and corporeal aspects of wrongs and victimization.[12] Such a reconstructed rape law would 'specify [the] conditions under which coercive, violent or degrading sexual encounters should be prohibited'. This would lead to a broader understanding of consent and one 'which assumes a mutuality of relationship and responsibility between victim and offender'. (p. 65)
2. A process open to a discussion of the different meanings of the wrong and of sexual victimization. This would mean that changes would have to be made to the rules of evidence 'so as to allow victims more fully to express their own narrative in the court room setting ... [without being subject to] an examination of their sexual history'. (p. 66)

In a claim which at first surprises the reader, but which is consistent with the idea of 'sexual integrity' as a 'project' not an 'end state' (p. 67),

Lacey argues that 'the criminal law of rape should express an unambiguous commitment to the positive integrity as well as the full humanity of both rape victims and men accused of rape' (p. 66). She assumes that defending 'a value of sexual integrity' via criminal law is largely a symbolic, not instrumental exercise. She acknowledges the limits of criminalization in securing 'relational autonomy' and 'bodily and sexual integrity'. By viewing 'integrity as a project' (p. 67), Lacey wishes to avoid the problem of defining 'personhood' too restrictively. Ultimately, she imagines that the rape trial might 'become an – always risky – space for recovery rather than for continued victimization', where women can 'tell their stories' and 'be heard' (p. 67).

Lacey alerts us to the ways in which the harm of rape is contained in criminal law, that the harm is effectively silenced because law abstracts and disembodies it. Unless this containment is addressed, any justice process will be inappropriate, and indeed, it may create more injury. While Lacey concurs with Smart (1989) that women's experiences of rape are disqualified in the criminal process, she believes it may be possible to reform criminal law and procedure. She imagines that in a reformed legal process, the harm of rape can be revealed through narratives by the victim and the offender during the trial. Precisely how the trial process as a 'political space [for the] contestation of meanings' (p. 62, note 48) would unfold in a traditional courtroom is uncertain. Moreover, in Lacey's formulation, there appears to be no way that women can tell their stories of victimization when offenders plead guilty and their case does not go to trial. Perhaps an informal process, of the sort used in conferences, may offer a more effective political space than the process in a traditional courtroom. In an earlier paper, John Braithwaite and I gave examples of how this could occur (Braithwaite & Daly, 1994). We said that feminists needed to be involved in the conferences themselves and in the training of coordinators to ensure that conference scenarios were subject to feminist interpretation. The place of 'caring men' in conferences may also be important in containing misogynist voices and in reducing men's re-victimization of women. Thus, restorative processes (like conferences) may have some relevance in responding to gendered harms, and sexual assault, in particular.

Lacey expressly limits her discussion, saying that it centres on rape law in England and Wales, and it concerns adult men and women (p. 53, note 19). She does not address the 'special cases such as offences relating to children, where the normative framework of autonomy remains to some extent inapt' (p. 52). The next section considers such cases, asking whether we perceive the harm of rape differently when the offence involves an adult male offender and adult female victim, as compared to an adolescent male offender and a younger female victim.

Point 3: Consider harms concretely, not abstractly,
when considering just responses.

Be aware of the different meanings and contexts of gendered
harms.

At the Canberra conference in July 2000, a recurring gap emerged in
what victim advocates were referring to when speaking of domestic or
family violence and what restorative justice advocates imagined was the
content of these harms. To Ruth Busch and other victim advocates, the
accounts of violence they had in mind were of men's abusing women in
the most profound ways and of women's enduring violence for many
years, and thus, they had in mind the most serious forms of gendered
harms. Victim advocates have rightly critiqued the assumptions of
restorative justice advocates of an incident-based way of imagining
domestic or family violence (among other critiques, see articles by
Stubbs, Coker, and Busch in this volume). However, neither group has
discussed the varied contexts, degrees of seriousness, and varied potential for restorative processes in these offences. *It is crucial that both groups*
come to terms with the fact that gendered harms range from less to more seri-
ous, and that some harms will be less and more amenable to restorative
processes. To clarify, I assume that *any* crime may be amenable to a
restorative process (whether as diversion from court, pre-court sentencing advice, or post-probation or post-prison meeting), but in many
cases, victims may not want to participate in a face-to-face meeting with
an offender. It is useful to keep in mind that restorative processes need
not involve face-to-face meetings of victims and offenders, and victims
need not be present, but can be represented by others. Restorative
processes can also be used for victims alone, when, for example, an
offender has not been identified. All of these contexts and possibilities
need to be considered when contemplating the uses of restorative justice in responding to gendered harms. Victim advocates often assume
that only a face-to-face meeting between victim and offender constitutes
a restorative process.

Sexual Assault and Conferencing in South Australia

I shall present 18 cases of sexual assault that were disposed of by a conference in South Australia during 1998. My aim is to show what kinds
of cases are subject to conferencing, and in particular, to give more con-
creteness to the sexual assault category. All 18 cases had juvenile offenders (males under 18) because conferencing is a court diversion option

only for juveniles, not adult offenders in South Australia.[13] For background and context, I draw from a paper by two South Australian Youth Justice Coordinators, Ben Wallace and Marnie Doig (1999) and from data published by the South Australian Attorney-General's Department, Office of Crime Statistics (1999, 2000) on the disposition of sexual assault cases in 1998 and 1999.[14] Such cases are rare in the juvenile system in that they feature in about one percent each of conference and court cases (South Australian Attorney-General's Department, 1999: 111, 136). A striking feature from the 1998 and 1999 data is that more sexual assault cases were disposed of in conference (N=38) than were 'proved' in court (N=19) (South Australian Attorney-General's Department, 1999: 109, 136; and 2000: 118, 140). An analysis of the 'proved' rates in the Youth Court clarifies matters. For all offences disposed of in the court during 1998, 72 percent were proved; the rest were dismissed or withdrawn (South Australian Attorney-General's Department, 1999: 136). For sexual offences, the proved rate is substantially less than the average, at 33 percent (p. 136). For comparison, the proved rate for robbery is 46 percent; for assault, 62 percent; for burglary, 65 percent (p. 136).[15] Driving offences, by contrast, have a much higher proved rate at 89 percent.

My statistical exercise should give victim advocates some pause. For those who believe that a traditional court process may be better for victims, if only that the harm is vindicated and treated seriously in court, these statistics suggest otherwise. For victims whose cases went to court, these South Australian data suggest that *just one-third* will have the satisfaction of finding that the offence was proved. In light of how the conference process is triggered in these youth justice cases, that is, it cannot go forward unless the young person admits to the offence, victims who participate in the conference process have the satisfaction of knowing that an offender has made such admissions.[16]

At present, it is unclear why the police refer some cases to conference and others to court. In addition to evidentiary matters, the referral decision may vary by victim–offender relationship and an offender's official offence history. Of course, an offender's admission is one crucial element. Wallace and Doig (1999, p. 6) find that offenders going to court are older than those in conference, but other than this, they find no other major differences.

In reflecting on conferencing in sexual assault cases, Wallace and Doig (1999, p. 8) say that

[These conferences] tend to be more intense for participants [than those for other offences] because the effects of the offence have usually been severe for the victim and his/her family; and the disclosure of the offence has usually had consequences for the offending youth and his family prior to the conference. ...

The indications for us are that family conferences are useful in dealing with sexual offences where there is a past, and potentially a future relationship between the young offender and the victim and that the process does achieve resolution for the victim and appropriate outcomes for the offender.

These Youth Justice Coordinators therefore see a value to restorative processes in cases involving victims and offenders who know each other. The coordinators also say that compared to other offences, they spend more time preparing these cases, and they share their 'experiences of these cases with each other frequently' (p. 8).

The Family Conference Team provided me summaries of 18 sexual offence cases that were referred to conference by the police or the court during 1998.[17] Here is an overview of the kinds of cases handled.

- Of the 18 cases, 14 involved indecent assault, and four involved sexual intercourse or rape. One case had six offenders, but the rest had one each.
- All the offenders were non-Indigenous males.[18] Their ages ranged from 11 to just under 18 years, and the median age was 14.
- There were a total of 26 victims of these offences; all but three were female. The victims' ages ranged from three to 50. One offence was by a young man who exposed his penis to both older and younger women. Excluding that case (and the four victims over 18), the median age of the victims was six years.[19]
- Thus, the average offence involved a 14-year-old male against a female who was six.
- Of the 18 cases, eight involved brothers and sisters (or step relations), and a further six involved cousins, family friends, and other friends they played with. Three involved offenders whom the victims knew from school. Just one case involved a 'stranger'; however, as the local town flasher, he was 'known' to people in the town.
- In five of 18 conferences, the victim attended; in those conferences where victims were not present, their views and experiences were represented by other people such as the mother of the victim.
- Several victims were concerned that brothers would be sent away, or they felt responsible for reporting what happened.
- Except for some offenders in the country areas, all the offenders participated in the Mary Street Program, an Adolescent Sexual Abuse Prevention Program (described below), as part of their undertaking, normally for 12 months. Six had to do community service, and the number of hours was substantial, much higher than other offences, ranging from 50 hours to 240 hours.[20] In South Australia, the maximum length of an undertaking is 12 months.
- Twenty of the 23 offenders carried out their undertaking.

The Youth Justice Coordinators say that without the Mary Street Program, they would be more hesitant to use conferencing in sexual assault cases. Mary Street is headed by Alan Jenkins and is based on his 'invitations to responsibility' theory (Jenkins, 1990). The program is highly regarded not only by the coordinators, but also by Youth Court judges and magistrates, who rely on it when sentencing youthful offenders. Mary Street workers prefer to have several sessions with an offender prior to his attending a family conference, and some youth may be in the program for some time before attending a conference. Because Mary Street workers are familiar with the conference process, they can prepare an offender (and his family supporter[s]) for it. Among other things, they are concerned that apologies to victims are thought through with a great deal of care and not made prematurely. Thus, in some cases, Mary Street workers may advise against a verbal apology at the conference. The timing of a conference may be determined, in part, by how far along the offender is in the therapeutic process. Unlike conferences for other offences, those for sexual assault have a heightened degree of symbolism in that they mark a stage in an ongoing therapeutic process. Conference outcomes in sexual assault cases may not always involve the Mary Street Program mainly because it serves the Adelaide metropolitan area, not the entire state. However, coordinators may consult with program workers to determine what the most appropriate regional service is, or program workers will liaise with other regional services.

From the case information provided me by the Family Conference Team, I am able to summarize each offence, although I admit to discomfort in presenting the offence 'facts' for several reasons. First, the summaries provided me are sketches of the offences, containing little on the individuals' biographies and familial contexts. Second, as noted by Bumiller (1990) and Smart (1989) in analysing rape trials, the recapitulation of offence details can be read as a form of pornography.[21] To appreciate the variety of harms, I grouped the cases into those I perceived as being 'more' and 'less' serious. I am aware of the problems in any effort to classify seriousness. I do not know how the offence was discussed at the conference, and I do not know how individual victims experienced the assaults, except when this is revealed in some case summaries. While it was difficult to categorize the offences, I classified six as 'less serious', five as 'more serious', and seven as 'most serious'. I used these criteria in classifying the offences: whether it was one incident or a pattern of incidents, whether it was rubbing genitals or genital penetration, whether or not the offender used devious methods to manipulate victims, whether or not the offender threatened the victim if she disclosed to others what he did, and the degree of emotional impact the offence had on the victim, as this was described in the offence summary.[22]

Cases 7 and 13 are indicative of 'less serious' cases, which appear to be 'one-off' events, with the offenders touching victims and rubbing themselves against the victims, but not penetrating them:[23]

> *Case 7* (one count of indecent assault)
>
> The young person, who is 12 years old, admitted to having 'played games' in bed one morning with his half-sister, age three. He touched her and rubbed her 'private parts' while they were in bed, and he said he did this only one time. The boy lives with his father, but visits his mother and sister on weekends. The mother thinks that the boy is being abused and this might explain his behaviour.
>
> *Case 13* (one count of indecent assault)
>
> The young person, who is 16 years old, placed his hand down the victim's underpants and touched her vagina. The victim is his sister, age four. The incident occurred while the mother was out shopping, leaving her son, daughter, and other children at home. The boy was honest in admitting the offence to his mother after his sister told her what had happened. This appears to have been the only time he did it.

Cases 8 and 12 are examples of the 'more serious' cases, where offenders lure victims to secluded places, threaten them or use force in some way, and where there appears be a pattern of sexual abuse, although not involving penetration.

> *Case 8* (one count of indecent assault)
>
> The young person, aged 15, bribed his four-year-old cousin with an ice cream to come into the garden shed, where he asked her if she'd let him touch her vagina. She said no, but he did it anyway. He touched her for some time until their uncle saw them and reported the incident. When the boy was interviewed by a social worker, he admitted that he had done things like this before. He is described as 'intellectually backward' for his age. When the victim was interviewed by the police, she disclosed that another cousin was sexually abusing her [a conference was also held for this boy]. The offender is part of a large family with many uncles, aunts, and cousins. Police suspect that there is an incest pattern in the family.
>
> *Case 12* (3 counts of indecent assault)
>
> The young person, 14 years old, pulled down the shorts and underpants of his foster sister, age nine, while they were in the computer room. He touched her vagina with his fingers. He did it twice again on the same day, putting his hand down her pants and pulling her toward him. The girl reported the

incidents to her mother several weeks later, but she was worried that her disclosure would result in her foster brother being removed from the home, and she didn't want that to happen. The boy, described as having a 'slight intellectual disability', made 'full and frank' admissions to the police. The mother was concerned that he did not see his behaviour as serious. The children live with their foster parents, having been removed from their biological families some time ago because of neglect or abuse.

Cases 3, 4, and 6 are examples of the 'most serious' offences, where offenders penetrate victims, have been abusing victims for some time, and have threatened victims not to disclose the offence, and where victims show many indications of emotional harm caused by the offence.

Case 3 (three counts of unlawful sexual intercourse and two counts of incest)
The young person said that he put his 'willy' into the victim's (his sister) vagina. He was 12 and a half years old, and she was seven. He did this in the bedroom and in the bathroom. The victim said she felt sore as a result of what her brother did. When their mother learned what happened, she said she wanted to kill her son. Initially, she thought that both her sons were involved. During his interview with the police, the offender also disclosed forcing oral sex on his sister. He said he wanted to experience sex, and he threatened his sister with 'trouble' if she told anyone. The file suggests that the offender appears not to be concerned with the impact of the harm on his sister.

Case 4 (three counts of rape)
The young person admitted 'doing sex' with the victim, his sister, at least three times. He was 14 and she was three. He said he chose her because he wanted to try sex and thought he could control her. He said he knew what he did was wrong. He told his sister that it was a game, and she mustn't tell anyone. Their mother caught them. The mother, who was a heroin user, said that she began using again soon after the disclosure.

Case 6 (6 counts of indecent assault)
A group of six young people (males) followed two victims (females) along the beach, onto the bus, into town, and continued following them through a park until they reached home. The boys harassed the girls verbally, assaulted them in the sea while they were swimming, pinched their breasts and genitals, slid their hands under the girls' blouses and down their pants while on the bus. At one point, a young person put

his hand over one of the victims' mouths when she tried to scream. This occurred during school holidays; the boys ranged in age from 11 to 15; the girls' ages were estimated on the file as being '14 or 15'. The victims said that they felt 'very dirty' when they got home. One victim said that the other victim vomited in the park when she was trying to scream. Both girls were taken to the hospital; they had bruises on their legs, breasts, stomachs, and cuts on their feet and legs. They had trouble sleeping and wouldn't go out of the house after the incident for a long time, up to when the family conference was held, six weeks later.

When one absorbs the character of these offences, and their varied seriousness and meaning in the lives of offenders, victims, and their families, it is not easy to make glib or generic claims about 'how sexual assault cases should be handled'. One major axis in judging the harm of sexual assault is the age of the offender. With all these offenders under 18, we might say that their behaviour is not as entrenched; it is more exploratory and less serious. However, the victims were quite young, and in the sibling and family cases, the victims were used as sexual practice by their brothers or cousins. One could argue that some of these cases are even more serious than those involving adult offenders and victims because these juvenile offenders acted as if their victims had no bodily or sexual integrity at all.

The information supplied to me does not indicate what happened in the conference itself, for example, the degree to which offenders minimized or denied the harm, or the degree to which offenders began to appreciate better that what they did was wrong. Wallace and Doig (1999: 13) do make clear, however, that answers to questions such as 'what made you do that?' are typically not forthcoming in conferences. 'The question of why the youth has committed the sexual offence is not one that youths at family conferences for sexual offences can ever answer to anyone's satisfaction.'

Wallace and Doig (1999) also emphasize that the conference provides an *opportunity* for the stories of victimization to be heard, and it sets in motion (or consolidates) a long-term plan, normally of six to 12 months for counseling the offender. However, they do not expect that participants will want to reconcile or that victims can ever forgive the offender or even that offenders will feel remorse for their actions:

In cases where there has been real deception by the offender, and if the abuse has been taking place for a long period of time, and when there are serious questions from the victim's parents that they can trust the youth again ... people are more likely to reject reintegrative notions in favour of totally cutting off the relationship with the youth. In other words, the conference may provide an opportunity for remorse and forgiveness, but it's up to the participants to decide whether to feel remorse or to give forgiveness. (Wallace & Doig, 1999: 13)

One step in developing a feminist-informed criminal jurisprudence would be to gauge the nature of the harm, not from the law's point of view, but from that of an embodied victim who has emotions and feelings, as Lacey (1998) has proposed. However, it is uncertain how one moves from a detailed knowledge of these embodied experiences to a consideration of what appropriate sanctions would be, assuming that defendants are found guilty or plead guilty. We would benefit first from a consideration of what are 'more' and 'less serious' forms of sexual assault, and of gendered harms, more generally. That discussion is a necessary prerequisite for subsequent decisions about appropriate responses (censure and sanctions, safety plans, etc) and sites of response (court or conference). There is, however, a problem with my recommendation. The dynamics of gendered harms provoke us to consider additional questions, which are not as relevant for other offences. These emerge in Lacey's discussion of the harm of rape and in victim advocates' concerns for victim safety. How can justice system responses impugn the normative supports for boys' and men's violence toward girls and women? How can victims be safe from these forms of violence?

Conclusion

When considering the viability of restorative justice in cases of sexualized violence (or other gendered harms), we confront a justice problem that cannot be solved. The challenge for restorative justice is *how to treat serious offences seriously* without engaging in hyper forms of criminalization. I have argued that if retribution is made part of the restorative process in an explicit way, then the problem of taking offences seriously may be satisfactorily addressed. I am persuaded by Hampton's argument that restorative justice must ultimately be concerned *first* with vindicating the harms suffered by victims (via retribution and reparation) and then, *second*, with rehabilitating offenders. Currently, the use of conferencing as a diversion from court in Australia and New Zealand is skewed more toward diversion as a form of rehabilitation. (Using conferences to advise the sentencing judge in New Zealand youth court cases may be an exception.) Perhaps because the offenders are juveniles in these diversionary conferencing schemes, this skew toward rehabilitation is appropriate; but if restorative justice is to be applied to more serious cases and to adult offenders, then the process, and underlying philosophical premises, may have to change.

A second challenge for restorative justice is whether it can incorporate a new understanding of the nature of gendered harms, which includes the emotions and bodies of victims. Because restorative justice processes are tied to extant criminal codes, practices may suffer from treating gendered harms abstractly. However, a restorative justice process typically involves a more free-ranging discussion of the nature of the harm than is possible in a courtroom, and thus, it may provide a satisfactory 'political space [for the] contestation of meanings' that Lacey (1998: 62, note 48) imagines. With a space for contestation comes the danger, however, that old ways of thinking about sexualized violence (and gendered harms) would be reinscribed. This is the major concern for victim advocates who see in informal processes a high probability for the re-victimization of victims unless the proceeding is prepared and managed well.

One can neither fully endorse nor disparage restorative justice processes in responding to sexualized violence or other gendered harms. A generic position is premature and ill-advised (see also Coker, 1999, on this point). If we consider diversionary conferences as one kind of process, they may be appropriate in the handling of some offences, especially when this entails offenders' admissions of wrongdoing and perhaps when offenders are viewed as 'immature'. For other cases, however, face-to-face meetings may be totally inappropriate, especially when offenders are not remorseful for what they've done and have a history of violence. Restorative justice advocates need to be mindful of research on violent men: the threat of penal sanctions as a 'back-up' appears to be especially important in changing patterns of entrenched abuse toward their partners (Dobash, Dobash, Cavanagh & Lewis, 2000). While we might wish it were possible to engage in moral education without relying on the threat of incarceration, that is naïve.

In calling for the need to think concretely, not abstractly, about harms, I am not proposing that justice is best served by an entirely individualized response to crime, as some might infer. At the Canberra conference, John Braithwaite said that my first and third points seemed to be contradictory. Specifically, he asked, how could I propose to rehabilitate retribution at the same time that I suggest the need to think concretely about harms? I take his question to mean, how can you be a retributivist who says we need to examine cases individually? My answer is as follows. Retribution is a term that has several meanings: it is a justification for *why* we punish (because it's right to do so, to vindicate victims' suffering or the inequality created by the offender harming the victim) and for *how much* we should punish (that is, in proportion to the harm caused). Hampton addressed the *why*, but not the *how much* of retribution. *What form* retribution should take is yet another matter, and

I have proposed that at a minimum, retributive censure be made a much more explicit feature of a restorative justice process; otherwise, it cannot be distinguished from a civil proceeding. Following Hudson, I have suggested that one potential way forward is to separate the censuring of the act from the sanction. In my first point, then, I lodged a critique of the oppositional contrast of retributive and restorative justice: the contrast fails on empirical grounds, and elements of retribution (that is, at a minimum, *censure*) must be part of a restorative process. I was not discussing retribution *as proportionality* in making my first point.

In calling for the need to think concretely not abstractly about harms, and by sketching the offending in 18 sexual assault cases, my aim is that scholars and activists become more aware of a diversity of harms that fall into the sexual assault or domestic/family violence categories, and compare these against the scenarios in our minds and experiences. We require a full appreciation of what harms we are talking about, their seriousness, and impact. Subsequent discussions about whether the sanctioning (or reparative) process ought to be radically individualized (with upper limits) or related in some proportional way to the offence harm are further down the road. We have learned our lessons about the failure of 'just deserts' to deliver a more superior justice than 'individualized' justice, but we must remember why just deserts made good sense in the first place: the failure of individualized justice to appear fair to a broad constituency. Restorative justice (or new justice practices more generally) will not be able to resolve that long-standing justice problem either.

Notes

1   This paper relies on summaries of sexual assault cases, which were disposed of by a family conference in South Australia in 1998. My thanks to Youth Justice Coordinators, Marnie Doig and Grant Thomas, for gathering and assembling the data, and to Carolyn Doherty (Senior Coordinator) for her help in moving the project forward. My appreciation to Brigitte Bouhours for her research assistance.

2   I refer to *criminal* harms, which include both a *public* wrong that must be recognized (and censured) and a harm that might be compensated. The definition of restorative justice normally includes the idea of 'repairing the harm', which may lead one to infer that it is no different from a civil process. Antony Duff has clarified the importance of censuring the wrong in a restorative process; it is central to his position (and mine, see Daly, 2000b) that 'Restoration is not only compatible with retribution and punishment: it requires retribution ...' (Duff, 2001: 2).

3   Such arguments were made more than a decade ago by myself and others (Daly, 1989; Daly & Chesney-Lind, 1988: 522–24; Harris, 1987), but only seem now to resonate with a wider feminist audience.

4 Yet, as Coker (this volume) correctly points out, it is unclear whether an increasing criminalization of domestic/family violence has played any significant role in increasing rates of incarceration for minority group men.

5 I use sex/gender to signify the importance of each term, sex and gender, and their interrelationship. Recent feminist work on the 'sexed body' suggests that the distinction between sex and gender, which had been made formerly, can no longer be sustained (Gatens, 1983, reprinted as chapter 1 in Gatens, 1996; see review in Daly, 1997, and readings in Naffine & Owens, 1997, especially by Davies, 1997).

6 My claim is of course contextual (i.e., within a neighbourhood or city) and historically and culturally specific. It would be wrong to assume that women as a group are (or will be) more law-abiding than men as a group or that women are less likely to be criminalized across time, place, nation, and culture. One needs only to examine rates of arrest for US black women and white men in certain crime categories (see Chilton & Datesman, 1987).

7 While some women also physically and sexually abuse women, men, and children they know, I shall use the masculine and feminine pronouns throughout this article to denote, respectively, the typical relationship of a male abuser and female (or child) victim.

8 By traditional, established, or 'old justice' practices, I refer to contemporary forms of courthouse justice, not to pre-modern forms.

9 My focus is on the response to sexual assault at the point of its detection or reporting to legal authorities. There are other contexts in which restorative processes may be used, for example, when adult women confront men who abused them when they were children or when community members wish to meet a man convicted of sexual offences upon release from prison (see Yantzi, 1998).

10 Harry Blagg raised this point during question time at the Canberra conference. It raises difficult questions for how to analyse gendered harms committed by males under 18 years of age. Should they be viewed as 'less mature' and hence less blameworthy for their acts? Andrew von Hirsch (2001: 232–33) argues that compared to adults, penalties for young offenders should be 'substantially scaled down' on normative grounds: young people should be seen as less culpable, the 'punitive bite' should be less, and society should have a 'special tolerance' for young people who offend.

11 I work through Hampton's arguments in some detail, often choosing to use her words rather than my summary of the argument, because her words are so strong and well chosen.

12 She prefers to use the value of bodily-affective 'integrity', drawing from Drucilla Cornell (1996), rather than the value of 'autonomy', which is at the heart of consent. She also draws on Jennifer Nedelsky's (1989, 1995) development of the concept of 'relational autonomy'.

13 South Australia was the first Australian jurisdiction to legislate conferencing as a diversion from court; the Young Offenders Act was passed in 1993, and conferencing began in February 1994. See Wundersitz and Hetzel (1996) and Wundersitz (1996) for a review of the history and first several years of conferencing in South Australia.

14 The sexual assault category includes rape (and attempts), indecent assault, unlawful sexual intercourse (and attempts), incest, and indecent behaviour or indecent exposure.

15 I have calculated these rates from the data given in the South Australian Attorney-General's Department statistical report (1999: 136). My calculations do not include those cases where the major charge was not proved, but there was a finding of guilt to a lesser-included offence. About six percent of all cases fell into this category (p. 45).

16 It would be important to compare the offence facts in the court and conference cases, including how strong the state's case was.

17 The sample includes those cases referred to the Family Conference Team in 1998 (and established in their registry as a 1998 case) for the offences listed in footnote 14. Missing from the analysis is a small number of cases, which the Youth Justice Coordinators could not easily access from the archives.

18 Data on sexual assault offences disposed in court and conference (including cases withdrawn and dismissed) from 1995 to 2000 show this racial/-ethnic breakdown: for court cases, 13 percent Aboriginal, 77 percent non-Aboriginal, and 10 percent unknown; and for conference cases, six percent Aboriginal, 84 percent non-Aboriginal, and 10 percent unknown (data provided to me by the Data Technology Unit, Adelaide, South Australia).

19 The Youth Justice Coordinators report that counseling for victims is often addressed prior to a family conference by the family itself. In Adelaide, referral for counseling and support can be made to several providers such as Child Protection Services at the Women and Children's Hospital, and the Yarrow Place program. The Coordinators say that families of very young victims may elect not to seek intensive counseling assistance. If a case is referred to conference, but it appears that counseling or support services have not been utilized, the Youth Justice Coordinators will suggest appropriate referrals, depending on the victim and family's wishes.

20 A family conference in South Australia can impose a maximum of 300 hours community service, but this rarely if ever occurs.

21 Youth Justice Coordinators say that this can also be a problem in recapitulating the offence in a conference, where the offender may take some pleasure in hearing or discussing the offence details again.

22 Of the six cases I judged to be less serious, in three cases, offenders received community service; and of the seven cases I judged to be most serious, in just one case did the offender receive community service. Thus, there seems to be little connection between my seriousness judgements and whether offenders receive community service.

23 I am aware that offenders may trivialise or deny their assaults by saying it was 'just touching' (see Yantzi, 1998).

5   Children and Family Violence: Restorative Messages from New Zealand

Allison Morris

Introduction

New Zealand is sometimes presented as having endorsed restorative justice to a greater extent than other jurisdictions. There is certainly considerable support for restorative justice there: 104 of the 113 submissions made to the discussion paper on restorative justice prepared by the Ministry of Justice (Ministry of Justice, 1995) were broadly supportive of a restorative approach (Ministry of Justice, 1998). However, the issue of whether or not family violence should be dealt with within a restorative justice framework was addressed in only 11 of these 113 submissions and only five saw a positive role for it. The range of arguments presented against the use of restorative justice included power imbalances in the family, the trivialization of crimes against women and the reinforcement of misogynist attitudes.[1]

I will return to these arguments briefly later in this paper. At this point, it suffices to say that, in my view, criminal justice responses have offered little protection to women who have experienced violence at the hands of their partners. Only a small proportion of the women who experience such violence rely on the law, police or courts to deal with it; even when the police are called, few men are actually arrested; and, even where men are arrested, criminalization and penalization may well increase the likelihood of future violence (for more detailed discussion, see Carbonatto, 1994, 1995 and 1998; Braithwaite & Daly, 1994; Buzawa & Buzawa, 1996; Martin, 1996; Stubbs, 1997; Hudson, 1998, Snider, 1998).[2] For these reasons, I have argued elsewhere for consideration of the use of restorative justice as a means of dealing with violence against women by their partners (Morris and Gelsthorpe, 2000).

This view was shaped by the fact that New Zealand has had a system of restorative justice which deals with some forms of family violence for more than 10 years. That is to say, sexual or physical violence by young offenders, including sexual or physical violence within the family, is dealt with by family group conferences and young people who are the victims of physical or sexual violence within the family may also experience a family group conference. Care and protection and youth justice family group conferences do have very different objectives: youth justice family group conferences are concerned primarily with holding offenders accountable and making amends to victims; and care and protection family group conferences are concerned primarily with the victims' safety. Critical for both, however, is giving victims a voice and meeting victims' needs. Both also focus on taking steps to prevent the recurrence of the offending or victimization. Thus they share a common restorative core.

This paper describes both youth justice and care and protection family group conferences and claims that they both provide examples of how to deal with violence in the family by and against children in a restorative way. However, it also goes a little further: it uses the practice of family group conferences in New Zealand as a way of exploring whether or not restorative justice could deal with family violence generally in a way that offers more to both victims and offenders. Thus it specifically challenges claims that restorative practices inevitably reproduce power imbalances in the family, trivialize violence in the family and reinforce negative attitudes.

Basically, it seems to me that if we can show that restorative processes and practices 'work' for children, then it can be argued that they might well 'work' for women too.[3] By 'work', I am referring to the two main issues which advocates of using the criminal justice system to deal with violence against women by their partners promote: the need to hold men accountable for their actions and the need to ensure that victims are safe. As I have already said, I see little evidence that the criminal justice system does either of these effectively. I argue in this chapter that restorative justice offers more potential for achieving both. I have tried to base this argument on empirical data, but such data are not always available. As a result, the debate between proponents and critics of using restorative justice in this area runs the risk of becoming little more than the exchange of rhetoric. Both can point to examples of where events went tragically wrong. But for me the two key questions are: what has the criminal justice system *actually* achieved for the victims of family violence? And what *might* restorative justice achieve for the victims of family violence? Hooper and Busch (1996) present a detailed critique of restorative processes as a method of dealing with 'domestic' violence, their term. I hope to address some of their concerns in this chapter. What they fail to do, however, is to show that the criminal justice system better serves women who have experienced abuse at the hands of their partners.[4]

Describing Conferencing

Both youth justice care and protection family group conferences have certain common features. In summary, these are:

- involving those most affected by the issue in determining appropriate responses to it;
- decision-making by agreement;
- the relative informality and flexibility of the process; and
- the use of a facilitator.

Thus the family group conference is an opportunity for all the parties concerned in a particular case to participate in decisions about children and young persons whether it be about their offending or their safety. The intent of The Children, Young Persons and Their Families Act 1989 is to encourage family and whanau (extended family) responsibility, through recognizing family strengths, through enabling the family to take the principal role in decision-making and through providing support to families. Professionals are expected to play a different role – for example, to provide support, information and resources. Solutions to the problem – where the child should be placed to ensure his or her safety or how to address the offending – are expected to be located in the 'communities of care'. One of the reasons for this shift from professional to family decision-making was the belief that families' decisions were likely to be better than those imposed by external agencies. It is also expected that these decisions take place in a forum which is respectful of all the participants, is non-stigmatizing and does not blame or shame either the family or the child or young person.

There are three distinct stages in a family group conference:

- all the parties coming to some sort of consensus about what has happened and exploring options for dealing with the offending or for making the child safe;
- private time during which the family discuss what they wish to come out of the meeting;
- coming together again to reach agreement about recommendations and plans for the future.

More than 90 percent of family group conferences result in an agreement about how to ensure the child's safety or about how to deal with the offending.

Youth justice family group conferences and restorative justice

Youth justice family group conferences in New Zealand are held for all medium–serious and serious offending, including violent and sex offences. This, of course, means that they are used, as I said previously, for violent and sex offences committed by young people within the family. There seems to be a broad agreement that youth justice family group conferences do, indeed, reflect restorative values, represent a restorative process and work toward achieving restorative outcomes (NACRO, 1997; Dignan, 1999; Morris & Maxwell, 2000). Clearly, for example, youth justice family group conferences bring together those most affected by the offending – the offenders, their victims and their communities of care – to decide how best to deal with the offending. There is a statutory requirement to pay regard to the interests of the victims and hence to try to make amends to the victim by healing the damage that has been caused (symbolically through apologies and directly through reparation or community work). There is also a statutory requirement to hold the young person accountable for his or her offending and to address the offender's well-being.

Generally, research in New Zealand has shown that, through family group conferences, young offenders can be held accountable for their offending in meaningful ways;[5] the voices of their victims can be heard; victims can feel better as a result of their participation in conferences; and outcomes which address both victims' and offenders' needs or interests can be reached (Maxwell & Morris, 1993). In particular, research shows examples of victims and offenders being reconciled. For example, I have observed victims and offenders shaking hands at the end of conferences, victims inviting offenders and their families to dinner and victims offering to attend court to provide support for offenders. There are also examples of the offender agreeing to live with the victim's family for a while and of a victim and an offender setting up business together. Maxwell and Morris (1999) also found that aspects of restorative processes – especially the expression of remorse[6] – can reduce reoffending.[7]

Critics of restorative justice have used Maxwell and Morris's (1993) research to challenge these claims. They point to the fact that not all victims participated in conferences,[8] that about a quarter of the victims who did participate felt worse as a result of their participation and that about half of the victims interviewed expressed dissatisfaction with the outcomes. These research findings, however, indicate not the failure of family group conferencing, but rather the failure to implement the values, processes and objectives of restorative justice adequately and the existence of poor practice.

Case studies

I cannot offer any statistical data specifically on the frequency with which young people who have committed sexual or physical violence in the family were dealt with by family group conferences or how effective the family group conferences were in these cases. The 1999 police statistics show that six percent of violent offences attributed by the police to young people were referred directly to a family group conference and that a further 16 percent were referred to a family group conference by a youth court judge. This means that, taken together, more than a fifth of violent offences went through a family group conference. The figure for sex offences was somewhat similar: 20 percent (this was made up of 10 percent directly referred to a family group conference and 10 percent referred to a family group conference by a youth court judge). The remaining violent or sex offences were dealt with by police warning or by referral to Police Youth Aid.

However, the following case histories from a number of sources make it clear that violent and sex offending within the family can be appropriately addressed through restorative conferencing. They also make clear another point which seems relevant in debates about restorative justice: the close connection between childhood victimization and offending (Maxwell & Robertson, 1996; Fergusson, 1998) and the need to address both if further offending is to be avoided. The first group of cases come from Levine et al (1998: 36–38).

Andrew, the victim of very serious intergenerational abuse, was arrested and charged with kidnapping his girlfriend and a young family member, wilfully setting fire to a property, assault, assault with a weapon, and wilful damage – all the result of a drunken episode. The family group conference was well attended by Andrew, his parents and whanau, kaumatua, the victim and the Youth Aid officer, but, early on in the conference, Andrew deliberately and seriously injured himself. He was taken to hospital but returned and the conference continued. In the words of one of the professionals present, this had the effect of 'shocking the family into reality'. Andrew apologised to the victim and he and his family agreed to make reparation. Everyone agreed that a custodial sentence was inappropriate and that Andrew needed counselling to help him deal with his abuse, alcohol problems and anger. The plan, therefore, addressed the needs of the victim, made Andrew accountable for his offending and dealt with the outstanding care and protection issues. Incidentally, the probation officer who had been present at what was by all accounts a very moving and emotional family group conference recommended a custodial penalty to the judge, demonstrating the continuing hold of criminal justice values. The judge, however, accepted the plan put forward by the conference and agreed to by the police.

William had been known to social services since the age of 13. Immediate family members had abused him. He also had a history of offending. At the age of 16, he was arrested for 23 burglaries, 3 thefts and 4 charges of male assaults female (his partner with whom he had a child). A number of family group conferences were held involving the whanau. Eventually, a 3 month supervision with activity order was made. This included writing an apology to all the victims, doing 180 hours community work and undertaking drug and alcohol counselling, anger management, and courses in parenting and life skills. The victims' views were taken into account, but the plan focussed on giving William assistance to move ahead with his life.

Alex had a long history of care and protection problems which the youth justice coordinator described as 'shocking'. He had come to the attention of the police before but the first time he appeared in court was at the age of 15 on a charge of male assaults female. The victim was his mother. Prior to the family group conference, Alex spent some time in custody. The offence carried a possible two-year jail sentence. The conference participants included the young person and his lawyer, his mother, seven whanau and a number of professionals. They decided an holistic approach was necessary and that it was necessary to address Alex's problems at every level: spiritual, emotional, cultural and physical. As part of this, the young person, the whanau and the victim spent a period in retreat during which they participated in sessions with a tohunga [priest or learned person] to allow healing to begin and to develop a detailed plan for Alex. This included one module on whanau development, one on personal development and a set of long term educational and career goals. The judge was impressed with the plan and accepted the conference's recommendations in their entirety.

Each of these case histories took account of the victims' views, went some way toward meeting the victims' needs through making an apology and addressed the offending in a way that might prevent further offending (and hence further victimization). It is difficult to imagine what might have been better achieved through further penalization of Andrew, William or Alex. It is this which makes me see conferencing, in an appropriately adapted format, as a useful way of dealing with violence in the family more generally. Indeed, in some areas and on an ad hoc basis, family violence cases are already being dealt with in New Zealand through restorative processes.

Bowen and Consedine (1999), for example, present seven case histories of adults who have experienced restorative conferences prior to sentencing as an aid to the judge. Three of these relate to sexual or physical abuse within the family:

Frank was charged with the sexual violation of his grand-daughter. The family moved from a position of 'shoot the bugger' to a belief that imprisonment would not only damage the grandfather but also the direct victim who was very fond of her grandfather and also other members of the victim's family who were also, of course, members of the offender's family. The conference recommended a suspended prison sentence with supervision and certain conditions. The judge, who said that a sentence of 15 months imprisonment would normally have been imposed, accepted this. This family came together in the conference and afterwards to support both victim and offender.

Mary was charged, among other offences, with threatening to kill her de facto partner. Mary had consumed a considerable amount of alcohol at the time of the threat to kill. She expressed her regret at the conference and her partner made clear that he forgave her. Both wanted her to have counselling and the conference recommended that Mary should undergo a psychiatric, alcohol and drug assessment and attend an anger management course. The judge accepted this and placed Mary under supervision for 12 months.

Barry was charged, among other offences, with male assault female (pushing his wife in the stomach) and with assaulting the man she was now associating with. Barry expressed remorse at the conference and his wife acknowledged there that he had previously apologised to her. She also said that she did not expect him to be violent then or in the future. The conference recommended anger management counselling for Barry, that both Barry and his wife agree to attend counselling arranged by the Family Court counselling coordinator and that, if both of these recommendations were complied with, there was no need for further punishment and that Barry could be discharged. The judge agreed to this and Barry was subsequently discharged.

A number of family violence cases were dealt with by Project Turnaround, a program in which a community panel, based to some extent on restorative values, deals with referrals from court and, if the offender successfully completes the outcome agreed to at the meeting, the police request the judge to discharge the offender. Within Maxwell et al's (1999) sample were a 63-year-old man charged with assaulting his 84-year-old female partner, a 27-year-old man charged with assaulting his wife, a 42-year-old woman charged with assaulting and threatening to kill her de facto male partner, and a 27-year-old woman charged with assaulting her partner. They report two cases of family violence which were dealt with by Te Whanau Awhina, a similar program based on a marae and following kaupapa Maori.

Both Project Turnaround and Te Whanau Awhina were evaluated by Maxwell et al (1999). This involved comparing the reconvictions after one year[9] of a sample of 100 adults who had taken part in these pilots with those of a matched control group who were processed through the courts.[10] Although I cannot say specifically that those involved with family violence offences and processed through the restorative justice pilots reoffended less frequently than those involved in similar offences and processed through the courts,[11] at both six months and after one year, generally speaking, those referred to both schemes were less likely to be reconvicted than their comparable control groups and the results of the survival analyses showed that participants at both pilots were statistically less likely to be reconvicted of an offence than their matched control group. If the pilot participants did reoffend, they were also less likely than the court samples to reoffend seriously.

*Care and protection family group conferences and
restorative justice*

Care and protection family group conferences have not, so far as I am aware, been conceptualized as restorative, but, as I noted previously, the victim's interests are central as are ensuring the victim's safety and preventing re-victimization. The basic purpose of The Children, Young Persons and Their Families Act 1989 with respect to care and protection is to protect children from abuse and neglect and to ensure that they are safely looked after. Section 5 of the 1989 Act refers to the family participating in decisions about the child, maintaining and strengthening the relationship between the child and the family and giving consideration to the wishes of the child. Section 13 refers to removing children from their families where there is a 'serious risk of harm' and also states that, where a child is removed, the placement should ideally be within the extended family, should maintain family relationships and should be for the minimum period possible.

Thus the principal responsibility of the family group conference is deciding on the appropriate placement of the child to ensure his or her safety and not on the responsibility of the offender or making amends to the victim for the harm done.[12] The criminal courts continue to deal with the behaviour of adult offenders, including where the abuse or violence is within the family, though often, of course, such prosecutions fail to take place because of the lack of evidence (due, for example, to the child's young age).[13] Making amends to the victim for the harm done is the province of the counseling services and here too children's special status is recognized to some extent. This paper does not address either of these processes. Instead, it documents the extent to which practice in care and protection family group conferences reflects restorative values, meets restorative objectives and reaches restorative outcomes and, in so doing, ensures the victim's safety.

The work of care and protection family group conferences

An average of 10 children a year in New Zealand die as a result of family violence. A further 250 are hospitalized each year as a result of the injuries they have received. However, these children represent only a small proportion of the children exposed to violence in the home

(Ministry of Social Policy, 2001). There is no doubt that much of the work of care and protection family group conferences relates to the abuse of children by family members. In the year to June 2000, more than 26,500 notifications were received by social workers and just over a quarter of these resulted in a finding that abuse – emotional, physical or sexual – or neglect had occurred (Ministry of Social Policy, 2001). We cannot tell from these statistics how many were attributed to family members. However, other sources give some indication. Basher (1999) documents the characteristics of abusers arising from over 1000 investigations of the alleged abuse of children: 51 percent of the alleged offenders in cases of sexual abuse were family members and a quarter were family friends; in cases of physical abuse, 83 percent of the alleged offenders were family members. Indeed, in almost a half of these allegations, the alleged abuser was a parent. This means that care and protection family group conferences are dealing with some forms of family violence and that an examination of the practice of care and protection conferences, to the extent that they are restorative, contributes to debates about the appropriateness of using restorative justice as a way of dealing with family violence. In 1996–97, almost 3,000 care and protection family group conferences were held (Department of Social Welfare, 1998).

I do not plan to describe further care and protection family group conferences except to note a few points that are relevant to this discussion. Obviously, some children are too young to participate effectively: babies are not immune from abuse. In such cases, they must rely on others – in particular, family members, but perhaps also professionals – to ensure their safety. In most conferences, however, the children are present and can participate.[14] Indeed, such is the value placed on this that conference participants may decide to exclude the family member who is the (alleged) offender if his/her inclusion would silence the child (victim). This only happens rarely, however, since value is placed on having the abuser present.[15] This may encourage abusers to accept responsibility, but it certainly enables assessment of the risk the abuser presents to the child and of how the child may be kept safe. Another way of ensuring that the child is safe is that the referring agents – usually social workers – must agree that the family decisions will protect the child. I want to turn now to an assessment of how these conferences work in practice.

Evaluating care and protection family group conferences

A number of evaluations have been carried out on care and protection family group conferences in New Zealand. Though none specifically addresses restorative justice issues, they can be drawn on to provide a basis for this discussion. Hassall (1996: 31–32), for example, sets out eleven anticipated advantages in holding family group conferences:

- continuity (maintaining continuity in a child's life while bringing the abuse to an end);
- pride (creating a sense of identity, belonging and pride in one's family by encouraging families to respond to the child's needs);
- ownership (the family taking ownership of and responsibility for resolving the problem);
- extension (extending solutions beyond the child in question to others in the family);
- meaningfulness (ensuring the processes are meaningful and understandable);
- learning (allowing participants the opportunity to hear, learn and understand – for example, about the nature of the abuse and the level of support available for the victim);
- satisfaction (giving the family and the child the opportunity to speak and be heard and to feel vindicated by the participants' condemnation of the offender);
- repair (initiating better communication, cooperation and supervision within the family, bringing families together and restoring legitimate authority);
- truth (challenging evasions, prevarications and lying by those familiar with the offender's behaviour);
- privacy (the advantages just listed assisting the fact that the proceedings are private) and
- effectiveness (the family, knowing its members, making plans which might work).

All of these seem to me to be consistent with a restorative value system.

However, Hassall (1996: 32–33) acknowledges that the principal risks associated with family group conferences can be summarized under these headings:

- continuity may mean no real change and that the abuse may continue though it is perhaps better concealed;
- pride in the membership of an abusive subculture may be reinforced;
- outcomes might be dictated by the professionals rather than 'owned' by the parties themselves;
- if effective solutions are not found the result will be the reinforcement and perpetuation of failure;
- participants may fail to take the proceedings seriously;
- families with an entrenched dysfunctional way of operating may learn nothing;

- victims may feel trapped and helpless if authority is given to the family which abused them;
- the process may reopen old wounds so that family divisions are worsened and prolonged;
- *the conference may fail to arrive at the truth and privacy may result in injustice;* and
- the family's plan might be unrealistic and impractical.

None of these risks can be disputed at a theoretical level and, of course, negative consequences may also result from more conventional decision-making approaches, from inaction and from poor decision-making by professionals. However, as Hassall (1996: 33) rightly says, it is the responsibility of the care and protection services to 'maximise the advantages and minimise the risks'. This leads me to the research that has been conducted on care and protection family group conferences to assess whether or not, in practice, the advantages claimed for them outweigh the risks. Paterson and Harvey (1991), in their early evaluation, found that families did participate in decisions; agreements were reached; and most of the professionals involved in the study expressed support for conferencing as a means of resolving care and protection issues. Walker (1996), also drawing from research in the early years of conferencing, commented on the improvements in and strengthening of family relationships, the opportunity given to children and young people in the conference to express their views, and the partnerships created between families and others to resolve the issues at hand. On the other hand, Paterson and Harvey (1991) raised concerns about the lack of monitoring and follow-up of the agreed safety plans, the inability of some families to make sound decisions to safeguard their children, and the wishes of families taking precedence over the needs of the child. Overall, Robertson's (1996) review of research on care and protection family group conferences concluded on a fairly positive note though he also expressed concern about the lack of follow-up data and monitoring. These concerns are, however, again primarily related to poor practice and point to the need to ensure that restorative values are fully implemented. They do not provide fundamental objections to using care and protection conferences as a way of ensuring children's safety.

Case studies

Because of the lack of data on precisely how conferences 'work' for children who have been the victims of family violence, I have again drawn from case histories. O'Reilly and Bush (1999) present the case of the ABC family. The following summary highlights the key features:

The ABC family presented an alarming history of family conflict, violence and child abuse with evidence of severe and on-going extreme physical punishment of three young children ... The family were referred for a family group conference after ... the children had been removed from the parents' care [into the custody of the Child, Youth and Family Service on the basis of an interim custody order]. Initially, the social workers and education and health professionals ... were doubtful any agreement could be reached at the conference since the parents did not accept that their treatment of the children was unusual or harmful. They were angry and hurt that their children had been taken from them, whereas ... social workers believed that the children could not be returned to parental care. Because of the poor relations between the parents and the social workers, the care and protection coordinator suggested a mediated meeting between the parties. Both claimed that the other side never listened to their point of view, but agreed to participate with the coordinator acting as mediator. During this meeting, the reasons for the maltreatment became clearer and the parents spoke of the use of physical punishment in their own childhood. Family members were also spoken to prior to the family group conference and placements were available there if the parents agreed. At the conference itself, the coordinator used a strategy which explored any gaps in needs and services to focus discussion on the children. At the conference, the parents talked [openly] about what had happened to the children and were clear about what they wanted for them in the future. The parents then left the meeting and the family decided how to put their decisions into practice. When the parents met with the social workers later, they said they were satisfied with the plans.

What happened here was that the family had been able to face the reality of their abuse and neglect of their children and to plan for their future without pressure and, arguably, without blame. The parents were able to shift from outright rejection of a placement within the extended family to acceptance of it. The children were in a safe place and were no longer at risk.

Fraser and Norton (1996: 41–44) describe the S family's experience in detail. The following summarizes the key features:

The mother of the S family ran away from home as a teenager ... Her birth family has a history of alcoholism ... The eldest child in the family is A. He is 15 years old and had been involved with a troublesome group of teenagers. [Referral for a family group conference] was precipitated by the school's notification that A had arrived at school with a black eye and severe bruising as a result of excessive disciplining by his father. There are two other children in the family ... medical reports indicated that these two children were undernourished and developmentally delayed. The mother told the social worker that she had been hitting the children out of frustration and feelings of despair ... The mother was beaten by the father two weeks prior to the referral. Both were intoxicated at the time ... There were further concerns about the family's financial and living situation ... The first stage of the meeting ... was very difficult and tense as the extended family members were angry that they had not been informed earlier of the difficulties faced by the S family. They expressed anger and shame about the situation and strongly challenged the right of the various agencies to be involved ... Instead of the professionals telling the family what to do, the family began to use the professionals' experience and knowledge to extend their understandings so they could go on to make good, safe decisions for the children. [The professionals withdrew for the second stage – the family's private deliberations.] The family's discussion took a full day to work their way towards achieving their goal and there were many tears, recriminations and challenges during this time. The plan for son A was for him to live with his paternal grandparents in the Pacific Islands for at least a year ... The family wanted [the two other children] to be returned to the care of the parents with close family and agency monitoring and support. They also asked that appropriate counselling be arranged for the parents to address the issues of violence, alcohol use and parenting ... Finally, the family requested that the family group conference be reconvened in six months to ensure the plan was working and progress was being made.

Addressing Concerns

A number of concerns have been raised about restorative justice (Morris & Young, 2000; Ashworth, 2000; Crawford, 2000b). Not all are relevant here. I want to address specifically those of most relevance in the area of family violence. As I said earlier, it seems to me that if these concerns can be resolved or minimized when the offender or victim is a child, it seems likely that they could be resolved when the victim is a woman and the offender is a man (and vice versa for that matter).

Power imbalances

There clearly are power imbalances between children and adults and between children and parents. Young people (and families) participating in the New Zealand research on youth justice family group conferences were asked a number of key questions: 'Did you feel that you made the decision?' 'How involved were you in reaching the decisions?' and 'In your view, who really decided?' About a third of the young people said that they had felt involved in the process. If responses indicating that the young person felt 'partly' involved are added to this, then nearly half of the young people said they felt involved in some way. They were able to say what they wanted to and to speak openly without pressure. However, almost a half felt that they had not been involved in the family group conferences and that decisions had been made about them, not with them.[16] Technically, outcomes have to be agreed to by all the parties at the conference, but the young person's voice, on occasions, seemed to have become subsumed within the family's.[17] The reason for this was often that the young people's views were not valued over the views of adults. Young people, therefore, need to be actively encouraged and supported to speak and adults (families as well as professionals) need to be encouraged to listen. Good restorative practice would ensure this.

There are even greater power imbalances between abused children and abusive parents, where relationships are characterized by submission (by the abused child) and dominance (by the abusive parent) and where there is a conspiracy of secrecy and silence. How can it even be suggested, therefore, that abused children can assert their needs or wishes in such an environment? In practice, power imbalances in care and protection family group conferences are addressed by supporting the abused child and, sometimes, by challenging or excluding the abuser. Thus the extended family can provide a supportive basis for the voice of the child to be heard or may speak for the child.[18] In a promotional video prepared by the then Children, Young Persons and Their Families Service in which a young girl made allegations of sexual abuse against her stepfather, the girl wrote about her feelings and her placement in a letter read to the conference participants by her grandmother. In this case, the stepfather denied the abuse but was initially present at the conference. The girl wanted him to be there to face her whanau and she spoke to them about her wishes through her grandmother.[19] Professionals also have a role to play in preventing power imbalances in that they can provide general oversight and should not agree an outcome which is clearly at odds with either the child's wishes or their professional judgement about what is required to protect the child and to keep him or her safe.

I recognize that abusive relationships between men and women are characterized by dominance (by the abuser) and submission (by the abused) and, consequently, that women on their own may not be able to assert their needs or wishes (see, for example, Martin, 1996; Stubbs, 1997). However, the simple lesson from both youth justice and care and protection family group conferences is that it is at least *possible* to develop strategies to address power imbalances. I agree that violent men may be unable to 'hear' their female partners, but they are likely to find it more difficult not to hear the voices of concern from their friends, their parents, their partner's parents, their siblings and so on. Thus power imbalances between abused women and abusive men could be addressed by ensuring procedural fairness, by supporting the less powerful, and by challenging the powerful. Examples cited by Braithwaite and Daly (1994) include mobilizing the support of men who are anti-violence or women with experience in highlighting the effects of violence against women. On the other hand, Hooper and Busch (1996: 109), on the basis of 'extensive experience as a mediator', argue that these process changes can 'compensate for minor differences in power, [but] are not capable of re-establishing equality where violence has occurred'. I do not agree with this; it must depend on what actions are taken – for example, the man may be silenced throughout the process. Also, reducing power imbalances is certainly not an objective that the criminal justice system either aspires to or achieves. Arguably, by making decisions for women, it disempowers them further. Hooper and Busch may be referring to re-establishing equality in a wider sense. Again, the criminal justice system does nothing in this regard and restorative justice processes would at least put this on the agenda.

Putting children at risk

Early critics of care and protection family group conferences described the kinds of families whose children came into the care and protection system as 'dysfunctional' (Geddes, 1993; Connolly, 1994). There has been no real evidence of this. Paterson and Harvey (1991) report 20 mentions by the professionals interviewed as part of their research of problems created by families (such as intergenerational sexual abuse or heavy drug or alcohol use), but they also stress that many of the professionals who made this type of comment also said that such dysfunctional families made up only a small proportion of the families coming into the system overall. For example, Paterson and Harvey quote one worker who described one family as 'very dysfunctional' but went on to say that 'you can't say the whole of the principle isn't right because of that family' (1991: 68). It is possible too that the nuclear family might well be 'dysfunctional' and finding it difficult to cope at a particular point in time because they are in crisis or have recently experienced traumatic events. But this does not mean that there are no strengths which can be tapped into in the extended family or that the family would not be able to cope in the longer term, especially with extra support. Indeed, it can be argued that extended families are far better placed than professionals to prevent the recurrence of abuse, to arrange networks of support and surveillance and to monitor safety plans. They can visit more frequently and call in on the child uninvited. Again, therefore, the conclusion has to be that restorative justice processes can devise procedures to minimize risk. Indeed, some programs which are dealing with men who have been violent toward their partners have already incorporated similar meetings specifically geared to creating safety plans for the woman and any children and to monitoring these plans (McMaster et al, 2000).

Trivializing abuse in the family and perpetuating negative attitudes

Abusers commonly deny responsibility for their behaviour or place responsibility for it onto others, including children. Families may well share in this. For example, four coordinators interviewed by Paterson and Harvey (1991) did say that sexual abuse was difficult to deal with in conferences and they quoted one coordinator as saying that the family can be 'unsupportive or blaming of the child. All too often the family protects its men to the cost of its women and children' (1991: 68). However, care and protection family group conferences can challenge these attitudes and behaviour and can encourage the abuser, if present, to take responsibility. Others in the family may also raise their concerns about the abuser's behaviour, perhaps revealing the existence of intergenerational violence. However, as previously noted, the primary purpose of the care and protection conference is not the allocation of responsibility. The criminal justice system still deals with this, as best it can, though, as some of the case histories referred to earlier made clear, there is no reason why restorative justice processes could not be used here too. Where the offender is a young person, this already happens: holding him or her responsible is a key part of the youth justice family group conference, as is allowing victims to confront their offender with the consequences of his or her actions.

The use of restorative processes for men's violence against their partners would not signify its decriminalization. The criminal law remains a signifier and denouncer, but it is my belief that the abuser's family and friends are by far the more potent agents to achieve this objective of denunciation. Arguably, by challenging men's violence, their denial that it is unacceptable, their tactics of victim blaming and their techniques of neutralization, the message of denunciation is loud and clear for those who matter most to the offender. The potential impact of this challenge by whanau, friends, men's groups, victim advocates, or professionals if not by the woman herself in signifying to men the seriousness of their violence against their partners should not be underestimated. Indeed, in this way, restorative processes also have the potential to challenge community norms and values about men's violence against their partners.[20] There is also nothing in a restorative justice approach which prevents the police from arresting violent men or which prevents them and other agencies from educating the public that men's violence against their partners is wrong.[21]

Conclusion

New Zealand already has a system of restorative justice for dealing with some types of abuse within the family. From a review of the research on family group conferences – both youth justice and care and protection – it appears that many of the concerns expressed about restorative justice processes can be avoided by good practice and by a commitment to ensure that restorative values are given prominence and made a priority. The same can be said for the potential of community or restorative conferences dealing with adult offenders. It is these values and practices that will ensure that women and children are empowered and made safe, and that violence is denounced. There is little evidence that conventional criminal justice processes always ensure the safety of victims, hold offenders accountable and prevent reoffending and re-victimization.

Women who are experiencing violence from their partners rarely call the police; only about a tenth of the women participating in the New Zealand Women's Safety Survey reported that they had ever done so (Morris, 1998). Thus the prosecution of men who are abusing their partners is rare and, even if they were imprisoned for this (itself a rare occurrence in New Zealand), this penalization might only serve to brutalize them further. Police and/or court action also did not feature among the factors that the women participating in the Women's Safety Survey thought might change their partner's behaviour; 'losing me' and counseling were the most commonly cited factors (Morris, 1998). Women themselves, therefore, seem to be looking for solutions other than reliance on the criminal justice system. Restorative justice processes may offer a better way. Safety issues can be addressed, offenders can be held accountable in meaningful ways and both victims and their communities of care can be given a say in what 'works' for them.

Notes

1 It should be noted that, in these submissions, 'family violence' was taken to mean 'violence against women by men'. Other forms of family violence (such as violence by or against children within the family) were not discussed.

2   Police statistics in New Zealand show that the number of recorded offences for 'male assaults female' (the only offence other than homicide which gives an indication of the extent of men's violence against women) rose markedly from 1988 to 1994, but that the number has declined since then (although the 1999 figure is still higher than the 1988 one). The reasons for this are not clear, but it does not seem plausible to suggest that men's violence against women is declining.

3   I acknowledge that men can be the victims of family violence too, but most research suggests that it is (primarily) men who beat (primarily) women (see, for example, Young et al, 1998) and it is with respect to women that most concern has been raised about the possibility of using restorative processes to deal with family violence (see, for example, Hooper and Busch, 1996).

4   They refer, for example, to abused women being afraid to disagree with their partner in custody and access cases and in Family Court mediation and counseling because he might hurt her if she did, to abused women perceiving that their partner had more decision-making power than did non-abused women, to abused women's passivity and learned helplessness, to abused women's fear of their partners more generally and to abused women's unwillingness to assert their needs for fear of antagonizing their partners. They also refer to the failure of mediation to provide ongoing protection to women against abuse. They do not say how the criminal justice system prevents any of these happening.

5   Apologies and community service, including service to the victim, are common outcomes.

6   This included the offender feeling sorry for the offending and showing it.

7   There are no data on the extent to which conferences are more effective in reducing reoffending than the former court system. However, to the extent that the courts then generally failed to hold offenders accountable in meaningful ways – almost a half of young offenders were discharged by the courts – and did little to encourage real remorse, it would be unlikely that they produced lower reoffending rates.

8   However, Morris et al (1993) found that only six percent of the victims they interviewed said that they did not want to meet 'their' offender.

9   Criminal records for the participants were obtained up to the 21st January 1999. This meant that the period following completion of the scheme varied between individuals. Nearly all participants were followed up for six months, and most were followed up for one year. All the matched controls were followed for one year. A 'survival' analysis was undertaken using the LIFETEST procedure of SAS.

10 They were matched on offence type, participants and control subjects were matched on sex, age, ethnicity, number of charges and number of previous convictions.

11 Even if I could, the numbers involved would be too small to enable any general claims to be made.

12 The police and social workers do, however, tend to work together in this area and case conferences are held to share information and sort out areas of overlap. Although the primary purpose of this multidisciplinary coordination is to promote the safety and well-being of the child, other objectives

can be met, including assisting the offending adult to assume responsibility for their behaviour and to assist in the identification and prosecution of offenders (New Zealand Children and Young Persons Service, 1995).

13 Special procedures have been introduced in New Zealand criminal courts, as in many jurisdictions, in contested matters where the victim is a child – for example, the use of videotaped evidence, the use of closed circuit television and so on. The child's special status is recognized though there continues to be concern that these reforms have not gone far enough (Pipe & Henaghan, 1996).

14 Paterson and Harvey's (1991) early research found that children were present in 79 percent of the family group conferences concerning them.

15 Paterson and Harvey's (1991) early research found that five percent of care and protection family group conferences resulted in a family member being specifically excluded, usually because they were the alleged abuser.

16 Although about a quarter of the young people said they did not know who had decided the outcome, the group most frequently identified by them as the decision-makers was their family. This was stated by about a third. However, even these relatively 'low' rates of involvement in conferences are still considerably higher than young people's involvement in conventional court processes.

17 In South Australia, the police and the young person are specifically named as having to agree to the outcome. This may make a difference to young people's perception of their involvement. Research on this matter has not yet been published.

18 It could be argued that judges now in many jurisdictions routinely ask children about their placement in line with Article 12 of the United Nations Convention on the Rights of the Child. But it seems unlikely that children will open up to strangers in the same way that they will speak to whanau.

19 In the video's story-line, the stepfather subsequently pleaded guilty at court.

20 Hooper and Busch (1996: 118) say that 'in New Zealand at present there is no ... societal consensus about domestic violence ... [and] that an offender's abusive behaviour takes place within a social context which often legitimises, condones and even supports his use of violence'. They cite for this an unpublished paper by an Australian authority (Stubbs), but in fact New Zealand data suggest that it is a minority of men who think it is 'OK' to hit their partners (Liebrich et al, 1995). Thus this dominant support which challenges men's violence against their partners could readily be utilized in restorative justice processes.

21 And, of course, the availability of restorative processes does not prevent women who prefer to use the criminal justice system doing so. In addition, the criminal justice system can be used as part of an escalation of responses (on the lines proposed by Braithwaite and Daly, 1994).

6   Feminist Praxis:
Making Family Group Conferencing Work

Joan Pennell and Gale Burford

Family group conferencing can stop family violence. As we learned from our Canadian study, the question is not whether family group conferencing (FGC) works to stop domestic violence and child maltreatment but rather how it can be made to work so that all family members are safeguarded. In this chapter, we stress that FGC needs to build partnerships that respect the privacy of families while *promoting women's* leadership and ensuring protective intervention. Such partnerships can counter the isolation, fear, and entrapment that are imposed by recurring intra-familial violence, typically targeting women and children, and that is engendered by social conditions and practices marginalizing certain populations.

Our approach to FGC is influenced by the New Zealand FGC model in its emphasis upon the responsibility of the wider family group for their young relatives, rights of children and young people, affirmation of cultural diversity, and encouragement of community–state partnerships (Hassall, 1996). Our theory on FGC is indebted to the communitarian vision of child welfare and youth justice projected by Indigenous peoples in New Zealand (Rangihau, 1986) and Canada (Bushie, 1997; *Liberating Our Children*, 1992). And our perspective on FGC is shaped by multiple social movements, including those represented in this volume – feminist, Aboriginal, and restorative justice. This chapter elaborates the feminist perspectives that inform our work.

Feminists have insisted that protecting women and children means promoting their empowerment through creating just societies (Callahan, 1993). As this volume highlights, the women's movement has extensively questioned the capacity of state institutions, as currently structured, to advance justice, and their critique is consistent with those of activists from the Aboriginal and restorative justice movements. These latter movements have proposed alternatives such as mediation, sentencing circles, and family group conferencing (see chapters by Kelly, Bazemore, Blagg, and Pranis). Knowing the pressures placed on abused women to forgive their victimizers and reunite, feminists have approached with caution any strategies that bring together survivors and perpetrators while at the same time seeking to learn from these alternatives (see chapters by Behrendt, Busch, Coker, Daly, and Stubbs).

Through making links within and outside the women's movement, we propose that feminists, who are by no means a homogeneous group, can interrupt their and others' pre-set conceptions and can generate alternatives to stop family violence. We have chosen to place this chapter within a feminist praxis of 'links, interruptions' because in our experience in Canada, the United States, and England, women so often provide the leadership vital for making FGC work in situations of family violence. Their leadership is evident as community activists in initiatives to establish FGC programs and as family members and service providers in deliberations at the conferences and in carrying out the plans.

This chapter begins by briefly reviewing the positive outcomes of the Family Group Decision Making Project in the Atlantic Canadian province of Newfoundland and Labrador. Given questions about the applicability of FGC in situations with grave power imbalances, we devote the bulk of the chapter to examining the role of feminist praxis in conferencing. This section begins by defining feminist praxis and reviewing recent Canadian and US developments in stopping family violence. From these developments, a feminist praxis framework of 'links, interruptions' is constructed and then employed to conceptualize FGC as a means of resolving family violence. General findings and examples from the Canadian Project are used to illustrate the design and implementation of an FGC program along the principles of feminist praxis.

Outcomes of the Newfoundland and Labrador Project

The outcomes from the Family Group Decision Making Project establish that FGC can be an effective strategy for stopping child maltreatment and domestic violence (Pennell & Burford, 2000a). The findings from the three study sites further demonstrate that the model can work in quite different cultures and regions: a northerly Inuit settlement; a rural peninsula with people of French, English, and Micmac heritage; and an urban centre with residents of primarily Irish and British descent.

Over a one-year period, 32 families took part in conferencing. In all, 37 conferences were held, 32 first-time and five reconvened conferences.

Although these numbers may appear limited, the participation rates provide a different picture. The conferences had a total of 472 participants, of whom a substantial majority were family group members (384) rather than service providers (88). These figures indicate that conferencing is a broad-based community initiative that goes well beyond the nuclear family.

The referrals came primarily from Child Welfare but also from Adult (Parole and Probation) and Youth Corrections. The Project requested that the most difficult situations be referred, and for the most part, the referring workers were only too pleased to comply. Because of Child Welfare's mandate, most families were referred for child abuse and neglect or youth unmanageability and, thus, masked the prevalence of women abuse and sexual abuse. These other concerns became apparent during FGC preparations or at the conferences. During this period the FGC coordinators documented the presence of an adult abusing an adult in 21 of the 32 families, with nearly all of the violence committed by males against females. Although only three of the referrals were for child sexual abuse, such abuse surfaced in another seven families during the preparations or at the conference.

To measure the impact of FGC on family violence, the Project adopted a quasi-experimental design: the non-random assignment of families to the Project and comparison groups, application of a treatment (FGC), and comparison of pre-test and post-test measures. Validity and reliability were enhanced by collecting the data through diverse methods (e.g., interviews, file analyses), from a range of perspectives (e.g., family, community, government), and by comparing quantitative and qualitative findings. Families were followed for a one-to-two-year period after conferencing. All Project families were included in the review of Child Welfare and Police files. In addition, 31 comparison families were selected through an independent consulting group (Andy Rowe Consultants, 1997) for the Child Welfare file review. The majority of families took part in follow-up interviews: 115 individuals from 28 families were interviewed about the impact of conferencing. For a complete overview of the evaluation measures, see Burford and Pennell (1998a).

Notably all of the data sources agreed that in general FGC benefited the families. The major findings for the Project families were:

- a reduction in indicators of child maltreatment and domestic violence;
- an advancement in children's development; and
- an extension of social supports.

These findings pose the question: Why did the Project work? We now turn to our argument that a feminist praxis of 'ties, links' was crucial for its effectiveness.

Feminist Praxis and Stopping Family Violence

Praxis refers to thought and action reshaping each other through engagement in social change (Lather, 1991). This approach to creating knowledge has intellectual roots in the Marxist dialectic and the Pragmatist 'learning by doing' (Ritzer, 1992) and has served as the epistemology of modern emancipatory movements (Freire, 1968; Friedmann, 1987). At their heart is a contradiction about identity: in resisting oppressive categories such as class, 'race' (using the term as a social construction) and gender, social movements unify people around these same identities. This is an unresolvable tension for the feminist movement, which simultaneously deconstructs (takes apart) gender as a category and constructs (joins together) a common sense of identity as women (Elam, 1994; Phelan, 1993).

Feminist praxis is particularly concerned with the politics of gender identity. This mode of critically reflective action *interrupts* assumptions, including about gender identity, while still fostering the *links* necessary for working together to end injustices based on gender and other oppressive categorizations (Ristock & Pennell, 1996). In our view, a feminist praxis of 'links, interruptions' is a useful framework for conceptualizing gender dynamics in the context of family groups making plans to stop family violence. We hold this view, in part, because feminists have been instrumental in identifying how family ideology has been used against women.

Feminist analysts have observed that in English-speaking policy circles, the term family has often been employed as a code word for mother (Thorne, 1982: 10), with gender and 'race' obscured and family and nation accentuated (Williams, 1989: xiv). Although ostensibly focussing on family and children, social welfare and child welfare have been crafted so as to support and control women as caregivers for dependent family members (Ursel, 1992) and, thus, limiting their capacity for paid employment or civic participation (Pateman, 1989). Their caring labour is enforced through social and legal sanctions while being unpaid in the family or poorly compensated in the workplace (Baines, Evans, & Neysmith, 1991). The result has been to leave women and their dependants trapped and at risk not only of poverty but also abuse (Callahan, 1993).

Not surprisingly then many feminists have condemned the private and hierarchical family for breeding family violence (Yllö & Bograd, 1988) yet at the same time affirmed personal space, attachments, and home (Eisenstein, 1983). Especially as the voices of women of colour were heard, culture was seen as integral to ideas of family (Harrison et al, 1990; Hoop, 1986). For most, the goal was not to end the family but rather to reconstruct the family in a way that its boundaries protected a sense of privacy and identity without reinforcing abusive secrecy. Feminist efforts were not limited to critical analysis disrupting preconceptions of gender and family life. Feminist praxis pushed for overcoming the dichotomy between private and public life and uniting women in undertaking collaborative action to create women's places of safety.

Starting in the mid-1970s, one of the spin-offs of Canadian and US second-wave feminism has been the battered women's movement (Beaudry, 1985; Gilman, 1988; Schechter, 1982). Responding to women's stories of victimization, feminists helped women escape with their children from domestic tyranny, united women under one roof, and encouraged women to make decisions about their own lives and assume leadership roles. Notably the shelter movement offered an alternative child welfare system that kept mothers and children together (Callahan, 1993).

Concomitant with the rapid growth of transition houses, crisis lines, and support groups was the realization that women's lives remain threatened unless action is taken 'beyond the shelter doors' (Blackbear, 1991). Such a recognition propelled women's advocates to form alliances with various societal institutions and to call for a 'coordinated response' encompassing an array of services, including legal action, batterers' groups, and battered women's housing, advocacy, and support programs (Pence & Shepard, 1988). Although the proponents of a coordinated response wanted the reforms to expand beyond the legal system to community institutions (Pence, 1999), a number of factors converged to skew interventions toward police and court action.

In the mid-1980s in both Canada and the United States, greater legal enforcement was initiated in response to perpetrators. Because law enforcement had typically treated domestic violence as a private matter rather than a public issue requiring state intervention, policies and legislation were enacted that limited police and/or prosecutor discretion and stipulated charging offenders with or without victim cooperation (McGillivray, 1987). Support for these measures has come from feminists recognizing the necessity of state controls over perpetrators, the criminal justice system seeking to encompass victims' interests, and in the United States, the insurance industry concerned about liability of police departments.

Whether or not pro-arrest policies deter further violence remains a matter of controversy. Some claim that such intervention should only be applied to married or employed men who are most likely to anticipate costs from being convicted (Buzawa & Buzawa, 1996a). Others call for all criminal behaviour, including violence directed toward family members, to be understood in a construction of social and economic involvements and relationships (Fagan, 1993; Lackey & Williams, 1995). Pointing to US findings on victim outcomes, others have stressed that police intervention is both a resource and liability for survivors and that the women's involvement in employment and possibly family decrease recidivism (Miller & Krull, 1997).

While welcoming legal intervention, involvement of the police and courts remains a dilemma for women's advocates. On the one hand, the charges provide immediate protection for some women, make a symbolic and important statement that domestic violence is a crime and, more broadly, promote a social context in which women exercise greater autonomy over their lives (MacLeod, 1990; Stark, 1996). Canadian and US studies have found that survivors tend to report satisfaction with police intervention (Lacey, 1993; Martin, 1997; Miller & Krull, 1997). Despite racist police responses, a Canadian study found that Aboriginal women wanted criminal justice intervention to stop severe domestic violence (McGillivray & Comaskey, 1999).

On the other hand, the involvement of the legal system dominates over all other programs, leaving abused women feeling that they have little option but to prosecute (MacLeod, 1990). Within the adversarial legal system, survivors have been threatened with arrest unless they testify against abusers to whom they may still be tied emotionally and financially and from whom they may quite rightly fear retaliation. Their fears are justified: women's efforts to separate from abusers elevate the risk of lethal violence (Wilson & Daly, 1994). Moreover, police intervention can leave abused women with the perception of greater safety while in actuality intensifying some forms of domestic violence (Miller & Krull, 1997).

Indigenous, immigrant, and other disadvantaged women have expressed the greatest dissatisfaction with the application of pro-arrest policies (Martin, 1999; Nichols, 1991). 'Zero tolerance' of violence policies has meant that complainants may be charged if they defended themselves; counter-charging by perpetrators has discouraged abused women from reporting assaults (McGillivray & Comaskey, 1999). In US states disallowing a self-defence plea, partners have been held equally at fault and both arrested, but efforts are now being made to limit dual arrests through 'primary aggressor' policies and police training (Martin, 1999). The no-fault approach, however, has intensified in another protective system, child welfare.

Along with the greater reliance on legal intervention into domestic violence, child welfare in both Canada and the United States has become more legalistic in orientation. Despite initiatives to expand family supports and resources, the overall trend has been a narrowing from broad support services down to investigation and apprehensions (Kamerman & Kahn, 1997; Wharf, 1995). Within this procedural context, abused mothers are seen not as victims in their own right but rather as neglecting parents who fail to protect their children from abuse or witnessing abuse (Callahan, 1993; Lyon, 1999). Given the extensive co-occurrence of domestic violence and child maltreatment (Edleson, 1999; Jaffe et al, 1990; Straus & Gelles, 1990; S. M. Ross, 1996), reporting domestic violence places many mothers at jeopardy of losing their children (Phillips, 1992).

Such consequences, as dual arrests and removal of children from abused mothers, stem from strategies that focus solely on holding individuals accountable. The Canadian and US legal and child welfare systems are designed to take action against assailants or maltreating parents and, as a result, fail to hold families, communities, and institutions accountable for their part in sustaining family violence. In this chapter, we take the stance that ties to these collective resources are what make it possible for women to take charge of their lives and prevent further violence. And we make the case that a feminist praxis of 'links, interruptions' can generate a partnership-building approach to FGC that advances safety and empowerment.

As shown in the diagram below, feminist praxis opposed societal norms and practices upholding the private and hierarchical family by simultaneously denouncing gender norms and advancing women's leadership in stopping family violence. Working for safe homes and caring families, women's groups established shelters, support groups, and other programs that strengthened women's autonomy in making decisions over their lives and reconstructing their families. Recognizing the need for legal leverage over perpetrators, women's advocates urged police and court action. State intervention exerted controls over perpetrators but also abused women/mothers and in many ways contradicted efforts to advance women's leadership and the privacy of their homes. A coordinated response was envisioned as a way to move beyond using either women's programs or the legal system to stop domestic violence and to join together their efforts. The aspiration was to include other community institutions in the coordinated response.

In addition, we propose that FGC is a way to include families among these partners. Family–community–government partnerships are seen as a means to respect family privacy, advance women's leadership, and maintain state controls. Women want their homes to be free from unnecessary intrusions and their families and cultures affirmed; they want a say over their lives; and as needed, they want state agencies to provide protections. To achieve such multiple aims, a partnership effort is required for designing and implementing FGC programs. By placing these partnerships within a feminist praxis of 'links, interruptions', women's aspirations are not submerged under a masculinist and racist family ideology.

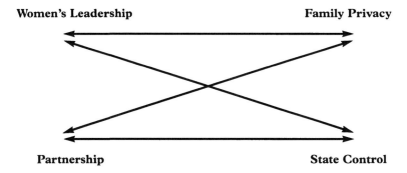

Figure 6.1 Women's Leadership, Family Privacy, Partnership and State Control

Designing an FGC Program

Principles for designing an FGC program can be teased forth from the Newfoundland & Labrador Family Group Decision Making Project, a trial demonstration of the effectiveness of FGC in stopping family violence. With some modification, Joan has found that the same principles apply to her work with the North Carolina Family Group Conferencing Project, which seeks to mainstream rather than test FGC (Pennell & Weil, 2000). Below are set forth a series of principles for using a feminist praxis of 'links, interruptions' in establishing an FGC program. These principles were applied within a context of 'crisis' catalysed by the reopening of investigations into child abuse at a Christian Brothers orphanage. The earlier failure of religious and public authorities to intervene, compounded by a dramatic increase in child abuse reports, generated an amenability of government and non-government leaders alike to look at alternatives.

Participatory co-leadership

Early in the 1990s, Gale and Joan formally and informally introduced the notion of FGC to provincial government and community leaders.

They worked together to encourage the adoption of FGC because of their experience as social work activists and their commitment to participatory decision-making. Gale's experience working in an organization in the 1970s that subscribed to the principles of Open Organization, or participatory decision-making, led to his doctoral research on the construction of team functioning in groups homes (Burford, 1990) and to direct practice approaches that included families in having a greater say over their lives (Burford & Casson, 1989). (His work in New Zealand beginning in 1989 brought him in contact with that approach to family conferencing).

Joan's interest in FGC came from her involvement in the women's and Aboriginal movements as well as her Quaker beliefs in making decisions within a 'unity of spirit'. As a founder of the first shelter for abused women and their children in Newfoundland & Labrador, she identified the necessity and limitations of such programs in ensuring safety and support. Her doctoral research on two feminist shelters diversified her strategies for participatory decision-making within funding and regulatory constraints (Pennell, 1990). Subsequently, her work with an Aboriginal family violence program educated her about community anti-violence approaches based upon cultural and spiritual traditions.

Diverse planners

Their participatory co-leadership fostered a climate in which other women and men could engage in dialogue and action on family violence. Within this context, women offered extensive leadership. Seated at the table or linked by telecommunications were representatives from public agencies, community services, advocacy groups, faith communities, and cultural/political organizations. Because of the commitment to testing FGC in different regions, the planners came from the three Project sites: the provincial capital, a rural peninsula, and the most northerly Labrador Inuit settlement. Evidence of broad collaboration and the inclusion of women and Native people facilitated leveraging funding from multiple sources.

Multiple funding

At the time that the Project was planned and carried out in the early and mid-1990s, FGC was considered an innovation in Canadian child and family welfare (Burford & Pennell, 1995) and qualified for federal funding as a family violence demonstration project. Thus, unlike family services programs in other countries, the early Canadian FGC funding was not directed solely at child welfare and was expected as well to address domestic violence. Eventually the Project was supported by six federal departments, three provincial departments, two Labrador Inuit organizations, and the authors' own university. Multiple funding sources further encouraged attention to a broad range of perspectives and collaboration by many public agencies and community organizations.

Firm principles

The multiplication of participants, project sites, and funding streams had the potential to destabilize the Project. The safeguard against entropy was a consensually developed statement of philosophy (Pennell & Burford, 1994). This statement affirmed that no child or adult should be abused, families in partnership with community and government can make and carry out plans to protect their relatives, and their solutions make sense in the context of their family, community, and culture.

Responsive policy

Putting these principles into effect required facilitation by provincial authorities around bureaucratic and legal obstacles, evaluation of the impact of policies on the safety and well-being of family members, and reshaping these policies as needed. A prime example concerned the referral of families to conferencing. Initially the Project accepted only voluntary referrals for which a parent had signed consent; the difficulty quickly emerged that abusive adults refused to sign although other family members wanted conferencing to proceed. With input from the three Project sites, the provincial advisory committee agreed that the protective authorities could make 'direct referrals' to FGC coordinators, who would then invite (not coerce) family group members to take part. Legal counsel advised that protective authorities could make such referrals where children were at risk. Women's advocates supported this approach because it removed the responsibility from abused women to sign the consent, thus, mitigating against the likelihood that her partner or their relatives would blame her for the conference.

Local ownership

Policies were adapted in each Project site by the local advisory committee to fit the region's conditions and cultures. These committees included representation from public agencies, women's groups, cultural associations, and other community organizations. One of their most important functions was to advise the project directors on whom to hire locally as the FGC coordinators and researchers. They were often far more aware than Gale and Joan of the applicants' commitment to ending family violence and sensitivity to local culture. At two of the sites, community panels were also instituted to provide guidance to the FGC coordinator on organizing the conferences for the referred families.

Implementing Family Group Conferencing

In reflecting back on the conferences, service providers referred to FGC as simply good practice with its emphasis on family strengths, cultural respect, and partnership building (Pennell & Burford, 1995). Likewise the feedback from family group members was overwhelmingly positive, with many wondering why this approach had not been used earlier with their families. Favourable feedback was the case whether the conference addressed primarily child maltreatment, domestic violence, or both. Their positive comment is particularly noteworthy given that the Project asked for the most difficult family situations to be referred and that families came from quite diverse cultures and regions. In-depth descriptions of conferencing are available for situations of family violence (see Burford, Pennell & MacLeod, 1999; Pennell & Burford, 2000b) and child sexual abuse (see Burford & Pennell, 1995). Below we highlight the manner in which the conferences enacted a feminist praxis of 'links, interruptions'. First, we overview the FGC process and then examine its movement from family privacy, women's leadership, state control, through to partnerships.

With some adaptation, the Project followed the New Zealand model for FGC (see Children, Young Persons and Their Families Act of 1989). This meant that once the FGC coordinators received a referral, they worked with the family group members to prepare them to take part in a safe and effective manner and consulted with a community advisory panel on these preparations (Pennell & Burford, 1995). To emphasize the centrality of the family group and create a de-professionalized atmosphere, the FGC coordinators invited a wide range of family group members, ensured that they outnumbered the service providers, and designed the conference in consultation with the family group. As a result, the conferences were typically held in a community setting, with chairs in a circle, familiar food selected, and transportation, childcare, and interpretation provided as needed. Close attention was paid to safety concerns. Family members likely to feel at risk during the conference were encouraged to choose a support person who would stay by them emotionally and to prepare in advance a statement of what they wished to say. The service providers were often uncertain about how to relate with the family group and required coaching from the FGC coordinators on how to dress for the conference and how to make their presentations.

Arriving at the conference with trepidations about the upcoming proceedings, the circle formation permitted family members to seat themselves next to kin and friends and reaffirm their family identities. The opening was geared to the family's customs and thus varied, from a senior family member welcoming each family member at the door to family members quietly taking their seats to an Inuit Elder leading the group in prayer. After a round of introductions, the coordinator reviewed the ground rules for the meeting and acknowledged the family group's feelings and hopes. At the conference, the protective authorities summarized the family's history and specified the concerns to address. Next community resources provided further information about the areas of concern and possible services to utilize in resolving them. Then the service providers including the coordinator left, and during their private time, the family group formulated its plan. The plan was to address each of the areas of concern and to establish a system of monitoring and evaluating its enactment. Before going into effect, the plan had to be approved by the involved protective authorities in regards to safety and resourcing. If new issues emerged or plans were not working, conferences were reconvened. At subsequent conferences, family group members and service providers were better prepared to work together and able to move quickly into planning.

Family privacy

In Project planning and training sessions, the image of family groups deliberating without a facilitator present evoked the most fears among service providers and coordinators. They were particularly concerned about situations of domestic violence and child sexual abuse and understandably worried that during the family's private time, the family group would blame the survivors, exonerate the abusers, or conversely attack the perpetrators. During the early conferences, the family group members, sensing their coordinator's trepidations, were more likely to urge the coordinator to stay in the room. In instances where the coordinators or other service providers remained, the group turned to them for guidance and the professionals 'took over'. At one such conference, the participants later complained that the well-intentioned service provider dominated their private time.

On finding that violence did not erupt at conferences and that family groups were able to develop constructive plans, coordinators began to trust the process. They identified that careful preparation and clear information were key to successful private time. The conferencing also revealed that the private time was crucial for the family group expressing their feelings for each other, challenging each other, sharing highly confidential information, and formulating plans that they saw as their own. A dramatic example was a conference in which an adult daughter confronted a male relative on his sexual abuse of her as a child. The researcher who observed the family's private time noted the exchanges among the 12 family group members.

During this family group's private time, a number of the mother's adult children expressed their pain at growing up with drinking and violence. In response, the mother said, 'You children are always blaming me or my boyfriend.' Looking back, she spoke of fleeing in the night with them from their abusive father (now deceased), and concluded by reiterating that she 'just want[s] the children to know that she loves them'. The children went on to acknowledge their caring for their family, but also an older daughter was able to challenge their male relative. The researcher wrote:

It's very quiet in here. A lot of tension. [An adult daughter] says that she'll go next, she's looking at [the male relative] and asks why did he do those things to her. And [the male relative] says that he was stupid at that time, and the [adult daughter] says that's why I don't like coming over to your house anymore ... [A son who had been physically abused by this same relative] then asks the mother, 'Did you know about this Mom? If you did, how come you never told us about it?'

The support person for the male relative helped to provide the reassurance for both this individual and the group that they could stay with the conference. In a 'more cheerful' although 'tired' state, the family group went on to develop an extensive plan. By this time, the mother was able to say that:

she hopes that something comes out of this conference ... She's glad that she came to this conference. She'd like to get her family back together.

Reflecting on the plan, the parole officer commented:

Overall it was a very good plan that covered most of the safety concerns and showed that the family was trying to reach out and get help.

He further noted, however, that the plan was not put into effect because Social Services delayed its approval:

The plan was then sent to Social Services for approval, they only approved [it] partially and sent it back to [the Coordinator], and [it went] back and forth, finally [it was] approved. But now most family members can't participate.

Given all of the ongoing upheavals in this chaotic family situation, the delay meant that the plan could not be implemented when finally authorized.

Nevertheless, the conference itself was viewed as helpful by the family. Eighteen months later in a follow-up interview, one of the children observed:

The family has been doing very well since [the mother's boyfriend] is gone ... [Our] relationship is closer to each other ... There's no fighting or drinking. It made the family better ... going to the family conference.

Given this family's lengthy and problematic involvement with Social Services and police, they required the private time to express their yearning for family and to reaffirm their kinship. The private time rather than silencing survivors offered an opportunity for voicing long-held hurts; and despite the delay in approving the plan, they made some strides as a family.

Women's leadership

One of the more exciting developments in the conferences was the emergence of women's leadership to stop family violence. The conference preparations and the information sharing broke, what Sandra Butler (1978) has termed, the 'conspiracy of silence'. No longer constrained by secrecy, the family groups were able to discuss and seek remedies for domestic violence and child maltreatment. A case in point is a conference that initially appeared antithetical to women's leadership and turned out quite the reverse.

The FGC referral came jointly from Child Welfare and Youth Corrections for 'a youth beyond parental control'. The older son was to be shortly released from a youth custody facility, and the workers and family anticipated that on his return he would continue to be a 'troublemaker' in the home and community. As the FGC coordinator wrote in her reflective notes:

[The older son] was diagnosed with ADHD [attention-deficit hyperactivity disorder] as a child ... The impression I got from speaking to people familiar with the history of this family ... no matter what program is in place [for the older son] – it is doomed to fail – because Dad is psychopathic. He is on the phone all the time [saying], 'What's wrong with you people – can't you do anything to help my son – he's driving this family crazy!' … Professionals commonly recognize [Dad] as someone who sets out to destroy any attempts at intervention while appearing to be cooperative and enthusiastic … Over the year, [the older son] has become a scapegoat in the family. As a result, he is a 15-year-old teenager with no motivation with regards to future plans, no social skills, very short fuse, very reactive in a violent way.

In organizing the conference, the FGC coordinator, well seasoned in both correctional and family violence work, became more and more alarmed about convening the family group. As a later file analysis revealed, her fears were not unfounded: in the year prior to the conference, the Child Welfare files had numerous indicators of child and wife abuse. Although the father had told the Child Welfare worker that he would 'cooperate' with the referral, the coordinator had difficulty reaching the family. Once contact was made, she and the student intern were permitted only to speak to the father and later the older son. Describing their first meeting at the home, the coordinator wrote:

We arrived on time – knocked on the door and were called into the house. The TV was extremely loud. The [younger] daughter, [younger] son, and Mom were sitting in the living room with their eyes glued to the TV. They did not look at us or acknowledge us in any way. Dad was sitting in the living room at the head of the table smoking and drinking tea (the lion in his den) … He seemed to understand everything I said. He appeared pleasant enough but made no request for the TV to be turned down – neither did I ask for him to do the same. I was feeling very, very intimidated … At the end of the conversation, he agreed to review the process with his family … We practically ran out of the house. We didn't say good-bye or nod to anyone. Both of us seemed to know instinctively that they were still glued to the TV and wouldn't acknowledge us anyway.

Shaken by the visit and suspecting that the family had far more problems than one 'troublemaker' son, the coordinator questioned holding the conference. Raising these concerns with the Child Welfare worker, she was asked to 'try to hang on to the family at all costs' – the conference was Child Welfare's last hope for the family.

Persevering, the coordinator continued to prepare for the conference despite obstacles generated by the father. Describing this stage, the coordinator wrote:

[The Dad and I] completed the Invitation List, which included all members of his family of origin, most of Mom's family of origin and two neighbours. He advised me upfront that Mom thought the whole process was a waste of time – she did not wish to speak to me or see me. As well he advised me his children were not interested in attending – only [the older son] was willing to speak with me … I returned to the [Social Services] office and spoke with the [Child

Welfare worker]. She advised me that the family are probably not allowed to attend and for their safety I should concentrate on the extended family.

Because of these safety concerns, the coordinator used an indirect avenue to reach out to the mother. A home care worker, quite close to the mother, served as the intermediary. The coordinator explained in her notes:

[The home care worker] advised the Mom is not allowed to attend FGC and very nervous about my approaching her. Between the two of us we decided [the home care worker] should do an informal needs assessment around Mom so plans could be made for her in her absence.

Her attempts to invite the extended family met with one refusal after another:

I made telephone contact with each member of Dad's family ... Each one individually told me they would not attend because it was none of their business, they could not help because they had nothing to contribute ... One brother more openly than the rest ... [explained that] they particularly avoid any contact with their brother because of fear. He said he could attend the conference but he would be unable to speak one word without repercussions.

Likewise the Mom's family declined because of their 'relationship' with the father, with one noteworthy exception:

[A sister of the Mom] was very keen on attending and welcomed the opening to re-establish ties with her sister.

This sister served as the conduit for information from the mother's other relatives:

I attempted to reach other members of the family by mail because they did not have phones – they did not contact me but did contact their sister and she relayed their views at the conference.

On the day of the conference, only four family group members attended: the father, the older son (his support person slept in and failed to arrive), the mother's sister, and the mother's home care worker. The three information providers, a school psychologist, Youth Corrections officer, and Child Welfare worker, summarized the family history, the strengths of the older son, and the issues of concern. Then the small family group moved into its private deliberations. Describing the conference, the coordinator wrote:

The conference lasted several hours. They did really well. They dealt with all of the issues presented. [The home care worker], as preplanned, included plans for Mom and [younger] daughter. Dad went along with everything.

The post-conference period, however, at first seemed doomed to failure as the father, utilizing his standard response repertoire to intervention, enraged the coordinator and the involved agencies:

Within a couple of weeks, Dad began manipulating [the older son] ... As well Dad began his crusade to acquire new eyeglasses through the project which weren't in the plan. Also Dad began setting up medical appointments for his son all over [the place] – some not necessary – in an attempt to make sure he used up the full [possible allocation of funding] ... It got to a point where I could not deal with this Dad. He made me very angry as I watched him set out to destroy the plan and continue destroying his son.

Nevertheless, the two women at the conference, in spite of or perhaps because of the father's manoeuvres, followed through on the agreement:

[The home care worker] and the [Mom's sister] were still doing parts of the plan with regards to Mom which was good. And [the older son] was still receiving counselling from a doctor.

The aftermath brought even greater changes to the family. In a follow-up interview approximately one year after the conference, the Child Welfare worker recounted that the younger daughter, now sufficiently trusting Child Welfare, had reported her father's physical abuse against her and was placed in foster care. The mother decided to leave the father and moved away with the younger son and was soon joined by the younger daughter. The mother's family was providing support to her and the children and helping to ensure that she and the children received counseling. In another interview close to two years after the conference, the Child Welfare worker relayed that the mother had moved out of the province, had a 'good boyfriend', and continued to live with the younger daughter. Rather than leaving the province, the younger son had opted to return to the father and was doing 'well in school'. The father to everyone's surprise had 'stopped drinking' and 'continued to go to group work and individual counselling'. Sadly but not unexpectedly, the older son was 'still in trouble with the law [and] in a group home'. Overall, though, the family had progressed. A comparison of the Child Welfare files, one year before and one year after the conference, showed a dramatic drop in indicators of child abuse and domestic violence.

For years, the father had succeeded in intimidating and manipulating his family, their relatives, and the involved service providers. The family group conference appeared likely to reconfirm the father's power and control. The conference, however, provided the opportunity for various women to band together across family and professional lines and to take leadership in undermining his influence. The first to start the momentum were the Child Welfare and Youth Corrections workers, both young and dedicated women workers. Secondly, the coordinator supported by the student intern persisted despite the father's numerous roadblocks. Thirdly, the home care worker had already established a trusting relationship with the mother and could ascertain and represent her interests at the conference. Fourthly, the determined sister agreed to attend the conference and became the conduit for information and support from the mother's family. And fifthly and most importantly, the younger daughter and mother had the strength to reach out for help and break away from the father.

State control

The two preceding family examples were used respectively to illustrate the importance of family privacy and women's leadership. These examples also testify to the essential role of state authorities in situations of family violence. Neither conference would have taken place unless Child Welfare and Parole in one instance and Child Welfare and Youth Corrections in the other were already involved and had decided to refer these families for conferencing. The pairing of protective authorities, as happened in these two examples, heightened the legal leverage over perpetrators. Following the previously described Project policy on referral, neither offenders nor victims in the families were given the responsibility for approving the referral. Given the source of the referrals, some Project parents probably felt pressured to attend. Nevertheless, no family member was compelled to attend; such flexibility was crucial for the mother and most of the children in the second example.

The influence of the protective authorities was also evident at the conferences. In reviewing the family's history and issues of concern, they set the stage for the family planning. In approving the plans, they ensured another safety checkpoint and also quite importantly authorized needed funding and resources. Whether or not a plan came out of the conference as in the first example, the protective authorities still maintained their role of monitoring the safety of family members. With an approved plan, though, the state authorities, community organizations, and family groups members could work together to resolve situations of family violence.

Partnership

Family privacy, women's leadership, and state control were not separate but instead interacting movements within conferencing. They all were integral to building the 'links, interruptions' for stopping family violence. In isolation, family privacy could endanger the safety of family members; women's leadership could once again place the burden of caring on the backs of women; and state control could undermine families and their communities. In working together, these three movements reinforced the purpose of conferencing: to form family–community–government partnerships to stop family violence.

Links, Interruptions

The second-wave feminist movements in Canada and the United States engaged in a feminist praxis that disrupted gendered expectations and uncovered the domestic tyranny behind the privacy of the family. This analysis led to creating safe places for women and their children and promoting women's sense of unity, autonomy, and leadership. Realizing that shelters could not protect women beyond their doors, women's advocates pushed for a coordinated response encompassing legal and human services. Their push for legal interventions was furthered by trends in criminal justice and liability insurance. Although disadvantaged women especially reported re-victimization by the state, overall women welcomed police and court intervention. At the same time in Canada and the United States, an increasingly legalistic response to domestic violence had other consequences. In particular, police and child welfare procedures led to arrests of both partners and removal of children from abused women. These consequences sprang from individualistic strategies rather than ones holding communities and public agencies, along with perpetrators, accountable for family violence.

As embodied in the 'personal is political', feminists have long identified the necessity of moving forward simultaneously with individual and collective change. They have sought to advance such two-pronged change through interrupting societal discourses that sever private and public life and enforce male control and women's caring. As a social movement, feminists have joined together to establish women's programs and in coordinated responses, allied with legal institutions and community groups, to stop family violence.

In our experience with the Newfoundland and Labrador Project, a feminist praxis of 'links, interruptions' can serve as a guiding framework for designing and implementing an FGC program committed to stopping all forms of family violence. The 'links' among people from varied perspectives served to 'interrupt' thinking on how to resolve family violence and, thus, made possible a broader vision and strategy. The 'links' also fostered the commitment and secured the resources necessary to carry out the program. Moving beyond reliance on state control and women's leadership, FGC provided a means of including extended family among the partners. The outcomes from the Project demonstrated that, within this context of 'links, interruptions', family group conferencing can stop family violence.

7 Transformative Justice: Anti-Subordination Processes in Cases of Domestic Violence

Donna Coker

Stopping domestic violence is hard work. Domestic violence is a social practice maintained by multiple systems that operate in the lives of battering men and battered women. For men in subordinated communities, social inequalities related to race, poverty, and Indigenous status, for example, operate in complex ways that are related to a man' s choice to use violence, though none is its single definitive 'cause'. The same intersecting oppressive systems operate in women's lives. For example, poverty increases women's vulnerability to battering and limits their *ability to escape violence; violence increases women's vulnerability to poverty.*

This chapter attempts to further the dialogue between restorative justice activists and scholars and feminist anti-domestic violence activists and scholars. My focus is on the struggle against domestic violence in subordinated communities. My aim is to address the need for justice strategies that account for the intersecting oppressive systems that operate in the lives of battering men and battered women who are members of these communities.

My discussion draws on theory and practice of both the feminist movement against domestic violence and the restorative justice movement. Feminist theory provides critical insights regarding the dangers of reliance on private mechanisms of control, the causes of male violence against women, the necessity of engaging the state on behalf of women, and the conflicting and ambiguous nature of that state intervention. Restorative justice theory offers critical insights regarding the way offenders' experiences with the criminal justice system influence their likelihood of reoffending, the importance of providing victims the opportunity to be active agents in developing responses to crime, and the importance of social networks of family and friends both in providing restraints against crime and in caring for victims of crime. I hope to lay the groundwork for a dialogue between feminist theorists working against domestic violence and restorative justice theorists. Building on the insights of both fields will enrich anti-domestic violence theory and practice.

I begin with a critique of the feminist analysis of liberalism's public/private distinction as it relates to anti-domestic violence work. Feminist efforts to construct domestic violence as a public issue rather than a private problem have been critical for gaining women's access to public resources, including criminal justice resources. But the discourse that constructs domestic violence as a public issue is subject to co-optation in ways that increase state control of poor women and women of colour. The critical dilemma for feminists who seek to empower battered women is to develop strategies for controlling the criminal justice system without increasing state control *of women.*

Restorative justice processes, on the other hand, threaten to re-privatize domestic violence in ways that are harmful to women. Feminist critics have warned of the dangers of restorative justice processes that privilege family and community forms of intervention, noting that family and community are often unwilling or unable to oppose domestic violence (Goel, 2000; Hooper & Busch, 1996; Stubbs, 1995; Stubbs, this volume). Indeed, family and community are often the *primary* supports for male control of women. I share these concerns of feminist critics, but I focus on a second manner in which restorative justice processes may be said to be 'privatizing'. The restorative justice critique of punitive criminal justice responses emphasizes the power of the state to do harm (Braithwaite, 1989), yet restorative justice proponents often construct the state as a distant and largely irrelevant party (Hudson & Galaway, 1996). This construction of the state elides state power and naturalizes state created crime categories and the operation of state crime control systems. Thus, restorative justice processes threaten to create a deeply privatized criminal justice process.

I identify two additional serious theoretical weaknesses of restorative justice theory as applied to domestic violence cases. First, it offers no clear principles for dealing with crimes, such as domestic violence, where majoritarian opposition to the crime is weak or compromised. Second, restorative justice theory under-theorizes criminal offending, generally, providing little foundation for a theory of male violence against women.

These weaknesses can be addressed by current feminist theory, critical race feminist theory, social science research regarding domestic violence, and the theoretical underpinnings of programs for men who batter. Incorporating insights from these theoretical and empirical sources can enable restorative justice theory to effectively address the complicated problem of domestic violence.

Finally, I call for anti-subordination processes that address the intersecting oppressive systems that operate in the lives of men and women in subordinated communities. These anti-subordination processes should seek to transform private relationships – the social networks that reinforce and support a batterer's controlling behaviour as well as the social networks that can assist battered women. A process that attempts to animate family and community to intervene against domestic violence need not result in re-privatizing domestic violence, provided the process seeks to transform the norms of family and community members, rather than rely on existing anti-battering norms that may be weak or contradictory. A focus on race and class subordination need not excuse domestic violence, provided that battering men are encouraged to connect their own experiences of subordination with their subordination of women.

In developing these processes I draw on Ruth Morris's concept of *transformative justice* (Morris, 1994, 1995). I expand Morris's model to include concepts from innovative programs, including batterers' treatment programs, that link a critical analysis of the racist, sexist, and classist practices of the criminal justice system with offender accountability to victims and communities. A process that incorporates insights from feminist and critical race feminist theory as well as restorative justice theory offers battered women and battering men the possibility of transforming communities as well as interpersonal relationships.

The Dilemma of Privacy: Battering as a Public Issue

The controversy about nation-wide implementation of mandatory arrest policies reflects the ambivalence with which feminists regard the police. On one hand, battered women's advocates want to hold the police accountable, as agents of the state, for carrying out the government's mandate to protect citizens. On the other hand, feminists realize that police often exercise their power in ways that reinforce the disadvantages already experienced by women, and in ways that reinforce the disadvantages experienced by members of poor and minority communities as well. (Sparks, 1997: 35–36)

Feminist challenges to the liberal distinction between the public realm of the state and market and the private realm of family and community have long been central to anti-domestic violence activism (Goldfarb, 2000; Schneider, 1991). In contrast to concepts of the family as a haven that fosters personal development and civic engagement, feminists have documented the extent to which families are sites of domestic tyranny marked by violence and coercion (Bartlett, 1999; Kelly, 1996). Feminists have further exposed the manner in which public/private ideology hides state action by making patriarchal families appear natural and inevitable (Fineman, 1995). Both positive law and the absence of law create family structures of dominance (Fenton, 1999; Miccio, 2000; Minow, 1990; Taub & Schneider, 1990). Constructing domestic violence as a *public* issue exposes the state's collusion with batterers, underscores the seriousness of the violence, and emphasizes battering as a civil rights issue.

By contrast, restorative justice scholarship presumes a largely unproblematized distinction between public and private life. Dominant methods of criminal processing are said to 'steal' the conflict from the parties (Braithwaite, 1999). As compared to state actors, community and family members are presumed to have a greater stake in responding to crime and to be better able to meet the needs of victims.

A number of feminist scholars have raised concerns about the privatizing potential of restorative justice processes (Busch, this volume; Hooper & Busch, 1996; Stubbs, 1995; Stubbs, this volume). When applied to domestic violence cases, reliance on mechanisms of the private realms of family and community threatens to reverse progress by pushing domestic violence back into the realm of the 'private' (Hooper & Busch, 1996; Stubbs, this volume).

Feminist critics also worry that processes like conferencing will 'domesticate' the violence (Cobb, 1997), couching it as mere conflict or as centred in unique relationship dynamics rather than as the result of the batterer's struggle to dominate his partner (Hooper & Busch, 1996; Stubbs, this volume). In addition, some feminist scholars are concerned that the moral educative function of criminalization may be lost when restorative justice processes replace retributive processes (see Daly, this volume). Public punishment marks the violence as serious and 'send[s] a clear social message that battering is impermissible' (Schneider, 1991: 989).[1]

The dilemma of privacy: limits of the public/private analysis

These critiques of the public/private distinction have been important to organizing public opposition against domestic violence, but feminists have paid too little attention to the dangers of a focus on making domestic violence a public problem. The feminist critique of the public/private distinction is an important but incomplete analysis of the relationship between battered women and the state. It is inaccurate to describe the state's response to domestic violence as a unified refusal to intervene in 'private' family matters. Race and class mark the history of the state's relationship to families in general, and to domestic violence, in particular (Gordon, 1988; Roberts, 1999; Siegel, 1996). As Riva Siegel's history of US law demonstrates, notions of family privacy eventually gave way to class and race based notions of white middle-class superiority (Siegel, 1996). By the end of the nineteenth century harsh penalties such as whipping were proposed for wife beaters who were characterized as 'lawless or unruly men of the "dangerous classes"' (Siegel, 1996: 2139). These 'dangerous classes' referred primarily to African-American and low-status immigrant men (Siegel, 1996). Linda Gordon's history of a child-saving organization in Boston similarly demonstrates that there was little objection to state intervention when family violence was understood as a problem of poor immigrant families (Gordon, 1988). The racist and classist beliefs of state actors may support intervention as well as non-intervention, but neither choice derives from beliefs about protecting family privacy. For example, the practice of police to refuse to intervene when violence is 'horizontal' – e.g., involving two persons of similar (and devalued) race and/or class (Ferraro, 1989; Hampton, 1987) better explains police refusal to assist battered women of colour than does their desire to guard family privacy (Ferraro, 1989).

Further problematizing an emphasis on domestic violence as a public problem is the fact that the lives of poor women and women of colour are often *under*-privatized (Fineman, 1995; Roberts, 1995; Roberts, 1999). In other words, women *need* privacy (Roberts, 1999; Schneider, 1991). US women who receive government assistance have little protection from state intrusion (Roberts, 1995). Families headed by single mothers are deemed suspect and 'may be thought of as "public" families, not entitled to privacy' (Fineman, 1995: 178). Suspicion about the mothering abilities of poor women and particularly of poor African-American women results in disproportionate numbers of their children in the US foster care system (Roberts, 1995).[2] The massive removal of Indigenous children by the governments of Australia, the US, and Canada eloquently demonstrates the way in which an ideal of family privacy has little relevance for the description of relations between the state and families in subordinated communities (Australia Human Rights and Equal Opportunity Commission, 1997; Kline, 1992; Indian Child Welfare Act of 1978).

In addition to state control of women as mothers, US women of colour and particularly African-American women who live in urban cores are subjected to significant invasions of privacy incidental to the 'war on drugs', renamed by some the 'war on poor people' (Bush-Baskette, 1998). This war is largely responsible for increases in the numbers of women in prison (Chesney-Lind, 1998) and the extraordinary increases in the numbers of imprisoned African-American women (Bush-Baskette, 1998).

The ways in which the state operates to control and disempower poor women and women of colour illustrates the value of restorative justice concerns with the state 'stealing conflict' from the community. Given a choice between the privatizing problems of community control versus the oppressive intervention of the state, some women will choose the former.

'Tough on crime' and domestic violence

Women's lives are subject to 'interlocking' (Fellows & Razack, 1998) and 'intersecting' (Crenshaw, 1991) sites for potential subordination. This reality shapes the effects and meaning of domestic violence intervention strategies. It should come as no surprise, therefore, that feminist discourse that regards domestic violence as a public issue is subject to cooptation. The language of public issue has been adopted by those whose agenda, unlike that of feminists, is not focussed on empowering women. If the problem belongs to the *public*, then individual women's desires need not be central to policy development (Mills, 1999). Further, given the trend in many countries, and especially the US, to enact increasingly harsh control and surveillance methods for dealing with social problems (Browne, 1995; Caplow & Simon, 1999; Fellows & Razack, 1998), domestic violence as a *public* problem has largely come to mean domestic violence as a *crime control* problem (Currie, 1993). Zero tolerance arrest policies and no-drop prosecution are popular in no small part because they resonate with this emphasis on punishment and control (Coker, 2001; Martin, 1998; Snider, 1998).

The dilemma for using the criminal justice system to empower battered women is to develop strategies for controlling state actors – ensuring that the police come when called and that prosecutors do not trivialize cases – without increasing state control *of women*. It is the dilemma of making domestic violence a public responsibility in the context of racist and classist public systems.

Aggressive crime enforcement policies that mandate arrest and require prosecutors to pursue domestic violence cases, even when victims are opposed to arrest and prosecution, are central to much of feminist law reform in the US, England, Canada, and Australia (Dobash & Dobash, 1999a). A primary reason for feminist support of these policies is that they increase the likelihood that police and prosecutors will act to protect women rather than trivialize or ignore their complaints (Stark, 1996).[3] For years, the problem with police intervention for US battered women of colour and Indigenous women was a problem of police refusal to intervene. Loretta Kelly (this volume) documents similar problems with police refusal to assist Aboriginal women in Australia. Thus, work to ensure that police respond when they are called and that they protect women when they arrive is central to justice for battered women. But mandatory policies such as no-drop prosecution and zero tolerance policing increase the potential for state interference and control in women's lives. This is particularly true for poor women and women of colour (Espenoza, 1999; Mills, 1999). As a direct result of these arrest policies, for example, more women are arrested for domestic violence (Hamberger & Potente, 1994; Zorza & Woods, 1994). Strong anecdotal evidence suggests that most of the women arrested are victims of battering who are acting in self-defence or who are responding to a pattern of abuse (Zorza, 1994; Hamberger & Potente, 1994). In addition to arrests for domestic violence, aggressive criminal interventions also threaten increased state control for those battered women involved in (other) criminal activity. Women's involvement in illegal drug activity and prostitution is often directly related to being in an abusive relationship (Daly, 1994; Richie, 1996). As noted earlier, the danger of identification, arrest, and conviction is much higher for women of colour and particularly African-American women who live in heavily policed 'drug zones'. In addition, domestic violence arrest mandates may aggravate racist and abusive police behaviours (Kelly, 1999; Rivera, 1994; Snider, 1998).

Zero tolerance arrest policies also create collateral harms for women. If a battered woman is arrested for domestic violence she may lose the protection afforded by special domestic violence legislation. For example, evidence of her arrest, even if she is not charged, may prevent her from benefiting from child custody laws that disfavour a violent parent (see, e.g., Florida Statute 61.30, 2000). In addition, police intervention and sustained prosecutorial presence increase state control of women through child protection monitoring (Pennell & Burford, this volume). In the US, many child protection agencies treat a child's residence in a home where domestic violence takes place as child abuse, even when the child was not present at the time the abuse took place (*Nicholson v. Williams*; Sengupta, 2000). Children are removed from the home and the mother's parenting is more broadly investigated (S. Dougan, attorney, personal communication, 1999). If both parents are arrested, children may be placed in temporary foster care.

In addition to these direct and collateral harms, the practice of denying women any voice in the criminal processing of intimates (or former intimates) raises questions regarding the legitimate role of battered women's agency (Mills, 1999; Minow, 2000).[4] These policies limit women's ability to negotiate the terrain between state control and private control (Ford, 1991; Harrell & Smith, 1996; Kendrick, 1998). Women, and in the US especially low-income African-American women, rely on the police to interrupt and prevent battering episodes

(Buzawa et al, 1999; Hutchinson & Hirschel, 1998). This does not necessarily mean that they seek prosecution and punishment. Some women clearly do, but others use the threat of prosecution to gain key concessions from the batterer. This kind of bargaining becomes impossible in jurisdictions with no-drop prosecution policies (Ford, 1991; Wittner, 1998).

In addition, mandatory criminal interventions reinforce pathological notions of battered women who do not want to assist prosecution and who do not want to separate from a partner who abuses them. As Martha Mahoney explains, women's 'failure' to separate is often understood as evidence that a battered woman is crazy, lying about the severity of the abuse, or both (Mahoney, 1991). 'Staying' is a socially suspect choice – often perceived as acceptance of violence ...' (Mahoney, 1994: 60). As Julia Perilla notes, 'a failure to leave the relationship is seen by many ... court systems as a woman's failure to do something for herself and her family' (Perilla, 1999: 124).

Thus, legal professionals in reform institutions in the US – judges who routinely hear protection order or misdemeanour battering cases, court personnel hired to work with battered women, prosecutors, police officers, probation officers, and court clerks – presume that women *should* separate for their safety (Coker, 2000; Fenton, 1999; Wittner, 1998). In fact, some actors refuse to assist women whom they do not view as serious about leaving their abusers. This problem is not unique to the US. Loretta Kelly (1999) similarly notes that Australian police sometimes refuse to assist Aboriginal women who make repeat police calls because they believe the women are uninterested in separating from their abuser.

Not only does this separation-focus 'devalue women's connections with their partner[s]' (Coker, 2000: 1019), it is based on the false premise that separation equates with safety. In fact, for some women separation increases their risk of death or serious assault (Mahoney, 1991). Further, the safety that follows separation is largely fictive for poor women who do not have the resources to relocate. If these women 'have managed to find low-cost or public housing in the inner city and to patch together support systems or social services which allow them to care for their children, they have no alternative but to remain there as sitting ducks for the abuser when he returns' (Bowman, 1992: 205).[5]

These are (some of) the harms of mandatory criminal interventions. However, this is only part of the story. 'The outcome of policing, and of criminal justice intervention more generally is likely to be varied, perhaps contradictory, and in part determined by context' (Stubbs, 1995: 262). This is true both because women's lives differ from each other in important respects, and because the implementation and consequences of criminal justice intervention policies differ from one location to the next.[6] These variances are shaped by conditions such as the nature of support services for battered women, the attitude of local law enforcement officers, the availability of programs for men who batter, the nature of the relationship between the police force and communities of colour, and the influence of the local battered women's movement (Coker, 2000; Pence & McDonnell, 1999). While the crime control agenda shapes feminist discourse, criminal justice systems are also shaped by feminist demands that '[r]edefin[e] the purpose of the system [by] ... attempt[ing] to shift its primary orientation from that of carrying out an abstract standard of justice to one of providing protection and resources ... [for battered women]' (Sparks, 1997: 36).

Feminists have long been aware of the ambiguous nature of their efforts to harness the power of the state for the good of battered women (Schechter, 1982). The results are varied and the impact is shaped by the different material and cultural positions of women. Women's positions are shaped in part by dominant ideologies that inform the availability and the nature of public resources. Battered women cannot afford over-privatized remedies that result in their inability to invoke state power for protection, nor can they afford remedies that give them no control while presuming to act in the public's best interest.

Three Theoretical Weaknesses of Restorative Justice Theory for Addressing Domestic Violence

Restorative justice proponents, for the most part, do not recognize this ambiguous relationship with state power. Categorical statements in restorative justice literature that presume sharp distinctions between criminal justice policies that are 'punitive' versus those that are 'restorative' fail to capture this varied reality (Daly, this volume) as does scholarship that depicts a singular victim and offender experience. Courtrooms may sometimes be 'nightmares' (Martin, 1998) for battered women, but sometimes women feel validated and empowered by court processes (Ptacek, 1999; Wittner, 1998). Arrest may cause some abusers to feel shame or rage or both (Braithwaite & Daly, 1994), but this experience may be moderated by subsequent respectful though firm treatment from the court (Ptacek, 1999) and treatment programs. Most men arrested for domestic violence misdemeanours serve little or no time in jail (Fields, 1994; Karan, 1999; Salzman, 1994) and many in the US and Canada are ordered to attend batterers' treatment programs (Dobash & Dobash, 1999a).

It is critical to engage the state on behalf of battered women, but we must do so in ways that are sufficiently protective of poor women and women of colour. Three theoretical weaknesses of restorative justice theory for use in domestic violence cases hinder its ability to provide this kind of protection.

Naturalizing state power: restorative justice and a theory of the state

We need to address the harder and more complex questions about how justice system practices are saturated and marked by racial-ethnic (and other) divisions, both past and present. (Daly, 2000b: 182)

The first weakness of restorative justice theory for dealing with domestic violence in subordinated communities is the manner in which restorative justice theorists often construct the state as a distant actor and thus elide the way state power suffuses all criminal justice processes, including restorative justice processes. I raise this concern not to argue for the superiority of formal justice processes – indeed, formal processes are clearly engaged in the same practices – but rather to argue for the modification of restorative justice processes.

Restorative justice scholars understand crime to be 'primarily ... a conflict between individuals that results in injuries to victims, communities, and the offenders ...' (Hudson & Galaway, 1996: 2). In restorative justice processes 'all the parties with a stake in a particular offence come together to resolve collectively how to deal with the aftermath of the offence and its implications for the future' (Braithwaite, 1999a: 5 (quoting T. Marshall, 1997, personal communication)). Thus restorative justice theorists construct the state as a distant or even irrelevant actor to restorative processes. The result is to elide the operation of state power that suffuses the processing of criminal cases. The legislature determines how crimes are defined and state actors within the criminal justice system determine how these laws are applied, to whom, and under what circumstances.

As some restorative justice writers have noted, the criminal justice system may not be the most likely arena for efforts to achieve large measures of social justice (Braithwaite, 1999a; Daly, 2000b). For example, John Braithwaite (1999a: 105) writes that the most important remedies for controlling crime 'are not reforms to the justice system' but rather 'reforms about liberty, equality, and community in more deeply structural and developmental senses'. The difficulty with this response is that restorative justice processes do more than simply fail to address the possible range of social injustices. They legitimate state power through reinforcing the behavioural norms reflected in the laws and through naturalizing the justice practices that bring the offender to the attention of the restorative process.

This legitimizing function illustrates a fundamental tension of restorative justice processes and the use of John Braithwaite's (1989) concepts of reintegrative shaming in those processes. (Perhaps, instead, it illustrates the inevitable tensions in partial reform.) A critical insight of Braithwaite's work (1989) (and restorative justice work more generally) is that an offender's experience of criminal justice processes may encourage future offending. Braithwaite (1989: 55) distinguishes between disintegrative (stigmatizing) shaming and reintegrative shaming. Reintegrative shaming involves 'expressions of community disapproval ... followed by gestures of reacceptance into the community of law-abiding citizens' (Braithwaite, 1989: 55). Braithwaite argues further that 'shame is more deterring when administered by persons who continue to be of importance to us; when we become outcasts we can reject our rejectors and the shame no longer matters to us' (Braithwaite, 1989: 55). In his later work on restorative justice, Braithwaite refers to the use of 'communities of care' composed of individuals who care about the offender, to provide reintegrative shaming in restorative processes such as conferencing (Braithwaite & Daly, 1994: 194).

Thus, reintegrative shaming requires that private individuals agree with and support the moral norms reflected in the penal laws (Braithwaite, 1989). It also requires that private individuals (implicitly, at least) acknowledge the moral authority of the state to create and enforce those norms. In essence, restorative justice and reintegrative shaming require an alliance between the state and 'communities of care'. Given the way in which crime policy is used to control poor people and people of colour, given the racist and classist practices of criminal justice officers, and given the way in which significant numbers of poor people and people of colour are locked out of electoral politics, establishing an alliance between the norms of an offender's community of care and those of the criminal justice system asks a great deal of subordinated communities. Further, unlike some community–police alliances (Kahan, 1999; Meares, 1997), this alliance does not offer subordinated people much in the way of control of the ongoing operation of the criminal justice system in their community. As Kathleen Daly (2000b: 174) argues, restorative justice 'must be tied to a political process [that includes] a process of engagement among and between the interests of political minority groups (for example, indigenous and feminist) and governments'. In other words, restorative justice must engage with political action directed at state inequalities; it must engage the state, rather than ignore the state.

Restorative justice theory and the lack of majoritarian opposition to domestic violence

The struggle to construct the meaning of domestic violence is no less present in 'communities' than it is in the larger society. The most important questions for thinking about the use of restorative justice processes in domestic violence cases are *'who* defines the problem?' and *'how* will the problem be constructed?' If community is, as Liz Kelly writes, the result of struggle and conflict over its identity (Kelly, 1996), then processes that are said to enact community norms cannot help but enter into that struggle. 'Community' practice cannot be neutral.

John Braithwaite argues that reintegrative shaming, of the kind proposed by some restorative justice advocates, requires that the law in question 'represent a clearly majoritarian morality' (Braithwaite, 1989: 14), but as Braithwaite and Daly note, '[f]ew societies ... contain a majoritarian masculinity that sets its face against violence' (Braithwaite & Daly, 1994: 190). Polls that show significant opposition to domestic violence are promising (Braithwaite & Daly, 1994; Klein et al, 1997), but such research does not capture the degree to which people are sympathetic to the 'the hapless man who must defend against a nagging, shrewish woman' (Coker, 1992: 110) or the cuckold husband who must defend his honour (Coker, 1992). Additionally, people often fail to condemn non-violent controlling behaviours such as threats to take children, control of money, isolation of the woman, and extreme jealousy (Pence & Paymar, 1993).

The question of the norms that will apply is even more complicated for restorative justice processes like conferencing that rely on family and supporters. In conferencing, the victim, offender, facilitator, and supporters of both the victim and the offender meet to discuss the crime and to develop a resolution that focuses on repairing the harm done to the victim. Thus, with conferencing, the relevant question becomes not what do *most* people believe, but rather what do significant people *in the batterer's (and the victim's)* life believe? Research with men who batter finds that friends and family often play important roles in supporting the batterer's view of himself as a victim rather than a victimizer (Bowker, 1983; DeKeseredy, 1990; Hearn, 1998a, 1998b). Jeff Hearn's in-depth interviews with abusive men found that their level of violence was positively correlated with *both* social isolation (few people with whom to talk over problems or socialize) *and* with having friends who tacitly or explicitly endorse their violence. Hearn concludes that '[i]t is likely to be the *nature* of men's contact with his friends rather than the volume as such that is most significant [in determining his level of violence]' (Hearn, 1998b: 151, emphasis added).[7] And what was the nature of this contact? Hearn found that most male friends either said nothing or actively supported the man's use of violence (Hearn, 1998b). For example, a man who stabbed his wife reported the following responses from his friends:

'What you've done, you've done something wrong, yes. And any man would have done something more or less similar, maybe not the same thing, or maybe not even anything related, but they would have fought for their children, sort of thing'. They said, 'And when children are involved in any sort of relationship or a man and a woman argument, it's a case of domestic and anything can happen.' (Hearn, 1998b: 154)

Whether because of familial loyalty, their own experiences with denying or excusing family violence (Gayford, 1983), or because they fear the abuser (Pennell & Burford, this volume), family members are also unlikely to actively oppose the batterer's violence (Hearn, 1998b). One man's report provides an example:

Q: Did any of your family or any of your friends know about the violence?

A: Two of my brothers knew. You know, they was blaming me for it, but they know different now. They've read everything what she's put down in statements and they know now that 99 per cent she started it. (Hearn, 1998b: 152–53)

In addition to micro-environments of family and male friends, the neighbourhood in which a batterer lives may shape his violence. Evidence suggests that men who live in the most intensely marginalized communities are the *least* likely to be deterred by arrest and criminal processing and their violence may escalate following arrest (Marciniak, 1994).[8]

The responses to offending that develop from restorative justice processes such as conferencing reflect the understanding of the causes of the criminal offence shared by those who attend the process. Thus the result is captured, somewhat, by the limits of the group's understanding. John Braithwaite's description of drunk driving conferences provides an example:

I have seen many drunk-driving conferences where the offender is a tottering alcoholic, but where no one in the community of care raises the need for a drug treatment program, sometimes because most supporters are also excessive drinkers. (Braithwaite, 1999: 69)

While members of the offender's support network may be willing to express (and even act on) opposition to the offender's driving while intoxicated, they are unlikely and unwilling to confront the root of his problem – his alcoholism. Similarly, without a process that deals with the beliefs and controlling behaviours that accompany domestic violence, conference attendees are likely to focus their attention solely on stopping the violence. The result is as likely to be encouraging the victim to appease the batterer by complying with his demands, as it is to support the woman's demands for autonomy.

Theorizing about domestic violence

I recognize that the violence was all about power, about wanting, I had to have my way, and by any means I would get my way. And usually the quickest means was violence. At the same time I always used to think that I never got my own [way] but in effect I did. I always got my own way ... (Hearn, 1998b: 170)

Restorative justice literature concerns itself more with the relationship of the justice response to further criminal offending than with the nature of offending, per se (Braithwaite, 1989). This under-theorizing of offending is a significant theoretical weakness for the use of restorative justice processes in domestic violence cases.[9]

Feminist work in domestic violence understands the violence as 'a way of "doing power"' in a relationship (Mahoney, 1991: 53 quoting Stets, J, 1988). Feminist criminology suggests that it is also a way of 'doing masculinity' (Braithwaite & Daly, 1994; Newburn & Stanko, 1994). Domestic violence is understood not as an eruption that follows 'conflict', but rather as part of a system of controlling behaviour. This is why reform systems require that battering men enrol in batterers' treatment programs that address a range of controlling behaviours that make up a battering system (Adams, 1988; Edleson & Tolman, 1992; Pence & Paymar, 1993). An emphasis on conflict resolution hides the struggle for control and the feelings of male entitlement that often create the context for 'conflict' (Dobash & Dobash, 1998; Fischer, Vidmar & Ellis, 1993).

Men who batter frequently describe themselves as victims (Coker, 1992). They equate women's verbal aggression or threats to separate with a physical assault requiring a physical response (Coker, 1992). A batterer's belief in his status as a victim is often tied to gendered conceptions of appropriate behaviour for his female partner. Her failure to prioritize his needs, her failure to make herself available sexually, or her failure to control the children are felt as attacks on masculinity and provide a rationale for violence (Dobash & Dobash, 1998). As described in the previous section, these beliefs find much support both within the larger culture (Mahoney, 1991) and within the micro-cultures in which the batterer operates (Bowker, 1983).

Lee Bowker argues that interventions with men who batter must be 'multidimensional' in order to address the multiple systems roots of masculine violence (Bowker, 1998). Those who urge an ecological approach to understanding battering make a similar argument (Dutton, 1995; Edleson & Tolman, 1992). This requires understanding the interactive links to battering that occur at the social, cultural, personality, biological, and economic system level (Bowker, 1998).

Part of this systems approach is to recognize the ways in which men construct masculinity and the relevance of that construction to violence directed at women. As Angela Harris writes, when men use violence or threaten violence it may be 'an affirmative way of proving individual or collective masculinity, or in desperation when they perceive their masculine self-identity to be under attack' (Harris, 2000: 781). Understanding the manner in which masculinities are shaped by race, class and ethnic identities and experiences may be central to successful intervention against battering. More privileged men are often better equipped to make their partner appear at fault (Waits, 1998). For example, when women leave, these men have the means to carry out protracted litigation that drains the woman's financial resources (Waits, 1998).

As Harris notes, men who are denied access to dominant forms of idealized masculinity because of hierarchies of race, class, or sexual orientation may create oppositional definitions of masculinity that are nonetheless shaped by the dominant model. For example, '[b]uilding on and subverting racist stereotypes, working-class and poor black men may aspire to a masculinity that emphasizes physical strength, mental control, and sexual prowess' (Harris, 2000: 784). Others may develop a form of 'hypermasculinity' which rests on 'exaggerated exhibition[s] of physical strength and personal aggression' (Harris, 2000: 785).

Battering is not only the product of the operation of systems in the batterer's life (Edleson & Tolman, 1992), it is also shaped by structural inequalities in the lives of women (Schneider, 1992). One of the key such structural supports for battering is the lack of material resources available for women (Coker, 2000). Some abusive men select women because they are economically vulnerable (Jacobson & Gottman, 1998).

Even were this not the case, battering men often ensure that women become and remain economically vulnerable (Raphael, 1995, 1996; Zorza, 1991). Access to adequate housing, employment, childcare, and health care are important determinants of women's victimization. Research by Cris Sullivan finds, for example, that when advocates assist battered women with access to material resources and community services, women experience less re-abuse than do women who do not receive the same assistance (Sullivan & Bybee, 1999).

Transformative Justice

Restorative justice processes do not generally address these sources of battered women's inequality nor do they address the subordinating systems that may operate in the life of the batterer. The concept of *restoration* suggests that a prior state existed in which the victim experienced significant liberty and the offender was integrated into a community; in many cases neither is true (Morris, 1995). Rather than restorative justice, battered women should have the option to choose processes that operate with a *transformative* justice ideal.

Some writers use the term transformative justice interchangeably with the term restorative justice (LaPrairie, 1995b; Porter, 1999), but Ruth Morris argues for distinguishing between the two concepts (Morris, 1994, 1995). Morris seeks to incorporate into justice processes the recognition that 'socioeconomic wrongs [are] at the root of our existing definitions of crime and punishment' (Morris, 1994: 290). She argues that while it is superior to more punitive models, restorative justice 'ignores structural causes of crime' (Morris, 1995: 72), which she understands to be 'an attempt to find power by the powerless and a negative response to pain by those in pain' (Morris, 1994: 291). She argues that when a crime is committed it presents an opportunity for the community to address its inequalities (Morris, 1995; see also LaPrairie, 1995a). Additionally, Morris adds the criminal justice system as a fourth player to restorative justice's focus on offender, victim, and community (Morris, 1995).

Morris's concept of transformative justice suggests possibilities for enhancing the capacity of restorative justice processes to intervene in domestic violence cases. Her vision of justice recognizes the criminal justice system as an actor and thus offers an alternative to the manner in which restorative justice theory and practice elide state power and naturalize criminal justice processes. Morris also recognizes the importance of identifying and addressing the links between the offender's experiences of subordination and his offending.

Despite these advantages, Morris's theory presents problems for application in domestic violence cases. Morris's single attention to structural explanations for crime results in what Jack Katz (1988: 313) refers to as 'sentimental materialism'. This structuralist approach fails to recognize the importance of how people construct the experience of offending (Harris, 1997). If applied to domestic violence cases, Morris's theory fails to address the importance of the gendered way in which batterers understand, explain, and experience their violence. Men who batter operate within constructs of masculinity that reinforce male dominance of women. Their explanations for their violence centre on women's perceived failures to live up to expectations for appropriate women's behaviour. Their violence is often directed at reinforcing male privilege and control of women's sexuality. Morris's structuralist approach also fails to acknowledge the role of offender choice and moral decision-making. As Angela Harris notes, 'crime does not simply emerge from structures of oppression and injustice; crime is committed by people who consciously make choices about their actions and how they wish their actions to be interpreted' (Harris, 1997: 42). This failure to attach clear moral blame may reinforce batterers' tendencies to blame the victim or others for their violence.

In addition, Morris fails to address the duality of oppression: the powerless in one context are the powerful in another context (Harris, 1990). The result is an incomplete structural account of crime. In reality, not only does inequality create crime, but crime (victimization) creates and maintains inequality. Domestic violence creates and deepens female poverty (Browne, 1995), it limits women's participation in civic and economic life (Zorza, 1994), and it debases and devalues women's lives in ways that deeply affect their emotional and spiritual sense of themselves (West, 1999).

An expansion of Morris's concept of transformative justice that is informed by feminist/critical race feminist theory would address both aspects of the relationship of battering to social inequality: the manner in which subordinating experiences in the lives of batterers relate to their decisions to batter and the manner in which their battering subordinates women.

This concept of transformative justice builds on research that demonstrates that batterers' networks are important supporters of battering behaviour as well as on restorative justice theory that emphasizes the ability of supporters to care for victims and reinforce non-offending norms in offenders. It differs from and expands upon restorative justice processes in several ways. First, rather than rely on existing community norms, it takes as its aim the transformation and creation of communities that support women's autonomy.[10] Second, it considers reintegration of the batterer important but secondary to enhancing the victim's autonomy.[11] Third, it offers an opportunity to recognize the manner in which systems of oppression in the batterer's life – 'including economic policies that result in an inability to support families, racist structures, substance abuse and addiction, and histories of horrific childhood abuse' (Coker, 1999: 50–51) – relate to, but do not excuse, his use of violence. A transformative practice challenges not only the state's monopoly on responses to crime, but also challenges racial and gender subordinating institutions, beliefs, and practices that support the crime of battering.

Examples of transformative processes

Current programs that work in subordinated communities provide models for a transformative justice process. These programs do not reject the use of coercive state power, but rely more prominently on changes in batterer networks, provision of support for battered women, and processes that link gender ideology and subordination with experiences of racial subordination and colonization. These programs aspire to meet the transformative goals of redefining gender expectations and norms and building more just communities to support these changes.

The Institute for Family Services in Somerset, New Jersey provides one such example (Almeida & Dolan-Delvecchio, 1999). The Institute works with Asian Indian-American families. Some abusive men are court-ordered to the program while others are voluntary participants. The program is based on the concept that 'it is essential to dismantle the power dynamics connected to gender in a way that does not simultaneously obscure and thereby collaborate with related systems of institutional oppression, such as racism and heterosexism' (Almeida & Dolan-Delvecchio, 1999: 657). Each client of the program is given a sponsor of the same sex whose job it is to 'connect the client to the collective experience of his or her gender, racial, and cultural group' (Almeida & Dolan-Delvecchio, 1999: 669). Through discussions of clips from movies such as *Sleeping with the Enemy* and *Straight Out of Brooklyn,* men in all-male 'culture groups' are encouraged to think about how differences of race and class affect the choices of the battered women in the films. The groups also encourage men to relate *their own* experiences of racism and classism to the issues of gender subordination. For example, 'one Muslim, dark-skinned Asian Indian father of three, who was referred for battering his partner and 12-year-old son, offered comprehensive ... analyses of racism ... He was challenged by his male peers ... to use his analysis of race to better understand their

requests for him to treat his female partner and his son nonviolently'
(Almeida & Dolan-Delvecchio, 1999: 678).

Couples sessions occur if the victim requests them and after the perpetrator accepts full responsibility for his abusive behaviour. These
meetings are attended by sponsors and therapists. In one such meeting
a man who had abused his wife and daughter read a letter in which he
accepted responsibility for his violence. The effect was to produce in the
wife and daughter '[feelings of] empowerment and dignity, as men and
women they had never met unequivocally held the abuser accountable
for his violence in a public forum' (Almeida & Dolan-Delvecchio, 1999:
679). The meeting was subsequently described to the man's culture
group where '[he] was supported by his peers for taking the first steps
toward establishing justice in his marriage' (Almeida & Dolan-
Delvecchio, 1999: 679). The entire process became what John Braithwaite refers to as a 'reintegrative ceremony' (Braithwaite, 1989: 102). It
provided the batterer with the opportunity to make amends and
acknowledge his responsibility for causing great harm to his family,
while also reinforcing the wife and daughter's sense of dignity and moral
worth. The process was also transformative because it reinforced the
emerging egalitarian norms of the men's culture group and in turn the
process in the group linked the struggle for gender equality with the
struggle for racial and economic justice. For women, the Institute provides support without requiring that women choose between cultural
identity or group membership and their safety and autonomy (Almeida
& Dolan-Delvecchio, 1999).

Other programs for heterosexual men of colour who batter similarly
focus on relating the experiences of racial/ethnic subordination to the
men's own use of power to subordinate their female partners (Carrillo
& Goubaud-Reyna, 1998; Duran & Duran, 1995; Duran et al, 1998;
Tello, 1998; Williams, 1998). All stress that the man's own experiences
of oppression do not excuse or justify his own oppressive behaviour. All
seek to enable men to redefine their masculinity in ways that do not
depend on oppressing women. These programs vary in the degree to
which they rely on defining masculinity in a manner that is overtly
oppositional to that of Anglo-European conceptions of masculinity.

In Navajo peacemaking, a process similar to conferencing, some
peacemakers use similar strategies in dealing with domestic violence
cases. These peacemakers employ traditional Navajo stories that contain
gender egalitarian themes (Bonvillain, 1989; Zion & Zion, 1993) to
enlist the language of cultural and political sovereignty to create conceptions of masculine identity that support gender egalitarianism
(Coker, 1999). Peacemakers use these stories to instruct parties regarding their gendered responsibilities to each other, including the

husband's responsibility to treat his wife with respect (Coker, 1999; Zion & Zion, 1993).

It is tempting to think of these processes as 'treatment' and therefore not 'law', but they are justice-*making* processes. These processes focus on education and organizing, not the individual psychology of the batterer or the battered woman. They rest on the realization that community is a project of political will and imagination (Harris, 1997; Kelly, 1996). Further, while processes such as those of the Institute do not directly alter the ways in which racial and class subordination shape crime legislation or criminal justice processing, they may form the basis for political action to attack those inequalities. Even if this were not true, they enable women in those communities to live less coerced lives.

We can also learn from justice programs that are not specifically focused on domestic violence. For example, Angela Harris's description of the work of the Prisoners' Alliance with Community (PAC), an informal organization operating out of Green Haven Prison in New York State (Harris, 1997), provides another example of transformative justice. The program operates with an Afrocentric and Latinocentric approach and 'places current statistics about the disproportion of African-American and Latino people in prison in the historical context of white supremacy ...' (Harris, 1997: 43). The PAC approach 'stresses "empowerment" rather than "rehabilitation": transformation of the offender and the community rather than a simple adjustment of the offender to the community' (Harris, 1997: 44). Harris quotes PAC material:

Inherent in the theory of rehabilitation is the concept that it seeks to 'correct' the individual such that it returns him or her to a state or condition that he/she was in, or should have been in, prior to the objectionable behavior ...[But] [t]he conditions for Blacks and Latinos prior to the objectionable behavior was one of a disadvantaged, second class citizen, in relationship to full and unobstructed access to the benefits, rewards and power in society. This lack of access clearly was a factor which contributed to the objectionable behavior. (Harris, 1997: 44)

PAC is not only interested in coming to understand the racial subordination that relates to choosing criminal behaviour, it is also interested in reconciliation with the community. This requires that prisoners acknowledge the wrongs they have committed. '[It] begin[s] with an apology and proceed[s] into five stages: recognition, responsibility, reconstruction, reconciliation, and redemption' (Harris, 1997: 44–45).

Harris does not note whether PAC specifically addresses crimes of violence against women, but the PAC approach of linking offender responsibility to the community while at the same time recognizing the injustices in the offender's life suggests the possibility for transformative processes that go beyond a 'program' and into the neighbourhood.

Principles of transformative justice process

A transformative justice project offers an alternative to the separation-focused interventions of the dominant forms of justice intervention. It helps women build a community that supports women's autonomy without forcing women to choose between their ethnic/racial communities and safety (Coker, 2000; Presser & Gaarder, 2000). Transformative justice processes must avoid the trap of 'privatizing' violence, but violence is not privatized when a man reads an apology to his wife and daughter in the presence of others, particularly when those others are in a position to monitor his future behaviour. In this way, transformative justice processes capture the benefit available in formal adjudication: that of a public repudiation of the batterer's behaviour and a declaration of unilateral responsibility for his violence (Fenton, 1999; Schneider, 1991). Needless to say, facilitators in a transformative process should not aspire to a neutral ideal (Umbreit & Zehr, 1996) but, like Navajo peacemakers (Coker, 1999) should make transparent the normative assumptions from which they operate (Freshman, 1997). These normative assumptions should not only oppose violence, but should support women's autonomy.

Contrary to some descriptions of conferencing (Retzinger & Scheff, 1996), a transformative process for domestic violence cases should *not* focus on eliciting forgiveness from the victim. The benefits of 'reintegration' for the batterer (Braithwaite, 1989) are found in enabling him to understand both his responsibility for his use of violence and controlling behaviour and his behaviour's continuity with the violence of racial, economic, and colonizing hierarchies. Reintegration does not require that the victim forgive him and certainly does not require that they reconcile, though it does not foreclose the possibility. Pressure to forgive places the victim in an untenable position of once again subordinating her own needs to those of the abuser.

Further, while public apologies from the abuser are important, there is a danger in placing too much emphasis on an apology. Some abusive men are quick to apologize, but slow to change (Coker, 1999). In order to guard against this kind of 'cheap justice' (Coker, 1999), a transformative justice process should include extensive fact-finding, planning, and enforcement. The kind of fact-finding that I have in mind is similar to the process of South Africa's Truth and Reconciliation Hearings (Minow, 1998), to interracial justice described by Eric Yamamoto

(Yamamoto, 1999)[12] and to the practices of some Navajo peacemakers (Coker, 1999; Yazzie & Zion, 1996). This fact-finding should ideally include the abuser's family and supporters, and at some point, the family and supporters of the battered woman. As the work of batterers' treatment programs illustrates, this takes time.

The focus in restorative justice literature on *symbolic* reparations is misplaced where the material resources available to the victim are directly responsible for her ongoing vulnerability to the batterer's control. Transformative justice should address the material needs of the victim whether through unencumbered access to crime victim compensation programs (Mills, 1999) or through direct transfers of money or services from the abuser or his family to the victim (Braithwaite & Daly, 1994; Zion & Zion, 1993).

Conclusion

Feminist critics are correct to worry that restorative justice processes may privatize domestic violence, creating a second rate justice that *offers little protection for battered women. Indeed, current restorative* justice processes seem largely inadequate to the task of addressing domestic violence. There are few restorative justice models that address the manner in which community opposition to domestic violence may be weak or non-existent. In addition, restorative justice literature offers little in the way of theory for understanding male violence against known women.

Restorative justice processes frequently involve a second kind of privatization, as well. Rhetoric that highlights the power of individuals to address crime may serve to make invisible the manner in which state power is deployed to define crime and to enforce criminal laws. Subordinated communities are poorly served if a discussion of social inequalities and discriminatory criminal justice practices are 'off-limits' for the restorative justice process.

Thus restorative justice processes may fail battered women because the particular dynamics of battering are poorly understood or because the process results in tacit approval of some measure of 'acceptable' male control of female partners. Restorative justice processes may fail both men and women in subordinated communities because of the failure to address their social context.

On the other hand, current anti-domestic violence strategies that focus on crime control measures create real dangers for women, and this is particularly true for women who are most vulnerable to state intrusion and control. Thus, women in subordinated communities must be concerned with both the coercive power of the state as well as the coercive power of battering men (Coker, 2001). The question is how to control the state – to ensure adequate protection for battered women – without creating increased state control of women.

Because '[w]omen live under conditions of unequal personal and systemic power that affect all aspects of our lives ...' (Mahoney, 1994; 60), we cannot presume that a singular response to domestic violence will be effective for all women. Rather, as Gordon Bazemore (this volume) writes, we need a 'menu of responses' to domestic violence that account for the structural inequalities of women's lives.

The transformative justice model sketched here is an attempt to further expand our 'menu'. This model addresses the structural inequalities that frame the battering experience for men and women in subordinated communities, provides material and social support for battered women, and holds men who batter responsible for their violence. Adoption of a transformative process does not mean that domestic violence should be decriminalized. Women must be assured that when police are called they will come, and that arrest takes place when women request arrest and the circumstances are legally sufficient for an arrest. But battered women risk not only that the police will fail to protect them, but that opening the door to state intervention will create additional sites for state control.

Battered women require transformation: transformation of their families, communities, and the state. Transformative justice processes can link with formal justice processes (Braithwaite & Daly, 1994; Presser & Gaarder, 2000) and create programs that centre on this transformation.

Notes

1   An additional privatizing concern not often mentioned by feminist critics relates to the private role of restorative justice facilitators and participants. Facilitators are private actors in ways that are not true of judges. They are not subject to removal under the same conditions, their decisions are less likely to be subjected to public scrutiny, and to the extent that their ranks are more numerous and their membership less well defined, they may be more insulated from reform measures such as domestic violence education.

2   The focus of state child protection agencies on the children of poor women of colour should be understood as part of a long history of US policies aimed at controlling the reproduction of poor women, particularly African-American women (Roberts, 1997).

3   These policies are also intended to 'shift the burden of confronting the abuser from the shoulders of the victim' to that of the state (Gamache & Asmus, 1999: 76; Hanna, 1996) and to 'hold the batterer accountable'.

However, 'holding accountable' may have different meanings. As Claire Renzetti writes, 'Could another translation of [holding batterers accountable be] ... "failing to adequately *punish* men for their violence?"' (Renzetti, 1998). Similarly, Laureen Snider suggests that feminist support for criminalizing policies confuses penality with social control (Snider, 1998).

4   Kathryn Abrams describes 'agency' as the partial autonomy women enjoy under systems of oppression. (Abrams, 1999). Martha Mahoney similarly notes that '[a]ll work with subordinated people confronts ... the challenge of analyzing structures of oppression while including an account of the resistance, struggles, and achievements of the oppressed' (Mahoney, 1994: 59).

5   Many battered women desire to separate from their abuser and these women need assistance and protection from the state. This assistance should address the desperate need many women have for additional material resources (Coker, 2000).

6   Activists with the Domestic Abuse Intervention Project, a model program that is often credited with the implementation of mandatory arrest and no-drop prosecution policies in the US and elsewhere, note that without a system-wide response that includes services and supports for victims, mandatory criminal policies can fail and even harm women (Pence & McDonnell, 1999).

7   Hearn provides a more detailed analysis of his study in his book, *The Violences of Men: How Men Talk About and How Agencies Respond to Men's Violence to Women* (1998a).

8   Tracey Meares makes a similar point describing the relationship between social disorganization and criminal behaviour in a neighbourhood (Meares, 1997).

9   An additional weakness of restorative justice processes and hence much of the theory that flows from those processes is that the majority of practice and research has focussed on juvenile offenders who commit property crimes. The leap from this context to work with adult offenders who commit violent crimes recommends caution in applying current research conclusions to domestic violence cases.

10 Carol LaPrairie (1995a) similarly notes that processes may be transformative because they have 'the potential for transforming communities by responding more realistically and effectively to community inequalities, needs, and conflicts'.

11 Presser and Gaarder similarly argue for restorative justice processes that make '[v]ictim well-being and safety ... the first priorities' (Presser & Gaarder, 2000: 186).

12 While Yamamoto describes a process in which communities of colour on both sides of a conflict engage in extensive fact-finding, soul-searching, apology and reparations, my focus is on the *batterer's* response (Yamamoto, 1999). Yamamoto describes 'the four "R's"' necessary for interracial justice: recognition (what I refer to as fact-finding), which includes investigating 'stock stories' that groups use to legitimate grievances against the other group; responsibility, which requires that the group 'assess carefully the dynamics of group agency for imposing disabling constraints on others'; reconstruction, which 'entails active steps ... toward healing the ... wounds resulting from disabling group constraints'; and reparation, which 'seeks to

repair the damage to the material conditions' and create 'material changes in the structure of the relationship (social, economic, political) ...' (Yamamoto, 1999: 10–11). He refers to reparations without changes in material conditions as 'cheap reconciliation'. I adopt Yamamoto's assessment and label as 'cheap justice' processes that over-value offender apologies without accompanying material changes (Coker, 1999: 85).

8 Balance in the Response to Family Violence: Challenging Restorative Principles

Gordon Bazemore and Twila Hugley Earle

Introduction

Though the response to violence, even among close acquaintances, is not problematic for restorative justice *per se*, power imbalance in the family context may present formidable challenges for restorative resolutions. The concept of balance may provide some guidance in the development of standards and dimensions for assessing the extent to which interventions are consistent with restorative principles. Although the idea of balance seems implicit in restorative justice, it has rarely been made explicit. In this chapter, we explore three types of balance to consider in the response to family violence. The underlying decision-making structure for achieving balance in a restorative approach is a consensus-based integration of mutual interests that emerges through pursuit of individual and collective outcomes. We conclude with a call for articulation of a core theory of the restorative justice process based on this structure and development of a research protocol to help observers gauge implementation and effectiveness of restorative justice interventions.

Although a great deal is known about causes and correlates of family violence, there has been little consensus about effective intervention approaches (Adler et al, 2000; McNamara & Kinnaird, 2000; Gondolf, 1997; Walker, 1999). While a growing body of empirical literature examines effectiveness in interventions for property offences, certain violent crimes, and substance abuse (e.g., Lipsey, 1992; Andrews & Bonta, 1994; Winters et al, 1999), empirically validated models of intervention for the unique problems of family violence are rare, and evaluation research in this field is in its infancy. Although there is much excitement about promising new approaches, the field of family violence seems also plagued by proliferation of unintegrated programs and limited by competing interests of system stakeholders (Adler et al, 2000).

In this context, the interjection of restorative justice processes may be welcomed by some, but can also be expected to add to the confusion and to be met with some degree of scepticism and resistance. One apparent reason for the confusion is that the various behaviors included under the rubric of family violence range all the way from murder to sibling fights. There is a natural and appropriate tendency to first think about the most lethal end of the continuum when considering the general idea of new approaches; specific programs, however, do not have to be designed or intended for all situations. An equally important obstacle is lack of clarity about what restorative justice intervention means. Here, two conceptual barriers hinder the development of restorative practices for addressing family violence.

First, there is the growing problem of a general misrepresentation of the restorative 'project' and 'vision'. For example, restorative justice has been alternately portrayed in recent critical commentary as primarily aimed at: getting offenders out of jail or prison, treating or rehabilitating the offender, giving sentencing power to victims, and shaming the offender (Arrigo & Scher, 1998; Delgado, 2000). Some of the same writers making these often self-contradictory claims have also said that restorative practice may have the following unintended consequences: increasing the likelihood that offenders will be incarcerated when they disagree with the victim's wishes or fail to complete a restorative agreement, coercing or manipulating victims to forgive offenders, widening the net of the justice system, denigrating due process, and exacerbating racial bias (Delgado, 2000; Feld, 1999; Immarigeon, 1999; Levrant et al, 1999). There is of course a great need for informed critique about the efficacy of restorative justice intervention in achieving a variety of aims, especially in application to harms such as those associated with family violence (see Stubbs, this volume; Coker, 1999; Polk, 2000; Zellerer & Cunneen, 2000). But as the more astute critics of restorative justice have demonstrated, there is no shortage of legitimate concerns without resorting to 'straw men' categorizations that typically assess these new alternative practices with little if any comparative reference to mainstream criminal justice process.[1]

Second, what may seem on the surface to be an obvious lack of fit between restorative justice and family violence may be due not so much to restorative justice concepts and principles as to their manifestation in specific program models. The best-known restorative justice program models have apparent limitations in the context of the dynamics of family violence. For example, neither the most widely used models such as victim–offender mediation, nor relatively newer approaches such as family group conferencing, were devised with family violence in mind. With few exceptions (Pennell & Burford, 2000a; Morris, this volume), these have yet to be widely employed in response to these problems. Hence, if restorative justice is thought of as a specific program model rather than a general response to crime focussed on repairing harm, it is easy to identify roadblocks to application in other contexts. Although program rules and protocols do not necessarily lead to rigidity, as programs are retrofitted into justice bureaucracies and become institutionalized, the rules of practice and protocol sometimes begin to take precedence over the needs and interests of those the program seeks to serve.[2]

To help shed practical light on conceptual issues, this chapter discusses the strategic problem of how those facilitating restorative processes may seek to balance potentially competing restorative objectives in family violence situations. We consider three specific 'balances' that are likely to be pursued in restorative processes and are likely to require difficult decisions and problem solving. First, *principle balance* considers how practical application of the core restorative principles of (1) repairing harm, (2) maximizing stakeholder involvement in decision-making, and (3) restructuring/transformation of the government and community roles in a way that empowers community as the primary 'driver' of justice solutions (Van Ness & Strong, 1997; Pranis, 1996) can sometimes create conflicts in which a strong focus on one principle appears to minimize the extent to which one can adhere to another. Second, *stakeholder balance* requires that we find the appropriate balance between participation and active involvement of victim, offender, their supporters and other community members in the restorative process. Finally, restorative processes must also seek a kind of *goal balance* between public safety, accountability, and reintegration/recovery.

Before addressing the challenges of each of the three balances in detail, we first briefly consider what is known about the viability of current family violence interventions and some implications for restorative approaches, and then address some problematic features of the idea of balance itself. We then conclude by suggesting that the fulcrum of the balancing process in a restorative justice intervention is a vision of individual and collective transformation of victim, offender and affected community as they integrate their different interests in repairing harm.

The Context and Dynamics of Family Violence

There is widespread agreement in the literature that current systems for addressing family violence are overloaded and under-resourced (Kaufman & Zigler, 1996; National Research Council, 1998). Current interventions are time-limited and inadequate for dealing with long-term needs for social support (Cameron, 1990; McCallion & Toseland, 1995; Pressman, 1989). Regarding offender programs, dropout rates tend to be high, and there is a critical lack of information about long-term results of interventions (Wiehe, 1998; Gelles, 1997; Gondolf, 1997). The Committee on the Assessment of Family Violence Interventions and the Board on Children, Youth and Families of the National Research Council and Institute of Medicine in the US reports that 'The duration and intensity of the mental health and social support services needed to influence behaviors that result from or contribute to family violence may be greater than initially estimated' (National Research Council, 1998).

We make no attempt to summarize or draw specific conclusions from the growing body of research on family violence (see Gondolf & Fisher, 1997; National Research Council, 1998). The most undisputed general conclusion in the research literature, however, is that the problem of intervention is complex.

Blockades at the door to restorative justice practice

The intervention response to family violence appears to be in a state of transition. As evidence that multidimensional factors contribute to family violence has mounted, collaborative or integrated interdisciplinary and community intervention strategies have increasingly been recommended and explored (Wolf, 1995; Fontana & Besharov, 1996; Kaufman & Zigler, 1996; Gelles, 1997; Wiehe, 1998; Wilson, 1997; Adler et al, 2000; Walker, 1999; Leeder, 1994; National Research Council, 1998). A general sense of urgency has seemed to speed replication of apparently successful or promising small-scale innovations. In some jurisdictions these interventions have been quickly incorporated into policy and practice without sufficient evaluation or reflection on the proper interpretation of context specific empirical findings to avoid problematic effects in broader or more varied settings (National Research Council, 1998).

Against a backdrop of cautious optimism mixed with a sense of confusion and a general climate of pessimism, a small 'open door' is being offered in some parts of the world to advocates of restorative justice practices in the arena of family violence. This context of general scepticism should, however, provide the basis for the exercise of great caution and care in experimentation with these generally very different approaches (Pennell & Burford, 2000a; Morris, 2000a). Moreover, several important differences in family violence cases pose serious challenges for restorative justice approaches. First and foremost, victim safety is both an immediate and long-term issue that does not manifest itself in quite the same way in other types of criminal cases, even those involving other forms of extreme violence. Second, as an abundance of research consistently shows, family violence cases typically involve a long-standing, chronic pattern of behaviour rather than a single incident. Offenders in these cases can by no means be generally included among those whose trajectory of behaviour is likely to be permanently altered through merely one-time or short-term interventions or interactions (Dutton & Golant, 1995 in Gelles, 1997; Gondolf, 1997; National Research Council, 1998). Third, patterns of relationships between victim and offender and between both victim and offender and the larger community are typically different than those that might be encountered with other kinds of cases. Whatever the quality of their relationships may be, victims and offenders in other kinds of cases can usually be expected to have families, friends and support systems that restorative justice processes can possibly bring together to explore needs, differences and common ground. In family violence situations, obviously victims and offenders are in the same family, and power dynamics within the family are typically already significantly inappropriate and entrenched (Wiehe, 1998; Wilson, 1997; Walker, 1989; Anderson, 1997). Intimidation can easily affect the voices and perspectives of adult victims (Walker, 1989; Gondolf, 1990; Connolly & McKenzie, 1999), and offenders may also harm or attempt to intimidate others who are close to their victim (Brewster, 1997; Walker, 1989). Effective inclusion of children's needs and points of view as victims is an even greater challenge in family violence cases. Furthermore, what is at times extreme isolation or insularity of the family from friends and other members of the community is typically part of the pattern (Cameron, 1990; Tifft, 1993; Pressman, 1989; Garbarino, 1977; Anderson, 1997; McCallion and Toseland, 1995).

Principles or programs?

Are there existing restorative justice practices that might be cautiously applied in the complex context of family violence? Is there potential for developing entirely new or hybrid approaches based on restorative principles? Those who view restorative justice as a general response to crime rather than a set of programs or techniques (Van Ness & Strong, 1997; Bazemore & Walgrave, 1999) might argue that there are, potentially, restorative *solutions* to any harm or crime, and that there is an appropriate path to reach those solutions. The best solution is not always evident and the path itself may be elusive. Such a solution may also employ traditional formal criminal justice safeguards such as incapacitation to ensure protection of victims and other co-participants in restorative processes (Braithwaite & Roche, 2000; Braithwaite & Daly, 1994; Bazemore & Walgrave, 1999). If it is to offer a useful response to family violence, restorative justice must be adaptable enough to offer an intervention that supports healing even when the path does not resemble typical restorative justice protocols. A restorative response will necessarily be guided by principles rather than program protocols.

Why such emphasis on principles (Van Ness & Strong, 1997; Bazemore & Walgrave 1999; Zehr & Mika 1998)? First, principles play an essential 'gatekeeper role' by grounding practice in certain values necessary to prevent a watering down of restorative justice. In doing so, principles reinforce norms of intervention, and also provide guidelines for evaluating individual and systemic, as well as programmatic, responses to crime in term of various dimensions of 'restorativeness'. Second, principles have been a primary factor in the successful adaptation of restorative practices to multiple settings and diverse community contexts (Bazemore & Schiff, 2000). If restorative justice is to be effectively applied to family violence in the same way that it is now beginning to be applied to a rethinking of school discipline (Reistenberg, 1996), teen courts (Goodwin, 1999), street-level police diversion conferencing, or conflict resolution in some residential treatment programs for offenders (Bazemore, 2000a), it is likely to be because principles have informed a transformation in current practice, rather than because new programs have been implemented.[3] Third, in the context of family violence, it is application of principles – more than anything else – that will help stakeholders guard against abuses and ultimately assess whether or not practices are actually implemented in a truly restorative manner. Here it is important to note that perhaps the most consistent value underlying the restorative justice framework is an overarching, primary commitment to meeting the needs of victims (Bazemore & Umbreit, 1995; Achilles & Zehr, 2000). This victim-driven obligation to repair harm provides the strongest basis for holding restorative policy and practice accountable and should be constantly emphasized in any application of restorative intervention in the family violence context.

When an assessment process is truly focused on Howard Zehr's three questions – what is the harm, what needs to be done to repair it, and who is responsible for such repair (Zehr, 1990) – the facts revealed will typically be difficult to reconcile with cookie-cutter solutions. Restorative processes, to the extent that they are principle-driven, may at times lead to highly unorthodox, individualized responses that are nonetheless more true to the complexity of crimes and harms. In encouraging a focus on developing more rigorous ways of applying principles, rather than expanding programs, we recognize that flexible and fluid approaches that rely less on rules and program scripts may also reduce procedural uniformity and among other things possibly invite legal challenge. Most importantly, such approaches put much more *pressure* on core principles and concepts to provide guidance in the response to unique stakeholder needs. Such guidance must then be translated into practical training and monitoring strategies to ensure that facilitators and all participants in restorative processes feel comfortable and confident with the lack of uniformity in response and with informal application of principles to a range of complex cases. The movement away from rigid program models, therefore, far from solving all problems of restorative justice, in fact, increases complexity. Indeed, the co-author of this chapter has suggested that restorative processes may be grounded in chaos theory in that higher order solutions arise from within the turbulence and complexity of the situation itself. This view theorizes that in human conflict, when sufficiently diverse viewpoints achieve high enough levels of interaction within the boundaries of a process conducive to mutual respect, non-linear dynamics can produce positive holistic change in the pattern of relationships. While the tone of the new pattern reflects the values of the process through which it arose, its specific contents cannot be predicted by knowing the viewpoints that preceded it since it is a result not of their sum but of their dynamic blending (Earle, 1998).

Ultimately, we believe that acknowledging the level of difficulty (and messiness) in a decision-making process that is indeed more open works against unrealistic hopes for restorative justice practices, and increases the likelihood that stakeholders will proceed with caution. The best way to discover whether restorative justice principles and theories-in-use are up to the task of improving on current practice is to examine specific contexts in which restorative principles and modes of problem solving are to be applied. Among other things, family violence is a difficult but highly relevant case study in the applicability and resiliency of restorative principles.

Balance in Restorative Justice Solutions

Strengths and limitations of the balance concept

Yogi Berra once said 'I'd give my right arm to be ambidextrous' and this comment should serve as a warning that the effort to find 'balance' may be more complicated than it seems and is possibly fraught with internal contradictions. Elmar Wietekamp has observed that 'Americans are obsessed with the idea of community because they have never experienced it.' Like the concept of 'community', 'balance' in the criminal justice context is a symbolic term that may be used as a marketing tool to build support for a wide range of policies. Balance is similarly an appealing metaphor in criminal justice precisely because there isn't much balance to be found in current crime policies. For policy-makers, supporting a 'balanced approach' can mean simply being against an 'unbalanced approach', placing oneself comfortably in opposition to the current system without making any particular policy commitment.

As a Western term and symbol, the idea of a 'balanced' criminal justice response may not resonate well with some Indigenous communities. Ironically, because the pursuit of balance in such communities at the individual and collective level is something akin to breathing, some Indigenous peoples might be sceptical about the need to talk so much about it. Although finding balance is part of the very definition of problem solving, including deliberations about the response to crime, it is more likely to be viewed as a natural part of everyday life, and clearly not something any *criminal justice process* would be expected to achieve (Melton, 1995). Regardless of the cultural context, however, participants in a restorative process attempting to respond to family violence are likely to encounter practical challenges about how to balance interests along multiple dimensions.

Applying the idea of balance to concrete restorative justice decision-making examples reveals both strengths and weaknesses of the restorative framework generally and its application to family violence specifically. This kind of balancing is not about merely throwing competing interests into a pot as if one were making stew. Nor does balance imply naïvely seeking to achieve absolute equality in the number of victim and offender supporters in each restorative encounter, equal devotion of resources to repairing harm versus engaging the community, or giving exactly equal attention to public safety, sanctioning and offender reintegration issues. Indeed, such crude prescriptiveness flies in the face of the restorative claim of an individualized response tailored to the needs and interests of key stakeholders, and would, like many retributive justice solutions, justify the charge that uniformity is being substituted for fairness and justice. What is needed therefore is more like a consensus-based *integration of mutual interests*. As we argue in the conclusion, in a restorative justice model, the pursuit of individual interests and collective outcomes for victims, offenders and communities through a focus on repairing harm is the path to the common ground, or fulcrum, upon which balance may be achieved. We focus first and primarily on the challenges of striking a balance in implementing core restorative principles. We then more briefly consider issues in balancing stakeholder participation and addressing standard criminal justice goals.

Principle balance

A restorative justice model is one that is intrinsically harm-focussed, rather than offence-driven. This means that vigilant pursuit of restorative principles will require that practitioners seek first to avoid doing additional harm. In addition, as Van Ness and Strong (1997) argue, because crime is more than law-breaking and is distinguished by the fact that it harms individuals and communities, justice must involve more than merely punishing or treating the offender. Based on this assumption, they articulate three core principles for restorative justice intervention.

1. *The Principle of Repair:* Justice requires that we work to heal victims, offenders and communities that have been injured by crime.
2. *The Principle of Stakeholder Participation:* Victims, offenders and communities should have the opportunity for active involvement in the justice process as early and as fully as possible.
3. *The Principle of Transformation in Community and Government Roles and Relationships:* We must rethink the relative roles and responsibilities of government and community. In promoting justice, government is responsible for preserving a just order, and community for establishing a just peace.

Although these core principles are logically linked and mutually reinforcing, even cursory examination of actual restorative practice reveals that conflicts frequently appear in attempting to fully implement each principle in the specific response to each case. In weighing the practical importance of core principles to particular instances of crime and harm, genuine principle balance requires a specific fit true to the actual situation rather than literalism in adhering to generalized ideals (see Figure 8.1).

Repair vs. stakeholder involvement

The involvement principle is important precisely because it defines the methodology for achieving repair: it is virtually impossible to repair harm without in some way engaging those individuals and groups who have experienced the harm. This principle implies that traditional criminal justice decision-making processes may need to be radically transformed in order to more effectively engage community members and groups, as well as victims and offenders (and their families and supporters), as stakeholders. Developing informal decision-making alternatives to adversarial processes in order to remove barriers to meaningful input, problem solving, the expression of emotion and feelings, and inclusive decision-making has been a primary source of

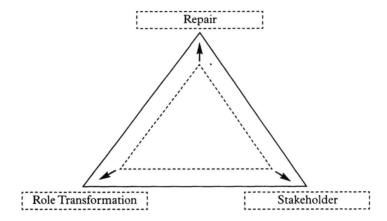

Figure 8.1 Principle Balance

creative tension and tremendous energy in restorative justice reform (Bazemore & Walgrave, 1999). Although restorative justice practice includes more than decision-making processes, the varieties of 'restorative conferencing' approaches should be driven primarily by the urgent need to provide more user-friendly, practical, informal forums for dialogue and input than those offered by formal justice processes.

However, as these approaches have evolved, many have realized that the process itself has tremendous transformative potential, independent of its value in helping stakeholders achieve a tangible settlement (Stuart, 1996; Umbreit, 1999). One dilemma for balancing the need to repair harm with the need to actively engage stakeholders as co-participants in the restorative decision-making process therefore comes when stakeholders appear to be pursuing a solution that does not seem in any way focussed on reparation. In the worst case, an offender-focussed solution might result in an agreement to simply punish or incapacitate the offender – an approach that would by itself have little to do with repair or attention to victim needs. Also problematic, however, is the case in which community members in restorative decision-making processes such as community or family group conferencing express great support for an offender and focus on addressing his/her needs without involving or adequately listening to the victim. When victims are not encouraged to speak about their own hurt or loss, participants may forget about the obligation the offender has incurred to make things right and may be insufficiently concerned about whether a victim has felt comfortable in expressing feelings and needs. Though the victim has the opportunity for input, are his/her needs addressed? Was the harm even identified?

A different kind of imbalance between repair and stakeholder involvement occurs when participants in a restorative process, perhaps guided by an overly dominant mediator or facilitator, rush to develop a reparative agreement without allowing sufficient time for dialogue and input. As Umbreit (1999) observes, such 'fast-food' restorative processes disempower participants, limit the flow of information to victims and victim input, and discourage the expression of emotions. They also tend to result more often in generic and superficial solutions, which, though they may offer some repair (through restitution for example), provide little opportunity for the expression of emotions, problem solving, healing, and relationship building. In the context of family violence, a tilt in the balance of emphasis on repair vs. stakeholder involvement should move in the direction of maximizing stakeholder voices, especially victim voices, and ensuring that adequate time is allowed for dialogue.

Repair vs. role transformation

The dilemma in the previous examples could play itself out in a number of ways that affect the balance between other restorative principles. Suppose that a local community agency strongly committed to restorative principles has noted that the various community conferences it sponsors are beginning to look, as suggested by the examples above, a lot like courts in some cases and therapy groups in others. Their dilemma is the extent to which the first principle of repair is being outweighed by the third core principle of restorative justice – rethinking and redesign of the respective roles of government and community in the response to crime (Van Ness & Strong 1997). While the principle of stakeholder involvement defines a justice *process* focussed on the goal of healing or reparation (i.e., inclusive and driven by stakeholders in the crime), the third principle defines the *organizational structure* and *relationship* between justice system and community, and specifies the roles and responsibilities of each. This new relationship is an emerging one in which communities and their justice agencies move through evolutionary stages beginning with the 'expert' model, and ending, in theory, with a more community-driven approach (Pranis, 1997).

This dilemma of repair vs. the community-driven stance is faced almost daily in programs like Vermont's community volunteer reparative boards where professionals in the sponsoring agency, the Department of Corrections, may be reluctant to challenge the authority of citizen boards. When not doing so means that boards pay little attention to victim involvement and recommend only standardized responses such as routine community service orders and apologies (Karp & Walther, 2000), empowering the community has created an imbalance that reduces the likelihood of repair. This dilemma of role transformation vs. the principle of repair is not unique to reparative boards and can arise in family group conferencing and circles as well as other restorative interventions. In the family violence context, where the risk of additional harm often makes the stakes dramatically higher, even more care must be taken to ensure that community assessment processes do not overlook or underestimate harms associated with an offence. This is especially important in that failure to protect after outcry reinforces intimidation and deepens silence (Walker, 1989). In Australian communities where Aboriginal women are 45 times more likely to be abused within families yet are often fearful of police, victims' advocates must struggle with the very practical question of whether community-driven solutions may offer these women less access to the protection of the state that can sometimes save lives (Coker, 1999: 57–58). Similarly, community leaders may struggle to honour Indigenous responses to crime, while seeking to limit violence associated with some of these 'customary practices'. As they acknowledge the practical and symbolic needs being met by such practices, they hope to redirect community members to other methods of censure that repair and strengthen relationships and, in doing so, strike a balance between community empowerment and repair.[4]

A second way this dilemma of balancing the focus on repair with role transformation plays out is in cases where the state may need to play a more assertive role in ensuring that some repair occurs. This generally happens when victims and other community members are incapable of giving input into this decision, or are for some reason unwilling to do so. Judges confront this balance every day in a mundane way when they order restitution, community service or other sanctions recommended by court staff or probation officers rather than by victims, offenders and communities. A more purist position might denounce any form of court-mandated repair as essentially retributive (McCold, 2000). The principle of repair would lead others to a balance that would include some repair for victim and community ordered by the court, if the alternative is no meaningful repair at all (Bazemore, 2000b; Walgrave, 2000a). In the family violence context, the state role in such repair might take the form of compensation or special bank accounts to support the temporary or permanent independence of victims from abusers (Braithwaite & Daly, 1994; Coker, 1999). Although such support might ideally be provided by the community, one may ask whether or not it is better for the state to either do nothing or simply follow the usual pattern of seeking jail or some other non-reparative form of sanction in cases where the community does not come forward. In the case of family violence, the default role of the state in ensuring protection of victims, as well as repair, may well become even more dominant.

The most convincing and strong opposition to restorative responses has come from feminists rightly concerned about the erosion of the hard-won recognition that family violence is a crime with public rather than simply private implications, and with practical examples of both restorative and system interventions that appear ambivalent to power imbalances. Ironically, the restorative justice movement seems to have been influenced by the feminist critique of patriarchal power as reinforced by retributive punishment, the notion of the personal as political, the questioning of adversarial systems and the women's literature on rape and abuse victimization (Harris, 1990; Bowman, 1994). The feminist critique of the authoritarian punitive paradigm has arguably influenced the restorative justice tendency toward inclusiveness, as well as its related challenges to hierarchical decision-making. Coker (1999), for example, describes a conflict that seems to require that the state play a more assertive role. The case involves a batterer who had committed several brutal beatings of his spouse. In the most recent incident, the spouse had thrown a flowerpot at him after he refused to answer her questions about why he had been away from home for several days. In a peacemaking session, the couple 'forgave each other' and agreed to 'love, trust and respect' each other so the 'dispute' would not reoccur. In Coker's view, equating the harm of one outburst of anger on the part of the victim with multiple brutal beatings on the part of the batterer (who was allowed in the session to also express his own anger with his spouse and to attribute tacit responsibility to her) seriously trivialized the harm (p. 15). Some might rightly argue that a more balanced solution could have been produced in this case by having other family and community members participate in the session to bring the asymmetry of the violence to the forefront of the deliberation (e.g. Braithwaite & Daly, 1994). Absent that, a court that chose to overturn or adjust the original outcome would be giving priority to ensuring meaningful repair and victim safety at the expense of empowering a community process. Coker (1999) is quick to note in her very even-handed critical analysis of Navajo peacemaking that abuser violence is typically taken seriously by peacemakers and other participants in the peacemaking process. The emergence of an active role for police officers in conferencing may well normalize and institutionalize conferencing by providing a guard against the kind of collateral abuse that may be feared in family violence.

For most restorative justice commentators, the community's assumption of a more active and directive role is essential (Braithwaite, 1999a; Bazemore, 2000a). Yet, contrary to some recent misrepresentations in the literature (Delgado, 2000; Feld, 1999), restorative justice advocates, including Van Ness and Strong, do not suggest that government abandon the justice process to community groups. Indeed, the state retains an important role in both peacemaking *and* maintaining order – while also functioning as a guardian of individual liberties and protection against tyranny (Pranis, 1997; Van Ness, 1993). The key change in the government role is in becoming a facilitator of the justice process, in relationship to the community as the 'driver' of such processes (Pranis, 1997). But expanding community control and limiting government assumption of responsibilities does not mean, for example, opposing expansion of formal law to control non-violent behaviour such as stalking, or use of creative charging decisions and prosecutorial strategies that limit the control batterers often exercise over their victims (Coker, 1999: 57). The key criterion is whether such government involvement is necessary to empower and protect disenfranchised parties to achieve a just solution and meet individual and collective stakeholder needs for repairing harm. Principle balance cannot be achieved by knee-jerk reactions that ignore the community role, nor by simply minimizing the government role.

For the most part, there has also been an 'absence of meaningful discussion of the parameters of "community responsibility", both in terms of offender rehabilitation and in terms of crime creation or maintenance', especially in family violence (Coker, 1999: 96). Furthermore, there has been insufficient discussion of the facilitative, problem-solving, community-building role criminal justice needs to play in order to mobilize a meaningful community response to crime. In the absence of analysis that may clarify the community's role in crime *creation* through factors such as economic and social conditions that impact the lives of women and children (Coker, 1999), restorative programs may be doomed to become little more than an appendage of a formal system that continues to weaken, rather than empower, community capacity to resolve conflict.

Stakeholder involvement and role transformation

The principle of stakeholder participation can conflict with community empowerment and role transformation objectives when the community itself is characterized by dysfunctional and/or oppressive power dynamics. Victims are not well served or protected, for example, when advocates for the offender dominate the restorative decision-making agenda. Getting the right power balance within the micro-environment of a restorative conference may be difficult or impossible, however, when dysfunctional power dynamics in communities result in the day-to-day oppression of one or another stakeholder and their supporters. This situation renders such dialogue dysfunctional if not overtly dangerous (Zellerer, 1996). Griffiths and Hamilton (1996), for example, describe small predominantly Aboriginal communities in Northern Canada in which a power elite of abusive Elders exercise dominant control and are in some cases themselves involved in violence against women. When such community groups gain control of the conference agenda, the interests of individual victims and offenders are likely to be ignored. In this case, the government must play its traditional protective role, though reformers might also use restorative justice processes to engage disempowered groups in community-level dialogue as a means of gaining support for more macro-reforms aimed at democratizing decision-making (Braithwaite, 1999). Griffiths and Hamilton (1996) identify examples of community members and groups playing the lead role in community healing processes.

Stakeholder balance

Achieving a balanced response to stakeholder needs does not mean that restorative justice begins with an assumption of symmetry between the situation of offender and victim. By virtue of the fact that the status and well-being of the victim have been reduced as a result of the material, emotional and other harms of the crime, an assumption of imbalance must drive intervention. This requires that initial attention to the needs of stakeholders is not necessarily in equal proportion because greater effort on behalf of the victim is needed to begin to move toward balance by bringing the victim up to a higher plane than the offender. To find a meaningful collective balance requires first an extensive assessment of the individual needs and interests of each stakeholder. The primary strategy for achieving this balance in an often-complex restorative decision-making process is a strategic representation of victims, offenders, and other community members including supporters of both (see Figure 8.2).

The importance of stakeholder balance

Conferences in which victim or offender supporters are badly outnumbered or overwhelmed by the political clout of the offender and his/her family are unlikely to achieve a just result that meets stakeholder needs. In the latter instance, achieving stakeholder balance is complicated when the various forms of power dynamics are considered.

The most common and obvious imbalance in restorative conferences

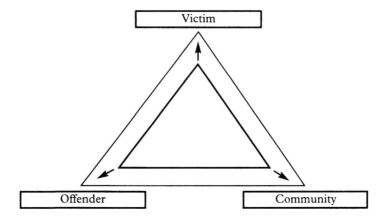

Figure 8.2 Stakeholder Balance

today remains the one between young people and adults (Braithwaite & Parker, 1999; Pennell & Burford, 2000a). Though restorative justice advocates are placing increasing emphasis on the importance of community and victim participation in decision-making, the potential for active meaningful participation by children and youth seems generally under-exploited in adult-centred restorative processes, and many restorative conferencing models too often find the young person in a relatively passive role (see also Morris's chapter). This imbalance in favour of adults in the decision-making process is especially troubling in light of the fact that teenagers and children are quite often secondary, if not primary, victims of family violence, even in cases that begin with a concern about spousal assault. If the traditional family environment is unsafe for women, homicide statistics on deaths of teenagers at the hands of parents show that it is increasingly lethal for young people. Moreover, young people are currently more likely to be the target of incapacitation, punishment, and certainly scapegoating as a result of recent repressive youth violence policy initiatives in some countries (Males, 1996). One example of this trend is emerging in Florida, where pre-adjudicatory detention criteria were expanded to require detention of teenagers arrested for alleged assault on parents or siblings. While this policy change has resulted in a dramatic increase in youths in detention awaiting formal hearings, detention workers and arresting police officers increasingly report that many of those arrested appeared to be responding to parental assaults or played a sometimes-unclear role in sibling fights. Although these harms must be taken seriously, such blunt-instrument use of law that disregards the community role and stakeholder involvement does not actually do so, and indeed may miss the target entirely by failing to perceive or address the underlying problem (see Daly's chapter on treating cases concretely). Another example is the fact that in general, criminal justice sanctions for young people involved in sexual abuse and assault against other young people are more severe than those for adults who perpetrate similar acts against juveniles. Such evidence suggests that the voices of young people are especially important in forming a more contextually accurate and balanced picture of the problems that need to be addressed and resolved in a restorative process. On the one hand, when young people participate in conferences primarily in the role of offender or victim in adult-led processes, their voices are often not heard because adults may not be capable of creating the proper space to invoke dialogue that is either respectful or relevant. On the other hand, conferences and circles are uniquely suited to bring forth the voices of young people if organizers accept the challenge of engaging adolescents in more empowered roles as friends, supporters, and even conference facilitators. Ironically, as has been demonstrated in the far less impactful – and generally un-restorative – practice of teen courts, it is possible to assign young people significant responsibility for decision-making.

The example of failure to empower youth in conferences can be extended to other stakeholders, and it illustrates a more generic problem of under-representation of other marginalized groups. Former offenders and victims are not typically among the participants in conferencing programs – with peacemaking circles standing apparently as a notable exception (Stuart, 1996). Having been an offender or victim may allow the conference participant to offer a credible voice of reason to move toward full acceptance of responsibility, especially in the family violence context, and also provide credible support and guidance to victim or offender. Couples who have resolved conflicts and families who have worked through problems successfully can be tremendous role models. Recovering adult survivors of family violence, including incest, can help speak for child victims unable to articulate their own needs and interests.

As a general requirement, restorative processes addressing family violence will need to be especially concerned with strongly presenting the perspective of the victim. The key to balance here is ensuring that community participation is adequate to ensure that knowledge of the abusive behaviour in question will be appropriately communicated, that support for the victim and protection by friends and neighbours emerges, and that protective roles are defined and agreed to by community members. Government and professional roles must also be clarified in this process as support and back-up for the community in a way that validates the important role of community guardians.

Managing the balance

Practically, how do conference coordinators and participants in restorative justice ensure that representation is adequate to ensure that stakeholder needs are brought to the table in the restorative process? Achieving stakeholder balance is often a result of strategic efforts to elicit dissenting views and bring the concerns of the less powerful and less vocal to the table. Braithwaite & Parker (1999) give numerous examples of how conference conveners may exercise great creativity in finding a support person for a young offender or victim who has been abandoned by immediate family and appears isolated from other community groups. A concern, however, is whether this important outreach function on the part of conveners or coordinators is sufficiently incorporated into actual practice. Proper resourcing and a clear role definition that makes getting the right players to the table a core achievable feature of the convener's job are necessary for balance to be ensured. Although practice in the area of strategic identification of support persons is steadily improving, the need for extended preparation and greater precision in conference design must become a more critical issue as conferencing professionals begin to address more complex cases.

Stakeholder balancing, when thought of as a balancing of *voices* rather than bodies, can also be used effectively by coordinators to decrease the likelihood of other imbalances. Though it may seem manipulative to some, conference coordinators may also prompt support persons to express concerns that flow out of other principle-based needs. For example, a victim supporter may be encouraged in a pre-conference meeting, or during the encounter itself, to express issues of harm and need for reparation when the victim herself seems reluctant to do so. This is crucial in family violence cases, as dynamics of intimidation require special advocacy for victims, including children.

An offender support person may also provide a reality check that helps the offender respond more appropriately to requirements being suggested by conference participants or encourage the offender to 'own up' to his/her responsibility in the offence. A young person supporting an adolescent peer so caught up in the web of family violence that she is unable or unwilling to speak to outsiders may play an important role in activating, or representing, the voice of the vulnerable young person. Finally, other families who have successfully worked their way through similar problems might be viewed as resources and used strategically in conferences to normalize the process and reduce stigma while also offering support and assistance.

Goal balance

Balancing goals acknowledges that there are intervention objectives that go beyond the needs of individual stakeholders in the restorative process. Communities have generic needs for their members to feel safe; to censure crime, impose obligations on the offender and enforce norms and tolerance limits (accountability); and to find ways to safely reintegrate not only offenders but also victims who may have been stigmatized or isolated in the aftermath of a crime (see Figure 8.3). Currently, the focus on these goals tends to be unbalanced in most criminal justice systems because the most common strategies for public safety, for example, are often not compatible with the effort to meet other needs. In the family violence context, there is usually conflict between the need to protect the victim – typically by incapacitating the offender, which the victim may or may not desire – and the need to somehow reintegrate the offender into appropriate roles and behaviours in the community. Competency in those new roles and behaviours must be developed for reintegration to be successful.

Although restorative justice commentary has had relatively little to say about traditional criminal justice goals, proponents must begin to articulate how public safety, sanctioning and integration might be reframed within restorative justice principles (Bazemore & Walgrave, 1999; Braithwaite, 1999a). For instance, in family violence cases as in other cases, communities and victims should be at least as safe in jurisdictions that make widespread use of restorative processes as in those that do not. Victims are no less vulnerable to abusers seeking to

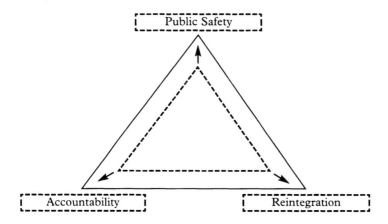

Figure 8.3 Goal Balance

perpetrate violence on the courthouse steps than they are in an informal restorative conference, where strategically it should be at least equally possible to include police officers and ensure police protection. Having affirmed the importance of not abandoning the resources of traditional criminal justice, it is possible to explore what could be achieved by reframing public safety and victim safety in a problem-solving approach informed by restorative justice principles. For proponents of a more holistic than programmatic approach to restorative justice, 'repair' implies not merely trying to balance traditional rehabilitation, public safety, and punishment or sanctioning practices, but rather meeting each of these goals in ways that are more compatible with each other. The key is reframing traditional goals in the light of restorative principles to create 'resonance' between strategies to achieve public safety, sanctioning/accountability, and recovery or reintegration so that these practices are mutually reinforcing. Braithwaite & Daly (1994) explore reframing the goal of deterrence. Braithwaite & Roche (2000) make use of the concept of 'active responsibility' to transform the idea of offender incapacitation to one of victim *capacitation,* operationalized by providing various forms of support, financial and otherwise, that create options and real choices for victims, including bank accounts and alternative living arrangements. An example of resonance occurs when operationalizing victim safety as support also enhances the goals of victim reintegration, trauma reduction and healing.

Coker (1999) and Stubbs (this volume) suggest reframing the notion of victim reintegration in the family violence context by moving away from the stereotypical categories of women as either agent (provocateur) or victim incapable of taking informed action. Viewing victims of abuse through these narrow, psychologized policy lenses (Bazemore & Terry, 1997) limits the potential for empowerment of women as *resources* in their own transformation and in the recovery and healing of others. Through the restorative justice lens, public safety and victim safety can be reconceptualized with the promotion of a sense of guardianship and active participation as a necessary component of safe, low-violence communities (Braithwaite, 1989; Sampson et al, 1997). Sanctions and accountability in such reframing become less about harming the offender, and more about making things right with victims and facilitating a community expression of outrage and disappointment that results in a kind of norm affirmation (Clear & Karp, 1999). Though anti-violence and anger management work are still critical for offenders, rehabilitation becomes a deeper and larger concept of recovery, less about simply completing treatment requirements and more about building long-term community relationships of support and guidance around the offender.

Toward a Restorative Theory of Process: Collective and Individual Transformation

This chapter has explored the practical task of achieving a restorative balance in the response to family violence and some of the challenges therein. The concept of balance is useful in illuminating the complexities of the task. We have also noted that simplistic efforts to achieve a crude proportionate balance between principles, stakeholder needs, and criminal justice goals are not sufficient. A clear understanding of the restorative justice vision is essential, along with a core theory of the restorative process. A research protocol informed by core theory could help observers 'know restorative justice when they see it' and begin to gauge the effectiveness of the process in achieving healing outcomes.

To move forward, a generic theory of restorative process is needed to distinguish restorative justice as a way of responding to harm caused by crime from any narrow association with specific program models, which may be appropriate in some types of circumstances and not in others. Rather, the consistent fulcrum of restorative balance is a consensus-based integration of mutual interests that emerges as common ground in the effort to repair harm and 'co-produce' individual and collective transformation. Since this fulcrum forms from within each specific situation, its particular aspects vary accordingly.

Common ground and mutuality

Unlike criminal justice responses which separate the parties in crime and conflict and assume that their interests are mutually exclusive, restorative processes seek to find 'common ground' in interests between victim, offender and community in a highly intentional three-dimensional focus that must give consideration to the roles and needs of each stakeholder (Stuart 1996). Although this common ground – where stakeholder interests intersect – is often a small 'plot', it is viewed in restorative justice as the most 'fertile soil' for achieving meaningful repair. The configuration of interests and the extent of overlap vary from case to case; for example, there may initially be little common ground between the interests of victim and offender, but significant mutual interests for victim and community. Especially in complex crimes such as those involving family violence, there is much opportunity for meaningful work toward restorative solutions in these initial dyadic relationships that can expand potential for more comprehensive solutions that may come later (e.g., working through some community and victim issues prior to engaging the offender). Such dyadic work is often a

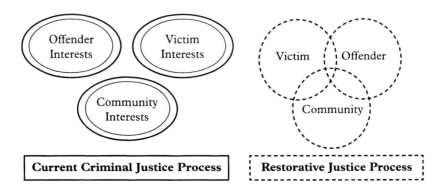

Figure 8.4 Stakeholder Interests and Common Ground

critical first step in a process that is nonetheless driven by the larger three-dimensional vision (see Figure 8.4).

Stakeholder Interests and Common Ground: Objectives of Alternative Decision-making Processes

A generic theory of restorative process might have as a key proposition that the best solutions and the most effective outcomes are achieved when the conferencing process seeks to address the interests and needs of all three stakeholders. Although finding common ground is often something that occurs idiosyncratically and certainly is unlikely to follow a linear process, Moore and McDonald (2000) suggest a four-stage process of emotional change in participants in restorative process-es. These stages, which involve individual and collective transformation, between individuals and the group, and between sub-groups and the larger collective, offer possibilities for the concept of using benchmarks to judge whether a conflict resolution process has been successful. For Moore and McDonald, the ultimate transformation that makes for successful resolution is shared group ownership of the conflict as a collective entity, a change that is initiated as relationships are built or strengthened.

Collective outcomes and social relationships

Most criminal justice interventions focus exclusively on individual change. Pursuit of both individual and collective outcomes (Van Ness &

Strong, 1997; Bazemore, 2000a) through mutually reinforcing individual and collective change is a key distinguishing feature of restorative processes. The necessary criteria for identifying and addressing mutual interests – ensuring that appropriate voices are heard and allowing sufficient time for the dialogue that includes these voices (Stuart, 1996) – often greatly increase the complexity of deliberation in restorative encounters. Such criteria may also greatly limit the range of restorative programs that are appropriate in the response to family violence. Yet, the focus on common ground and collective outcomes mitigates against the programmatic focus that has too often made coordinators and conveners content with routine outcomes such as apologies and expressions of remorse by offenders that may create a 'cheap justice problem' (Coker, 1999) which trivializes the harm of violent behaviour. However, the danger of privatizing (or re-privatizing) cases of domestic violence as individual incidents rather than patterns of oppression with collective roots and implications (Stubbs, this volume) decreases as collective outcomes are pursued and mutuality is recognized (Coker, 1999).

Much criminal justice policy related to family violence continues to focus on whether offenders should receive treatment or jail time as a primary response, and in doing so gives little attention to either the victim or the community context. In this context, restorative approaches could be especially appropriate to develop solutions that address both individual and collective needs in a way that essentially repairs relationships. The core concept of repair necessarily implies outcomes that include and also extend beyond impacts on individuals. Moreover, because the notion of finding common ground implies an attempt to engage mutual commitment to solutions, one manifestation of this collective outcome is the development of new social relationships or a restructuring and strengthening of existing relationships damaged by crime.

As suggested earlier, relationship building is a central long-term goal of the restorative process and a core aspect of the definition of repair (Van Ness & Strong 1997; Braithwaite & Parker 1999; Bazemore & Dooley, 2000). One approach to evaluating the effectiveness of a restorative process might be to ask whether or not the process and actions following up on conferencing agreements: created new positive relationships or strengthened existing relationships; increased community skills in problem solving and constructive conflict resolution; increased participants' sense of capacity and efficacy in addressing problems; increased individual awareness of and commitment to the common good; and created informal support systems or 'safety nets' for victims and offenders (Pranis & Bazemore, 2000). The importance of relationships in restorative conferencing processes is grounded in this sense of community as interconnected networks of citizens who have tools and resources to promote healing and reintegration.

In the family violence context, the focus on building or strengthening relationships engages what Coker calls the 'relational nature of choice' for women and other family members in abusive relationships. Restorative justice principles, appropriately practised, may also help over time to build the social capital needed in communities to offer both support and informal control in a helpful response to family violence. To the extent restorative processes are able to do so, they move beyond the realm of programs responding to individual needs, to processes that provide space and relational resources to support victims, offenders and communities in confronting and transforming problems of family violence.

Notes

1 Another misleading form of argument equates restorative justice with mediation – or at least a certain form of mediation associated with dispute resolution (Delgado, 2000). Although there are forms of victim–offender dialogue that have been conducted with a great deal of success as a response to victims of serious violence, most advocates of these practices have not recommended it for domestic violence cases (Umbreit, 1999). Portraying restorative justice as simple mediation sets up a 'straw man' to invite attacks on restorative justice. As critics rightfully oppose an intervention that appears to ignore the victim–offender distinction, they fail to address the victim blaming common in domestic abuse, and possibly reinforce subtle, or not so subtle, coercion (Coker, 1999). For responses to a range of other criticisms, see Bazemore, 1998; Bazemore & Walgrave, 1999; Braithwaite, 1999a.

2 This is usually less the fault of program staff than bureaucratic require-ments of justice systems that may place rigid boundaries on the range of flexibility in response to the needs presented in individual cases. It has often been the case that popular criminal and juvenile justice programs may take on a life of their own outside the context of principles, goals of intervention, and measures of effectiveness (Finckenauer & Gavin, 1999; Umbreit, 1999).

3 There are of course restorative conferencing programs that appear to max-imize flexibility for participants (Stuart, 2000; Pennell & Burford, 2000a), and it is possible to continue to adapt program models to the needs of clients. It is principles, however, that make practitioners attuned to the need for such adaptation. Hence, the challenge is not only to ensure that restorative justice interventions are adequately resourced, but also ade-quately conceptualized. Perhaps, as Pranis (this volume) and others sug-gest, what is needed is the development of new, problem-solving 'spaces' where stakeholders can safely work together to repair harm.

4 Response to question from audience in Restorative Justice and Family Violence conference in Canberra, 2000. Several other respondents placed

these sometimes violent community responses to crime in context by direct comparisons with the violence suffered by Aboriginal offenders in prison. Another illustration of this dilemma is apparent in the insensitive imposition of restorative and other conflict resolution processes in cultures whose own historical settlement processes have been devalued (Zellerer & Cunneen, 2000).

Lessons from the Mediation Obsession:
       Ensuring that Sentencing 'Alternatives'
       Focus on Indigenous Self-Determination

Larissa Behrendt

Statistical data have shown that Indigenous people in Australia are increasingly over-represented in the criminal justice system. At the same time, Indigenous families are experiencing high levels of violence. Hidden behind this trend evident in the statistics is the impact of colonization on Indigenous communities and of incarceration on the families of those coming into contact with the criminal justice system. Finding solutions to these already hard issues is made increasingly difficult by the cultural conflict that can occur when Indigenous people, as victims or offenders, come into contact with the criminal justice system.

This chapter seeks to consider the lessons that can be learnt from other attempts at seeking resolution to conflict between Indigenous peoples. It seeks to explain how cultural conflict arises in the legal system and in other alternative dispute resolution models, namely, mediation. It also considers the right to self-determination as an holistic approach needed for the breaking of the legacies of colonization, of which family violence is a factor. To this end, this chapter should be read in conjunction with the chapter by Loretta Kelly that considers the issue of family violence as a phenomenon in Indigenous communities in Australia in more detail.

When a legal system looks neutral on the surface, many will assume that it produces fair results. This assumption is incorrect, as the experience of Aboriginal Australians bears out, because:

• seemingly neutral institutions can often contain inherent biases;
• seemingly neutral institutions can generate biased results.

I want to use an Australian case study to explore and explain how seemingly neutral laws contain and create bias and how this cultural conflict extends to popular methods of alternative dispute resolution, particularly mediation models. I propose to discuss this in relation to mediation with the hope that these critiques will provoke some thought on how the same problems may occur and be avoided in conferencing and other more elaborated models of restorative justice such as the healing circles that draw on Indigenous experience in North America. It is my hope that these explorations will provide some basis upon which to explore the question posed by Loretta Kelly in her chapter, namely, whether restorative justice is culturally appropriate in the contemporary Australian context.

Historical Legacies

How seemingly neutral institutions contain bias

If court victories offer only sporadic and episodic protections, which are limited or overturned by the legislature's political will, the Constitution remains the last bastion for rights protection. But this area offers very few guarantees. Australia has no bill of rights and minimal rights are recognized in the constitution, though some have been implied.

The issue of whether the race power, which allows the Federal Government to make laws with regard to Indigenous people, could be used to deprive Indigenous people of their rights was raised by the plaintiff in *Kartinyeri v. The Commonwealth* (the Hindmarsh Island Bridge case). In that case, brought in a dispute over a development site that the plaintiff had claimed was sacred to her, the government sought to settle the matter by passing an Act, the Hindmarsh Island Bridge Act 1997 (Cth). That Act was designed to repeal the application of heritage protection laws to the plaintiff. The plaintiff argued, *inter alia*, that when Australians voted in the 1967 Referendum (Attwood et al, 1997) to extend the federal race power (s.51(xxvi)) to include the power to make laws concerning Indigenous people it was with the understanding that the power would only be used to benefit Indigenous peoples. The court did not directly answer this issue, finding that the Hindmarsh Island Bridge Act 1997 (Cth) merely repealed legislation. The majority held that the power to make laws also contains the power to repeal or amend them. This decision was seen as a victory by the Australian Government who saw constitutional challenges to amending legislation that extinguished Native Title rights as much harder to mount.

Many were shocked to contemplate that Australia's Constitution offers no protection against racial discrimination but one need only look at the intention of the drafters to see why it remains this way. In fact, a non-discrimination clause was proposed for inclusion in the Constitution when the instrument was being drafted. Proposed clause 110 was drafted to include the phrase:

'... or shall a state deprive any person of life, liberty, or property without due process of law, or deny to any person within its jurisdiction the equal protection of its laws' .

This clause was rejected. It was rejected for two reasons:

- it was believed that entrenched rights provisions were unnecessary, and
- it was considered desirable to ensure that the Australian states would have the power to continue to enact laws that discriminated against people on the basis of their race. (Williams, 2000)

If one is aware of these attitudes held by the drafters of the Constitution then it comes as no surprise that the Constitution is a document that offers no protection against racial discrimination today. It was never intended to do so and the 1967 Referendum in no way addressed or challenged those fundamental principles that remain entrenched in the document.

In a country where there is a racist Constitution, racist Native Title legislation and a government which cannot understand that there is a sector of the Australian community still hurting from the government practice of removing Indigenous children from their families to assimilate them into white society (Cunneen, 2000), the question of reconciliation between Indigenous and non-Indigenous people is going to be difficult.

How formal equality is a formula for inequality

In 2000 the United Nations Committee on the Elimination of Racial Discrimination issued a report critical of the present Australian Government's record on human rights protected under the Convention on the Elimination of all forms of Racial Discrimination (CERD). In particular, the concluding observations by the Committee included expressions of concern over the 'mandatory sentencing schemes which target offences committed disproportionately by Indigenous Australians, especially juveniles, creating a racially discriminatory impact on already high rates of Indigenous incarceration' (CERD, 2000).

The Human Rights and Equal Opportunity Commission's *Social Justice Report 1999* recounted the alarming statistics concerning Indigenous juvenile incarceration. According to the report, rates of over-representation of Indigenous youth in the criminal justice system are increasing. Indigenous people make up around two percent of the population but are around 20 percent of the prison population; for

Indigenous women and children, the over-representation is even higher. The Report cites the following figures:

- in 1993, an Indigenous youth was 17 more times likely to be detained in custody than a non-Indigenous youth. By 1996 this rate had increased so that an Indigenous youth was 21 more times likely to be detained in custody than a non-Indigenous youth;
- between June 1994 and June 1997 there was a 20 per cent increase in the number of young Indigenous people in detention. The correlative level of over-representation for that period increased from 18.9 times in 1994 to 24.6 in 1997. (HREOC, 1999: 84)

In the two jurisdictions that had mandatory sentencing schemes, in June 1999, 76 percent of all prisoners in the Northern Territory and 34 percent of all prisoners in Western Australia were Indigenous (HREOC, 1999).

These increases have occurred despite the lengthy and thorough recommendations of the Royal Commission into Aboriginal Deaths in Custody (1991). The legislation in Western Australia and the Northern Territory imposes mandatory periods of detention for offenders who commit prescribed property offences. These provisions focus on the punitive and retaliative roles of the criminal justice system, rather than on the rehabilitative and reformative functions (Roche, 1999). Nor do such provisions seek to address the underlying causes of the offending behaviour. The following two cases bear this out:

- an 18-year-old Indigenous man obeyed his father and admitted to police that he stole a $2.50 cigarette lighter. He was sentenced to 14 days in prison;
- a 29-year-old homeless Indigenous man wandered into a backyard when drunk and took a $15 towel. It was his third minor property offence. He was imprisoned for one year. (HREOC, 1999: 95)

These measures impact disproportionately on Indigenous people. In Western Australia, Aboriginal children constituted '80 per cent of the three strikes cases in the Children's Court of Western Australia from February 1997 to May 1998' (HREOC, 1999: 92). The HREOC Report noted that even though on the face of it, the legislation may not seem discriminatory, 'where a pattern of sentencing reveals that certain groups of children are more likely to receive the harshest penalties, sentencing is suspect' (HREOC, 1999: 92).

The impact of mandatory sentencing laws on Indigenous women has been particularly brutal with estimates, based on figures from the Northern Territory Correctional Services Department, of 'a 223% increase in the number of Indigenous women incarcerated in the first year of operation of the legislation. As of 30 June 1999, Indigenous women made up 91 percent of all women prisoners' (HREOC, 1999: 92).

The most contact that Aboriginal people have with the law is with the police. This contact also has an historical context since law enforcement officers led massacres of Aboriginal people and came to take children away. They are rarely from the Aboriginal community and often believe the stereotypes perpetuated about Aboriginal people and this has played no small part in the high levels of incarceration of Aboriginal people (HREOC, 1991). One in four of our men are in jail. Aboriginal people are 20 times more likely to die in prison than a non-Aboriginal person is. Aboriginal people are more likely to be arrested for a summary offence than a non-Aboriginal person. Aboriginal people are held in police custody for longer periods than non-Aboriginal people are.

Given these statistics, it is not surprising that restorative conferencing schemes begin to look attractive as an option since a young person may avoid a conviction and get a 'second chance'. This brings the emphasis back to rehabilitation and responsibility rather than punishment. It also allows a greater role to be played by victims, families and the community in crime prevention.

If most Australians do not question the fairness and neutrality of Australia's legal system, this is not true of Aboriginal Australians. The first encounter that Aboriginal people had with the law of the British was when Captain Cook claimed the continent of Australia for the British sovereign. The legal doctrine of *terra nullius* kept Aboriginal people dispossessed until 1992. The dominant legal system is an instrument of colonization that allowed the state to legitimate its control over the lives of Aboriginal people while failing to protect their rights.

Cultural Traditions and Dispute Resolution

Land has always meant different things to Indigenous and non-Indigenous Australians. We bond with the universe and the land and everything that exists in the land. As my father says: 'You can no more sell our land than sell the sky.' He would describe our relationship to the land in the following way:

Our affinity with the land is like the bonding between a parent and a child. You have responsibilities and obligations to look after and care for a child. You can speak for a child. But you don't own a child.

Even though Aboriginal people have been moved off their traditional lands, land remains an important need of Aboriginal communities. Even urbanized communities maintain links with their traditional lands. Traditional land is needed so sacred sites that remain can be protected. Non-Aboriginal Australians have destroyed and defaced Aboriginal sacred sites. Non-Indigenous concern for land is mostly economic.

The values and priorities of the Aboriginal community conflict with those of the dominant legal system at many points. While acknowledging that there is vast diversity between the lifestyles and cultural practices and values of Indigenous Australians it is also fair to say that several similarities exist. The notion of a creation period in which laws were created, a 'Dreamtime' is one such commonality. The interconnection with the land – whether it is called custodianship or ownership or guardianship – exists throughout all Aboriginal groups. Interconnection occurs with all living entities and people through a totemic or clan system. Our culture is oral; this is how law and responsibility were handed down. Learning is gained through the example set by others, leading to more respect for those with life experience and wisdom. This world view is much more focussed on the community rather than the individual. The smallness of groups and their reliance on each other to ensure survival facilitated a strong sense of loyalty and responsibility to the group that today still facilitates notions of cooperation and consensus. There was also no hierarchical structure in our communities in the sense that it occurs in the class structure of European society. In this sense, it can be asserted that Aboriginal culture was more egalitarian than European or Western culture.

These cultural values are reflected in the process by which conflict was resolved in pre-invasion Aboriginal communities. Grievances were dealt with in several ways. The following examples were taken from a specific area so there will be some elements shared with other groups and some that were unique to the area.

A group of Elders would make decisions for groups and would also intervene in disputes if they had not been resolved between family members. Meetings between Elders were usually convened when groups met for ceremonies. These groups were not judicially formed bodies; no one had a vested authority to decide the outcome. Decision-making was less formal and less systematic. Women had a prominent part in the process, having the power to make decisions if the person who had broken the law was a woman (Gale, 1986).

In an example from the lower Murray (Berndt & Berndt, 1981), two clans sought to settle a dispute in the following manner:

- Members of each clan sat facing each other
- Members were arranged around their spokespeople
- A general discussion was undertaken

• The aggrieved parties then spoke, including their family members and any other person with an interest in the proceedings.

In grievances between individuals, aggrieved parties were given the chance to express the way they felt – even through shouting, yelling and screaming. Open displays of anger were seen as part of the resolution process. Disputants were encouraged to spend time getting their emotions under control before they faced the person that they were in dispute with. Women were especially important in this process, playing an active role in the procedures. Facilitation of a resolution was aided by the use of the interconnection of the community. Social pressure can be very powerful in a small, close-knit and interconnected community.

From this example, several points of conflict with Australia's dominant legal culture and legal system become apparent (See Table 9.1) (Behrendt, 1995). The emphasis on speaking from the heart which is fundamental in Indigenous dispute resolution processes is given no place in the dominant legal system that seeks to put a version of events forward in a non-emotive and factual form. The Indigenous focus on feelings, hurt and perspective when speaking also runs into conflict with the formal rules of evidence that curtail the events that a disputant is able to put forward in court. The emphasis on speaking from the heart meant that disputants themselves presented their grievance, rather than through the words of an advocate as the dominant legal system seeks to do. These factors help to underscore the difference between a system that is based on oral evidence and accounts and law to a system that seeks to put everything in writing and record with the power of the word. The absence of these strict rules gives a feeling of informality to Indigenous dispute resolution processes that is missing from the formal and imposing processes and rituals of the dominant legal system.

Indigenous dispute resolution was based in an inherent understanding of the interconnectedness of all people in the community through family and kinship ties and responsibilities. Dispute resolution methods were thus based on situations where disputants had complex relationships with each other and would continue to have to live together, perhaps closely, within the same community. There are many matters that arise for resolution in the dominant legal system where the parties will not have a continuing and on going relationship and this has implications for the form resolution of the dispute will take. In recognition of the on going relationship between the parties, there was flexibility in process and no time limit on when the dispute would be resolved since it was understood that feelings may need time to settle down, that time out might be needed, before the parties were ready to resume their negotiations.

Indigenous dispute resolution processes, with this focus on inter-connection, encouraged participation by all those within the community who felt that they had an interest in the dispute and the outcome. Unlike the dominant legal system which has strict rules of standing, Indigenous dispute resolution processes take place in front of the family and community in a way that acknowledges the social context in which the dispute has arisen and must be resolved.

Another cultural conflict that arises is the emphasis on formal education and qualifications for participation in the dominant legal system. This lies in contrast to the emphasis on life experience as the indicator of knowledge and wisdom that is fundamental in Indigenous cultures and to the revered and respected role that Elders play in those communities.

Table 9.1 Aboriginal Dispute Resolution and the British Legal System

Aboriginal Disputes	British Legal System
Emotional response	Controlled response
Oral	Written
Disputants live together	Disputants often strangers
Experience as training	Formal legal training
No rules of evidence	Strict rules of evidence
Process in front of the community/family	Process in front of strangers
Disputants speak	Use of advocates
Time not an issue	Deadline intensive
Informal	Formal
Communal	Hierarchical

Cultural Conflict and Mediation

With these cultural conflicts endemic when Indigenous people have contact with the legal system, it is easy to see the attraction of mediation in these circumstances. Mediation was hailed as a way of alleviating these cultural conflicts and countering systemic racism and historical legacies. Mediation does recognize the inadequacy of litigation in certain circumstance that is costly and intimidating. It streamlines the court system and allows parties a better opportunity to express their opinions. Despite these benefits, there are still fundamental conflicts that arise in mediation models.

It is claimed that mediators are especially useful in dealing with disputes where there are cultural differences between the parties and that a mediator can reduce obstacles to communication through identifying cultural issues. It is asserted that mediation allows discussion of cultural beliefs and attitudes thus giving them importance and encouraging respect for those values without making people change their own values. Mediation assumes that people can resolve their issues. It allows disputants the control and the responsibility to decide the content of the conflict and the power to make a decision. In this way mediation encourages people to choose their own options for resolving disputes and in this way it empowers disputants.

This allows consensus in the outcome of the dispute and that means that it is more likely to be implemented by the parties involved. The obvious advantages with using mediation have made it the model used in pilot programs to implement alternative dispute resolution into the Aboriginal community, especially in areas related to families and land. It is also part of the process to review claims made under the Native Title Act 1993 (Cth) to the Native Title Tribunal.

Mediators have noted that mediation between parties from different cultural backgrounds can lead to specific types of problems in mediation. Proponents of mediation are quick to point to the following 'cultural issues':

- *Language issues* that lead to miscommunication and misinterpretation;
- *Incorrect assumptions* about diverse cultures;
- *Expectations* that others will conform;
- *Biases* against the unfamiliar; and,
- *Values in conflict* when the values of the dominant culture conflict with those of another culture. (Myers & Filner, 1993)

Training is the method by which most people working in mediation try to counter the cross-cultural bias. This is attempted in two ways:

- through 'cross-cultural' training;
- by training Aboriginal people as mediators.

Cross-cultural training sometimes includes components on Aboriginal culture and history but it is hard to believe that even a week of study could really allow someone to immerse himself or herself in an Indigenous world view. (Many cross-cultural training sessions to teach Aboriginal history and culture are a day or less.) This is inadequate to provide a thorough understanding of the weight of Aboriginal experience and perspective. These methods of trying to compensate for bias do not address the fundamental cultural conflicts in the mediation model and fail to alter the inherent bias in alternative dispute resolution.

Fundamental conflicts occur in the mediation model in the following ways:

- *The use of a neutral third party*: the mediation model relies on a neutral, impartial third party to facilitate. This poses a special problem for use in Indigenous communities in that it is counter to the philosophy of who has the right to speak within the community. Getting over the hurdle of having a stranger, an outsider, have the power to facilitate the dispute resolution is not something addressed within the mediation model.
- *The training of mediators*: the use of trained mediators gives rise to another inherent cultural conflict. It places the emphasis on formal training rather than life experience. This is a conflict with the value of life experience in Indigenous communities. It also inadequately 'trains' the mediator to have an understanding of Indigenous cultural and historical perspectives.
- *The power imbalance between the parties*: the mediation model does not level the economic or legal playing field.
- *Focus on the individual*: the mediation model is concerned with settling disputes between parties but deals primarily with disputes between individuals. When the dispute involves a community, the community usually resolves the dispute through representatives rather providing for a broad range of input.
- *Cultural bias*: the mediation process is not derived from Aboriginal and Torres Strait Islander methods of dispute resolution. Any cultural compatibility is purely coincidence. In fact, the logic of using mediation models in Indigenous communities derives from the belief by proponents of the mediation process that because they work well in other contexts they may work well in Aboriginal and Torres Strait Islander communities.

Mediation is really just an extension of the legal system and all its problems. This perspective is absent from proponents of mediation who are not conscious of or interested in challenging the fundamental aspects of that system. Their focus is usually on diverting Indigenous people from the litigation process. They are only interested in alleviating the impact of litigation. While that is a worthwhile pursuit that can have benefits for the Indigenous people who would otherwise be facing a court case, it has its limitations.

Although the training of Indigenous people as mediators is a better option and overcomes the problems of trying to give a different cultural perspective and experience to someone else, it is still flawed. It fails to get over some of the following fundamental conflicts in the model itself.

There are two points to note on the use of Indigenous mediators:

- They will not necessarily counter a cultural bias. An Indigenous person will be able to have a much better understanding of the Indigenous experience such as the way that the Aborigines Protection Board has permeated the lives of our people, and know what kind of racism is experienced by Indigenous people. But this may not be enough. Indigenous communities are not culturally homogeneous. These cultural differences may not all be countered if the person is not from the community in which the mediation is taking place.
- They may not solve the problem of a 'neutral' third party acting as facilitator unless the person is associated or in some way connected with the group, when the inappropriateness and distrust that may be generated by having a stranger come in to resolve a dispute may be alleviated.

The problem that many of those who embraced mediation as a better option to litigation – and I do not dispute the fact that it was a better option than going to court – was that it was implemented in a way that sought to take the model used in one environment and place it into another one with an attempt at 'cultural sensitivity training'. This of course did nothing to change the inherent imbalances within the system. This point was not picked up by those staunch advocates of mediation because they seemed to forget that mediation may have been an alternative dispute resolution process but it was not an alternative to the dominant legal system; it was only an extension of it.

A better way is a ground-up approach, one that starts with the community developing the process, not the process being adapted to the community. This ground-up approach has the added advantage of enabling Indigenous people to take control of dispute resolution in their own community; to, in a sense, exert self-determination.

The benefits for this will not only be a reinvigoration of those communities with the empowerment that comes over making decisions within and as a community, but it will also help to regenerate roles within the community – roles of family, roles for elders, roles for youth. Restorative conferencing should have a strong role to play if it can facilitate reconnection within the Indigenous community.

This is especially so in the role restorative justice models can play in relation to family violence. As Loretta Kelly argues (this volume), restorative justice principles are essential to the functionality and harmony of the community. Restorative conferencing programs need to understand that most Indigenous communities are engaged in a healing process and need to come to terms with the very personal cost of the colonization process. These legacies of colonialism – cyclical breakdown of families, substance abuse, unemployment and poverty – are often cited as the root causes of family fracturing and conflict. Such programs must not proceed with the same uncritical application that advocates of mediation have employed. The unquestioned placement of mediation models into situations where cultural conflict arises has shown that there can be more interest in the method and models than with the results.

Some restorative conferencing schemes have been subject to some criticism, including the extent of police involvement and the severity of penalties imposed. The HREOC Report also noted that despite 'chronic over-representation' in the juvenile justice system, Indigenous people are 'not being diverted from the system at the same rate as non-Indigenous children' (HREOC, 1999: 103). This may be due partly to the effect of prior records or the manner of the exercise of discretionary powers in some cases.

The Report identified the same problems of 'fitting' restorative conference models into Indigenous communities that have been identified as problematic in the employment of mediation models:

... some Australian models have been criticised because they lack commitment to negotiation with Indigenous communities and fail to recognise the principle of self-determination. Some have involved a 'one size fits all' approach, imposing a rigid model without due regard to the needs and circumstances of particular communities. In addition, there is potential for conferencing to increase the already high level of blaming and stigmatisation directed to young Indigenous people who come into conflict with the law. (HREOC, 1999: 104)

As well as recommending that Indigenous communities are able to develop and run their own conferencing models, the HREOC Report also emphasized:

- the desirability of diversionary schemes being administered by someone independent of law enforcement bodies, such as a judicial officer, youth worker or community-based lawyer;
- the need to monitor penalties agreed to in conferences to ensure that they are not significantly more punitive than those a court would impose as appropriate to the offence;
- the need to ensure that young people do not get a criminal record as a result of participating in conferencing;
- the need to monitor conferencing proceedings to ensure that they do not operate in a manner oppressive or intimidating to the young person; and
- the need to monitor the overall effect of conferencing schemes to ensure they do not draw greater numbers of young people into the criminal justice system.

Empowerment through alternative dispute resolution and sentencing processes is a small step forward in asserting the Indigenous self-determination that colonization has sought to curtail. However, even with this role, mediation or conferencing can only alleviate the ills, not solve them completely.

Conclusions: Empowerment through Dispute Resolution

If the high levels of family violence in Indigenous communities are a legacy of colonization, solutions to these extraordinary levels of conflict must match diversionary and specific solutions such as conferencing and alternative dispute resolution models with attempts to alter larger, institutional and contextual factors.

Indigenous people in Australia have not been given space within which to exert their own jurisdiction because there is no recognition of sovereignty. Control over decision-making is only acknowledged in circumstances in which ultimate control is still exercised by the dominant culture and its institutions and this takes place when all parties involved are Indigenous. Indigenous law and customs need to be recognized in subversive pockets of dispute resolution and decision-making *within* Indigenous communities but only when *all parties* involved are Indigenous.

This situation will only change if Indigenous sovereignty is recognized to an extent that allows Indigenous people jurisdiction and decision-making powers through the inherent right to self-government. To facilitate this, space needs to be made available for Indigenous communities and families to develop and exercise control over their own decision-making and civil and criminal processes.

Until real alternatives to the dominant legal system are provided for Aboriginal disputants, Australia's Indigenous communities are going to continue to be disadvantaged by institutional racism and biases within the legal system whatever band-aid, diversionary schemes are adopted. Empowerment through community-based dispute resolution processes is a small step forward in asserting the Aboriginal self-determination that colonization has sought to curtail. These principles of self-determination and empowerment need to guide any restorative justice strategy that seeks to navigate and negate the dynamics and forces that encourage family violence to flourish.

10   Restorative Justice and Aboriginal Family Violence: Opening a Space for Healing

Harry Blagg

Introduction

This chapter is based on a number of research and policy development projects undertaken principally in Western Australia on aspects of Indigenous family violence prevention, intervention and treatment (Blagg, 1998b, 2000a, 2000b; Indermaur, Atkinson and Blagg, 1997; Crime Research Centre/Donovan Research, 2000).[1] They were conducted against a background of increasing awareness that rates of interpersonal violence in Australian Aboriginal communities were significantly higher than in non-Aboriginal communities (Ferrante at al, 1996). While the quality of intervention and support for non-Aboriginal victims of domestic violence has generally improved over recent years, derogatory and racist stereotypes of Aboriginal women still continue to normalize abusive behaviour toward them (Blagg, 2000a). Aboriginal women victims of violence did not always receive equitable and timely support from front line agencies and courts, and that there is a dearth of appropriately structured and funded community-based prevention, intervention and treatment programs capable of mobilizing and engaging Aboriginal communities in the struggle against violence.

Indigenous people maintain that improving the situation for Indigenous victims requires an holistic process of community healing: a zero tolerance approach, based on the increased criminalization of Indigenous men, may simply intensify the cycle of violence in Indigenous communities. Restorative justice practices need to be developed that support community healing and genuinely empower Indigenous women. The content of restorative justice practices, as defined by non-Indigenous 'restorative justice movements', may not suit the needs of Indigenous people. Heavily scripted, single issue conferences, for example, convened and controlled by non-Indigenous parties, are unlikely to promote healing outcomes.

Living In Crisis: Family Violence in Indigenous Communities

Family violence is a major issue for Indigenous people; whereas property crime tends to be the obsession of white society, it is family-related crime that deeply concerns Aboriginal people (Homel et al, 1999). Since the mid-1980s, and particularly in the period following the Royal Commission into Aboriginal Deaths in Custody (1991), awareness of the scale of the problem has gradually increased (Atkinson, 1990; 1991; 1993; 1995a; Bolger, 1991; The Aboriginal and Torres Strait Islander Women's Task Force on Violence Report, 2000). Analysis of trends in Aboriginal offending, for example, identified dramatically escalating rates of sexual and physical violence by Aboriginal men during the 1980s (Broadhurst, 1987). An Australian Bureau of Statistics survey found family violence to be a significant issue for Aboriginal youth (Australian Bureau of Statistics, 1996).[2] Recent research suggests that Aboriginal youth are the most vulnerable group in Australian society to becoming the direct or indirect witnesses of violence and users of violence themselves – as well as having attitudes highly accepting of violence (Crime Research Centre/Donovan Research, 2000).

Some commentators have reported a 'break down in Aboriginal social order' (Atkinson, 1991: 4). While national attention was focussed on Indigenous deaths in custody, it was gradually becoming clear that many more Indigenous women were being killed by their partners than were dying in prisons (Australian Law Reform Commission, 1994: 20).

The scale of the problem in Western Australia

Aboriginal women in Western Australia are vastly over-represented in police statistics on violence. They were found to be 45 times more likely to be a victim of a serious 'domestic' assault than non-Aboriginal women, accounting for just under half of all victims (Ferrante et al, 1996: 34). Violence in Indigenous communities (including homicide and serious assaults) tends to be directed more toward intimates than strangers. While violence toward spouses represented 35.5 percent and 39.5 percent of homicides and serious assaults in Aboriginal communities in Western Australia, it represented only 19.8 percent and 7.5 percent respectively in non-Aboriginal communities. Moreover, the rate of violence directed toward 'family' in general was also higher – 22.6 percent of homicides and 17.2 percent of serious assaults, as opposed to 14.8 percent and 4.4 percent respectively in non-Aboriginal communities.

The scope of potential family violence victims is wide. Evidence from consultations with Aboriginal people in the Kimberley region of Western Australia (Blagg, 1998b) suggests that the victims (both direct and indirect) of family violence can include aunts, uncles, cousins and children of previous relationships. Similar dynamics are in evidence in the Northern Territory (Office of Women's Policy, 1996) and Queensland (Aboriginal and Torres Strait Islander Women's Task Force on Violence, 2000).

Domestic violence or family violence?

So, Aboriginal women are probably the most repeatedly and multiply victimized section of Australian society, and the main perpetrators of violence against Aboriginal women tend to be their own male kin. In many instances violence is excused or condoned by non-Aboriginal agencies, and many Aboriginal males, as a 'cultural' phenomenon, a notion hotly disputed by Indigenous women (Bolger, 1991; Aboriginal and Torres Strait Islander Women's Task Force on Violence, 2000). Yet, many Aboriginal women resist the annexure of this life experience to the discursive terrain of 'domestic violence' – where the behaviour could be rendered explicable as a manifestation of patriarchal power. Aboriginal women tend to talk, instead, about 'family violence'– a term adopted by Indigenous people to designate a constellation of harmful, exploitative, violent and aggressive practices that form in and around intimate relationships – not all of which could be designated 'domestic' in the strict sense of the term. The family violence paradigm represents a considerable shift – in both theory and practice – from the domestic violence paradigm, with its monadic emphasis on patriarchal power and narrow focus on criminalization as the main response. While not ignoring the need for men to take responsibility for their behaviour, the family violence paradigm stresses collective Indigenous experience of powerlessness and, at the level of practice, leans toward finding pathways to family healing, rather than new routes into the criminal justice system.

   Aboriginal people tell stories of family violence that encompass a wide diversity of personal and communal conflict. Aboriginal women in the remote West Kimberley region of Western Australia, for example, told researchers that family violence is:

family fighting. It happens when someone uses violence or threats to have power and control over someone close to them. This can be a partner or involve other family members. It includes family feuding. (Clarke & Varos, 1995: 2)

This definition concurs with that of Mow (1992), who included abusive behaviours such as 'beatings of a wife or other family members, homicide, suicide, and other self injury, rape, child abuse and child sexual abuse' (Mow, 1992). A group of Aboriginal women in Western Australia's Kimberley region add to the list 'jealousy ... emotional blackmail, racial or cultural abuse ... problems caused by too much alcohol, drugs or gambling' (Kimberley Domestic Violence Resource Directory, 1997). Northern Territory consultations found that family violence 'reverberates through the entire family' and is perpetrated by a range of family members against other family members, particularly women and children (Office of Women's Policy, 1996).

Aboriginal narratives on family violence: colonialism, deracination and trauma

Aboriginal narratives on violence are constructed within a 'context of difference' (Jackson, 1999) that situate the behaviour within the founding violence of colonialism. Atkinson (1991) describes a process of 'inter-generational trauma', tracing distinctive 'trauma lines' from first contact through to contemporary experiences of marginalization and dispossession. Blagg (1998b; 2000a) summarizes these narratives of loss as including, loss of land and traditional culture, the breakdown of community, 'skin'[3] and kinship systems and Aboriginal law, entrenched poverty, racism, alcohol and drug abuse, and the effects of institutionalization and removal policies on the 'stolen generations'. Canadian accounts also link family violence to the 'detrimental effects' of colonial policies (McTimoney, 1993: 2) and Canadian Aboriginal communities see violence against women 'as part of a history of violence against Aboriginal people' (Myers, 1996). A key narrative of loss focusses on the 'redundancy' of the Aboriginal male role and status that is often compensated for by an aggressive assertion of male rights over women and children (Blagg, 1998b; 2000a; Aboriginal and Torres Strait Islander Women's Task Force on Violence, 2000) as Indigenous men desperately seek to create a masculine identity.

Simply assimilating the family violence phenomenon into the domestic violence paradigm risks perpetuating traditional assimilation practices by eurocentrizing Aboriginal family structure, and risks essentializing the phenomenon as simply a variation on Western power dynamics. It also risks increasing already unacceptable levels of Aboriginal over-representation in the criminal justice system, including the victims of violence. Snider argues that the 'compulsory criminalization' of Aboriginal men had done little to increase the safety of

Aboriginal women and had only 'accelerated cultural genocide' in Canada (Snider, 1998; see also MacLeod, 1995). American studies reveal racial difference to be a factor in terms of willingness and capacity to access mainstream services for abused women (see Sorenson, 1996; Asbury, 1993; Peterson-Lewis et al, 1988; Joseph, 1997).

Aboriginal women are also suspicious of involvement with justice and welfare agencies. They see prisons and police lock-ups as part of the violence cycle, de-socializing brutalizing, de-skilling and sometimes killing their men and damaging community structures (Blagg, 2000a). 'Breaking the cycle' of violence in Aboriginal communities must include breaking the cycle of enmeshment in the criminal justice system.

Fighting women or helpless victims? Aboriginal women and violence

Culturally hegemonic definitions of a 'domestic' incident may actively work against the interests of Aboriginal women. They have tended to work by constructing a stereotype of a passive, helpless victim requiring rescuing by police. When police attend a disturbance in an Aboriginal setting the line between victim and offender may appear blurred. A distinguishing feature of Aboriginal family violence is the extent to which it crosses over the boundaries between the 'public' and the 'private/domestic' spheres.[4] Violence may take place on the street or on drinking grounds and spill over to include a range of people. Because of its public nature, and association with alcohol, and the diversity of parties mobilized by the event (immediate family and extended kin, neighbours, community members) the image presented may appear more like a brawl than an assault on a spouse or partner. Women victims of violence may, when they do not correspond to the stereotype, be charged themselves with public order and violence-related offences (Blagg, 2000a). Despite high rates of abuse, Aboriginal women are reluctant to access mainstream services and report incidents to police. It needs to be borne in mind that the criminal justice system – and especially the police, its gatekeepers – are not viewed by Aboriginal people, including women, as a 'service'. Aboriginal women tend to experience contact with the criminal justice system in extremely negative terms, influencing their willingness to use it when victims. Aboriginal women in Western Australia are almost 14 times more likely to be arrested by the police than non-Aboriginal women (Aboriginal Justice Council, 1999).

Racist stereotypes of Indigenous women continue to inform the response of justice agencies such as the police. Cunneen and Macdonald (1996) recount an incident in the Northern Territory where an Aboriginal rape victim was locked up with her assailants and – according to the Northern Territory Ombudsman's report on the incident – 'treated no differently from that of a normal suspect ... placed in a cell and ... [not] accorded the status of victim' when the police found an outstanding bench warrant in her name.[5] The inability of existing policing and justice systems to protect women on remote communities, 'the racist attitudes of police', and the inability of all aspects of the criminal justice system to deal with family violence in 'a culturally sensitive manner' has been identified as a serious problem by Aboriginal women in Western Australia (Aboriginal Women's Task Force and the Aboriginal Justice Council, 1995: 3) Recent consultations in the Kimberley (Blagg, 1999) found evidence of police down-playing the seriousness of violence against Aboriginal women on the grounds that it was 'part of their culture' and they were 'used to it'.

One worker in the Kimberley said:

They [the police] have learned that they can't get away with it any longer with white women but they can still treat Aboriginal women as less than human.

In an incident at Roebourne, in the Pilbara region, local Aboriginal women's groups were incensed when the local police demanded that a proposed new women's shelter should not be built near the police station on the grounds that they feared 'being used as security service' for Aboriginal women. This was a statement of breathtaking insensitivity, given that the town was in shock following the murder of a young Aboriginal woman on the street by her husband – no one had intervened to help her.

It is not surprising to find that physical resistance to violence may be the only avenue open to Aboriginal women given the 'pressures ... against the involvement of the police' (Cunneen & Kerley, 1995: 82–83). Resistance of this kind may also account, in part, for the alarmingly higher rates of injury sustained by Aboriginal women in Western Australia in abuse cases. They were more likely to suffer serious injury than non-Aboriginal women – in 23.5 percent as opposed to 11.4 percent of reported cases (Ferrante et al 1996: 35), supporting the assertions of other commentators that Aboriginal women are often imprisoned because of their resistance to abuse where this leads to the death of or injury to the abuser (Atkinson, 1990; LaPrairie, 1989; Langton, 1992).[6] Black women in the USA are also 'more likely than white women to fight back' (Joseph, 1997: 167), attracting a greater risk of severe injury – whereas White women are more likely to seek assistance from social services (Joseph, 1997: 167). Aboriginal women are unlikely to fit the gender stereotype of the docile, passive 'battered woman', and are, therefore, less likely to be treated leniently when resisting abuse.[7]

Also, recourse to non-Aboriginal agencies, particularly the police, may be seen as 'betrayal' by family members (Western Australian Task Force on Domestic Violence, 1986) leading to blame and 'retaliation' (Dodson, 1991: 381). Northern Territory consultations found that 'cultural obligations' and 'strong ideas of right and wrong in maintaining the family unit' ensure that women will often tolerate abuse (Office of Women's Policy, 1996). Aboriginal women are caught between a range of pressures to remain silent on family violence issues in the interests of community and family.[8] Similar patterns have been identified in Canada, where First Nation women do not want relatives to be jailed, and are pressured by relatives to 'forgive and forget' (Bopp & Bopp, 1997: 72).

When they do access the domestic violence facilities such as refuges, Aboriginal women tend to use them as places of immediate safety and respite rather than as exit points from relationships (Blagg, 2000a).[9] For Indigenous women from remote areas of Australia, who practise traditional law, dietary and avoidance laws may also influence access to refuges and shelters, when they infringe Aboriginal codes of behaviour and protocols (Hazel & Rodriguez, 1997). The police, when they are contacted, may be called in as a 'crisis intervention tool, to stop the abuse at a critical stage' but women may not necessarily want to press charges (Aboriginal and Torres Strait Islander Women's Task Force, 2000: 232).

Official inquiries in Western Australia have been alive for some time to the problems Indigenous women face when accessing the system. A review of restraining orders legislation argued that 'strategies currently adopted to protect victims from family violence have been based on the needs of people of European descent living in urban areas' (Ministry of Justice, 1995: 3). Similar findings informed an inquiry on gender bias in the criminal justice system, which recommended improved cultural awareness training for workers and better advocacy and legal support for Indigenous women. There is also a stress on counseling, family healing and programs and 'healing houses' as an alternative to the mainstream system (Malcolm, 1994).

Empowering Aboriginal women

Aboriginal women are at extreme disadvantage when dealing with the non-Indigenous criminal justice system. When given space to speak on the shortcomings of the system their message has been clear and consistent. A gathering of women in May 1995 (Aboriginal Women's Task Force and the Aboriginal Justice Council, 1995), for example, identified a host of shortcomings in the official response to family violence (referring to the phenomenon of 'domestic violence' as being one of them). The women's gathering argued that immediate attention needed to be paid to resourcing community education initiatives on family violence so that communities could devise local strategies and develop their own skill base (Aboriginal Women's Task Force and the Aboriginal Justice Council, 1995: 2). Government agencies, they argued, tended to see service delivery in 'programmatic' terms – wherein a problem was resolved by 'expanding the skills, expertise and resources of government agencies themselves to deliver a discrete service'. Instead, they argued, 'community infrastructure such as Aboriginal women's groups' should be nurtured and encouraged to work on the problem (Aboriginal Women's Task Force and the Aboriginal Justice Council, 1995: 2).

Before moving on to look at strategies, we may summarize the main elements of the family violence paradigm as encapsulating a preference for forms of intervention that stop abuse, cool out situations, and open pathways to healing, with minimum intervention by the criminal justice system. There is a clear preference by Aboriginal women, who are the main victims of violence, for strategies that change behaviour while maintaining family relations. Intervention strategies need to respect – rather than problematize – Aboriginal women's cultural and family obligations, even where these do not accord with the current orthodoxy on domestic violence intervention. Often, consultations with Indigenous women in Western Australia found the 'Aboriginality' of Aboriginal women was identified as an obstacle by non-Indigenous agencies (Blagg, 2000a). It needs to be borne in mind that, for many Indigenous women, choosing to leave 'family' – with all its complexly embedded ties of responsibility and obligation, connection with country and culture – is not an option. The capacity to exit family relationships (indeed, the very concept of 'choice' in such matters) – to repackage and reconstitute one's identity as an autonomous individual in some new location – is a profoundly eurocentric construction.

Once the considerable limitations placed on Indigenous women's capacity to abrogate responsibilities to family are accepted as the starting point – rather than the problem – in victim support, it follows that community-based strategies of diversion into restorative programs are most likely to satisfy the demands of Indigenous women and their communities.

Restorative visions and healing strategies

Healing, in the Indigenous sense of the term, is difficult to define and can appear to lack specificity. It has tended to be employed by

Indigenous people to describe a dynamic and unfolding process of individual and collective problem solving. It has a practical dimension, in relation to changing community structures and ameliorating social conditions, and a therapeutic dimension, in relation to changing the embedded negative value systems which have accompanied cultural marginalization and dispossession (for a Canadian discussion see Solicitor General of Canada, 1994).

I have argued elsewhere (Blagg, 1997; 1998a) that to be relevant to Indigenous struggles for justice, restorative justice movements need to extend their gaze beyond the single issue 'conference' as the *raison d'être* for intervention, and develop a 'restorative vision'. The restorative vision would inevitably necessitate moving, to borrow an apposite word from John Braithwaite, beyond the 'obsession' with petty juvenile crimes (Braithwaite, 1999a), and into areas of urgent concern to Indigenous people themselves. I have also been critical of the tendency of the restorative justice movements to 'claim lineage with the dispute resolution practices of Indigenous peoples' while remaining 'on the margins of debates about the contemporary social, economic and political aspirations of living Indigenous peoples' (Blagg, 2001). Supporting Indigenous initiatives on family violence in ways which promote Indigenous self-determination and community healing would be a restorative practice. The principle of self-determination needs to be placed at the centre of restorative initiatives because, as Cunneen maintains, the 'cultural and physical survival of Aboriginal people is dependent on self-determination' (Cunneen, 1999: 124).

Wherever possible models of intervention should work through existing community structures and be focussed on family violence as a community service rather than simply a criminal justice problem. It should be acknowledged that many Indigenous people are already working to end family violence in their communities. Restorative justice practices around family violence should 'add value' to these initiatives, providing a diversity of healing, peacemaking opportunities – and resist the temptation to capture the issue or impose non-Indigenous structures and solutions (Blagg, 1998b; Indermaur, Atkinson and Blagg, 1997). These need to be offered, wherever possible, as genuine alternatives to the non-Indigenous system, or, where this is not entirely possible (where there is no alternative to incarceration, for example), spaces need to be opened up within the non-Indigenous system for family-based healing. In other instances a degree of 'creative hybridity' may make possible restorative practices 'in between' the Indigenous and non-Indigenous domains. Actively constructing these 'in-between' or 'liminal spaces' (Blagg, 1998a) requires genuine dialogue and the equalization of power relationships between Indigenous and non-Indigenous people. Many forms of, so-called, 'consultation' aim simply to appropriate aspects of Indigenous governance when it suits the agendas of non-Indigenous agencies (O'Malley, 1996).

Interventions will only become meaningful when they actively reduce the reliance on non-Indigenous systems. Therefore – and this aspect of family violence intervention clearly goes against current domestic violence orthodoxy – intervention should aim to divert, wherever possible, men involved in family violence away from unnecessary contact with the formal, non-Indigenous justice system and into community-based Indigenous systems of control. Depending on the seriousness of the offence, and the willingness of the victim(s), diversion should be an option at a number of points in the system (front end, pre-court, court).

Morley and Mullender (1994) describe women's refuges as the 'success story' of domestic violence intervention. Given that the refuge system and its associated structures may be less appropriate in the area of Indigenous family violence, where can we look to for appropriate sites of safety within the Aboriginal domain? Which kinds of initiative should be 'value added'? Also, if the current zero tolerance-plus-criminalization approach raises serious problems – in terms of systemic racism, poor Aboriginal/police relations and an already serious problem of Indigenous over-representation (including both men and women) – how is it possible to police family violence incidents, stop the abuse and improve the quality of support? How can positive forms of diversion from the system enhance Indigenous self-determination and open up the space for healing?

I want to suggest that there are elements of appropriate community-based infrastructure in existence, albeit in an embryonic and fragmented form, in most Australian states. They include Aboriginal Night Patrols and Street Patrols in some country and urban areas, many linked to sobering-up shelters, Community Wardens schemes and women's grog patrols on remote communities, new Indigenous 'healing centres' and Aboriginal women's advocacy schemes. Properly resourced and supported these structures may provide the basis for new diversionary initiatives and become the 'success story' of Aboriginal family violence intervention. I will provide some illustrations of this potential new system and how it may open up space for restorative, healing practices.

Self-determining strategies around Australia: a brief review

Aboriginal women have become increasingly involved in policing their own communities through night patrols and community warden schemes: schemes in the Northern Territory have claimed dramatic reductions in family violence in Indigenous communities (Langton, 1992). The patrols have provided a local means of policing the anti-alcohol bylaws and ensured women's and children's safety (Mosey, 1994). Reviews of patrols in Western Australia by the Crime Research Centre (1995; Aboriginal Justice Council, 1999) have shown that patrols do become involved as an alternative to, or in cooperation with, police in family violence situations – both in public and domestic contexts. Sobering-up shelters are also used for 'cooling off' aggressive drunken men. The Salaam Shelter in Halls Creek, for example, has been identified as having had the 'spin off of protecting ... families from violent situations' (Togni, 1997: 75). In the Western Australian town of Geraldton, the Yamtji Street Patrol has developed an Aboriginal Women's Advocacy Scheme to supplement its family violence intervention. The advocates step in to assist Aboriginal women once the offender has been arrested by the police or taken to an appropriate place to cool off – 'cooling off' or 'time out' centres of various kinds are also in operation in metropolitan Perth.

I mentioned above that Indigenous women do not always feel comfortable using women's refuges and tend, when they have recourse to them, to use them as respite services rather than as ways out of relationships. Aboriginal women in the Derby area (West Kimberley), for example, rejected plans to build a women's refuge in their town and instead designed their own 'Family Healing Centre', based on Indigenous principles and culture (Blagg, 1998b). The Healing Centre now being built has four living areas surrounding an open communal space – women and small children escaping violence are to be accommodated in one section, with distinct sections for men, old people and the young men who have yet to go through 'law business' (there is a blend of victim safety and cultural requirements being met in this arrangement). It is hoped that once the immediate crisis has passed, the families can be brought together in the communal space, or 'camp fire', to resolve problems. It is also hoped that the work around the camp fire will be undertaken by Elders collaborating with appropriately skilled professionals (alcohol and drug counselors, family support workers, etc.). This model of a family healing centre fits well with principles of restorative justice and reveals that Indigenous people are capable of developing imaginative solutions from within their own cultural spheres.

In both remote Western Australia and the Northern Territory women have been retrieving and strengthening elements of traditional law to protect victims of violence. Women on small isolated communities find it difficult to escape violent men. One answer has been to construct shelters on women's 'law grounds' (barred to men) and placing sacred objects in shelters as a deterrent to violent men. These solutions directly empower Indigenous women both at the point of crisis and within their communities by reinstating the power of traditional women's 'business' as a living and dynamic factor in Aboriginal community life. The Northern Territory has also been brokering local partnering agreements between discrete communities or localities and a range of relevant government agencies. Local discussions led to the development of a plan or agreement committing the agencies and community councils to providing a number of services. One such scheme, The Ali-Curung Law and Order Plan, has claimed a 53 percent reduction in family violence incidents.

The Northern Territory Aboriginal Family Violence Strategy (Office of Women's Policy, 1996) also provides some valuable ideas, particularly in relation to intervention in remote areas. It stresses that the solutions to family violence need to emerge from communities in strategic partnership with government agencies. The Family Violence Strategy is intended to reduce family violence by assisting communities in designing and developing programs, ensuring context sensitive and culturally appropriate responses from service providers, and developing programs for men. The strategy acknowledges the importance of initiatives instigated by women on communities, such as the reinforcement of Grandmother law (where widows and senior women offer protection to victims and also become involved in dispute resolution) and the development of women's Night Patrols and community safe houses.

Community Justice Groups in Aboriginal communities in Queensland, such as Palm Island, Mt. Isa and Woorabinda, have developed local Family Violence projects. As in the Northern Territory, there is significant emphasis on reaffirming Indigenous customs and values and emphasizing the authority of Elders, including women Elders. Women tend to be well-represented on local Community Justice Groups and therefore family violence is seen as a high priority (Office of Aboriginal and Torres Strait Islander Affairs, 1998) Some groups, such as Kowanyama, deal with minor instances through mediation – most will contact the police in repeated or serious cases (Chantrill, 1997). The Community Justice Groups have an educative function within communities and attempt to create an harmonious environment. Family healing strategies have been in place in some Canadian communities for some time. In many emphasis is placed on the need to give adequate training to community caregivers. Also it is acknowledged that community leaders have to take a public stand on family violence – including adopting a 'formal declaration' on the issue which guides community businesses (McTimoney, 1993: 31). Martens stresses the need to situate family violence intervention within an holistic framework, which he calls a 'Community Wellness Program'.

Crisis intervention and restorative justice

Community development approaches are not quick-fix solutions: they require long-term commitment. Yet, many of our crisis intervention tool kits, developed in non-Indigenous situations, have been manufactured on the premise that a 'crisis' is a distinct event to be set against a background of relative stability and normality. Once the reasons for the crisis have been removed and temporary support provided then normality can be resumed. This belief system also underpins orthodox restorative justice practices, where a one-off reintegration ceremony 'resolves' the crisis created by acts of delinquency, and then everyone gets on with their lives (Blagg, 1997). The underlying assumption, here, is that those at the centre of the crisis have the capacity to change their social situation to the extent that such crisis will not recur. Aboriginal women and Aboriginal youths caught up in the criminal justice system, living in crisis families, subject to violence from within their communities and from within the criminal justice system, may have only limited capacity to change the social situations underpinning the crisis. The notion of a 'crisis' itself, therefore, may have to be rethought to accommodate the impact of a crisis event on people who may already to be gripped by multiple or 'compound' forms of crisis – relating to health, housing, employment, structural racism, poverty, bereavement and alcohol abuse. Restorative processes need to accommodate multiple forms of crisis. This means change may well be incremental and gradual – there will be few 'magic bullet' solutions.

Restorative justice practices will also need to consider the meanings attached to time from an Indigenous perspective, and be open to longer time frames for convening meetings, be willing to accommodate a potential plurality of different ceremonies, involving a range of significant others, which may not come to some neat and tangible resolution. To achieve this, restorative justice may need to free itself from the grip of the criminal justice process, and become actively aligned with community-building, rather than just problem-fixing, strategies. In many respects the potential for restorative justice exists most strongly in the context of community-based prevention initiatives.

Concluding Comments: From Narratives of Loss to Stories of Healing

Restorative justice in the context of Indigenous family violence should entail replacing the 'loss narratives' with stories of recovery and healing. Restorative justice will also need to come to terms with Aboriginal people's increasing demands for the acceptance of Aboriginal law as a solution to many of the problems existing in Aboriginal communities. The non-Indigenous system is viewed as 'fatally flawed, ineffective and unable to meet the challenges currently being presented' by many Indigenous people (Aboriginal and Torres Strait Islander Women's Task Force on Violence, 2000: xvii). Aboriginal law, as lived and practised by Indigenous people, may not necessarily correspond to those highly derivative and sanitized representations of traditional dispute resolution practices found in many restorative justice texts.

Notes

1   They were: 'Intervention at the Point of Crisis in Indigenous Family Violence', funded by the Domestic Violence Unit (Perth WA); 'Working with Adolescents to Prevent Domestic Violence', Parts 1 and 2, funded by National Crime Prevention; 'A National Study of Young People's Attitudes to Domestic Violence', Crime Research Centre/Donovan Research, funded by National Crime Prevention and DEETYA. Thanks are owing to Donella Raye, Rose Murray, Elveena Macarthy, Dean Collard, David Indermaur, Lyn Atkinson, Richard Harding, Keith Carter, Neil Morgan. Particular thanks are owing to the Aboriginal communities, organizations and individuals in Western Australia, who gave their time and presented their views in these various projects. This piece is dedicated to Glynis Sibosado (1949; 2001), Inaugural Chairperson of the Aboriginal Justice Council of Western Australia, strong Nyikana woman, champion of her people.

2   The survey found that approximately 45 percent of Indigenous young people they surveyed perceived family violence to be a common problem in their local area – the proportion was greater in non-urban areas. The survey also found that satisfaction with police intervention was lower for family violence incidents than for other categories of violence and crime (ABS, 1996: 59), generally because of the slowness of response and lack of understanding of Aboriginal culture

3   One effect of the forced 'Westernization' of family and marriage relationships in Aboriginal communities was the introduction of 'adolescence'. Whereas girls would previously have been married off according to 'skin' rules at the onset of fertility, they now faced a period of 'maidenhood'. Burbank (1988) saw this hiatus as one cause of new problems such as jealousy and family violence.

4   Of course this dichotomy itself is eurocentric and historical, based on Western construct of a gendered and economic division of labour, rather than a universal phenomenon.

5   Similar examples of police incapacity to see Indigenous women as victims abound in Canada. One incident included a women being handcuffed in a police van with her assailant on the way to court where she was to give evidence against him (McMullen & Jayerwardene, 1995).

6   Consultations also found strong anecdotal evidence from within the criminal justice system – including Aboriginal Legal Services, Legal Aid, magistrates and judges – that Aboriginal women charged with assaults, public order offences and murder were often resisting or trying to put a stop to family violence. As one ALS lawyer said, 'she may be the one who gets charged if she was the one struck the last blow, no matter what the provocation'.

7   In the case of *Osland v. The Queen*, Justice Kirby argues that 'as a construct' Battered Wife Syndrome may, 'misrepresent many women's experiences of violence. It is based largely on the experiences of Caucasian women of a particular social background' (pp. 213–14). Kirby goes on to cite arguments from Canada and New Zealand critical of the stereotype of passive, docile and helpless women, which excludes the experience of Maori women (whose experiences are shaped by racism) and 'women of colour' who have shown 'too much strength or initiative'.

8   There may also be other factors at work here. Aboriginal women take pride in their capacity to withstand hardship and maintain the family unit in the face of adversity – including violence. This does not mean they approve of violence, or consider it an integral aspect of Aboriginal law, rather that it represents one of the many crisis areas of life (Blagg, 2000a). Burbank (1994) maintains that many Aboriginal women see 'fighting' (though not unprovoked or extreme violence and abuse) as a relatively acceptable way to resolve issues. Indigenous women do not consider violence, sexual assault or incest to be in accordance with tradition or customary law (Bolger, 1991; Lloyd & Rogers, 1992; Smallwood, 1996).

9   Joseph (1998) suggests that Black women in the USA were also extremely reluctant to use women's shelters run by Euro-Americans.

11 Using Restorative Justice Principles to Address Family Violence in Aboriginal Communities

Loretta Kelly

Introduction

Many authors have commented that restorative justice has its roots in ancient culture. Wilkinson (1997), for example, argues that restorative justice dates back thousands of years. This chapter will discuss whether restorative justice has roots in Indigenous Australian culture and whether it is culturally appropriate in the contemporary Indigenous Australian context.

In this chapter I use the term 'family violence' rather than 'domestic violence' because '[d]omestic violence is one aspect of family violence. Using the term "family" in preference to "domestic" provides a greater contextual understanding of the inter-generational impacts of violence as its effects flow in-to and out-of our families' (Atkinson, 1996: 5).

At the outset I must note that I write from the perspective of an Indigenous woman and victims' advocate. I also write as a Goori[1] woman who sees my brothers, uncles and cousins imprisoned for perpetrating violence against my sisters and aunties. Too many Aboriginal men are in custody because of crimes against women. Aboriginal people are over-represented in the criminal justice system and the majority of Aboriginal people dying in custody are men.

According to Pam Greer, an Aboriginal woman, the Royal Commission into Aboriginal Deaths in Custody found that 53 percent of the Aboriginal men who had died in prison cells during the investigation period were there because of acts of violence (Greer, 1994: 65). The Royal Commission acknowledged that violence against women and children by young men in Aboriginal communities is a significant problem (Royal Commission into Aboriginal Deaths in Custody, 1991). At the same time, the figures show that Aboriginal women are more likely to be murdered by someone they know and in their own community than are Aboriginal men likely to die in custody. Pam Greer states that:

While too many Aboriginal men have died in custody, too many Aboriginal women have died in their communities. In two States more Aboriginal women have died from violence in their communities than all of the total national Aboriginal deaths in custody. (Greer, 1994: 65)

Family Violence in Aboriginal Communities is a Widespread Problem

Pam Greer comments that '[r]esearch concerning homicide in Australia provides shocking evidence of the extent of violence within Aboriginal communities, and demonstrates that Aboriginal women are at substantially higher risk of fatal domestic violence than are other women in Australia' (Greer, 1994: 64–65). Heather Strang's research on homicide found that 16 percent of all female victims of homicide in Australia were Aboriginal (yet we only constitute approximately two percent of the population): 21 percent of all homicide victims were killed by their spouse, yet 51 percent of Aboriginal homicide victims were killed by their spouse (Strang, 1992). Jenny Mouzos has also found that Indigenous women are at a far higher risk of homicide than non-Indigenous women and that Indigenous women were more likely to be killed by intimate partners than non-Indigenous women (Mouzos, 1999).

Pam Greer states that '[d]espite more than a decade of consultations, the violence remains commonplace and is escalating. I have yet to visit an Aboriginal community ... in which the violence is not rife – often being repeated in successive generations' (Greer, 1994: 75). This too has been my experience in visiting and working in Aboriginal communities in New South Wales. Greer makes an important point – we cannot assume that all Aboriginal communities have the same problems (Greer, 1994: 66). But my own work within Aboriginal communities leads me to believe that many Indigenous people do see family violence as an everyday phenomenon. This view was echoed in the 1981 report of the New South Wales Task Force on Domestic Violence concerning Aboriginal women which concluded that 'wherever Aboriginal women lived, domestic violence is an aspect of their lives which looms large'. Quotes from Aboriginal women included 'it's part of being black isn't it?' and 'it's so commonplace – there is nothing remarkable about it' (Greer, 1994: 67).

The Colonial Context of Violence in Aboriginal Communities

Family violence in these communities needs to be examined in the colonial context. Judy Atkinson, an Aboriginal researcher and community 'healer' states that:

over the last 208 years of colonisation our family and social relationships have been fractured and almost severed by the newly imposed English common law system called by some of us the white men's law. It is this law we are now being asked to turn to for protection from the violent assaults which are, in part, its product. (Atkinson, 1996: 5)

Without making excuses for male violence, we need to examine the factors that lead to such violence. Atkinson comments that '[s]uch behaviour becomes the norm in families where there have been cumulative intergenerational impacts of trauma on trauma expressing themselves in present generations in violence on self and others' (Atkinson, 1996: 7).

Family violence programs should be designed and implemented in a manner that acknowledges the post-colonial context of violence, but which protects the well-being and safety of women and children. Part of the result of being colonized (and consequently oppressed) is that we are forced to take on the laws and institutions of the oppressors. This law has been imposed on us, as no Aboriginal or Torres Strait Islander nation has ever consented to this law. Non-Indigenous people design and enforce oppressive and discriminatory institutions, which we are then expected to use to protect ourselves. It is therefore easy to understand that both Aboriginal men and women find that current domestic violence laws are not effective in preventing family violence in our communities.

Unique Concerns of Aboriginal Women

As background research for this chapter, I interviewed Aboriginal women advocates working with Aboriginal women victims of family violence. One of the questions I asked was: 'What are the unique concerns of Aboriginal women?' A common concern they expressed was their clients' fear of Aboriginal deaths in custody. One Aboriginal women victims' advocate said 'by far the majority of my clients are fearful of sending their men to gaol – they fear deaths in custody'.

Another concern is that, where Aboriginal women live in a close Aboriginal community on their traditional land, the women do not want to cause conflict within the community by taking action on the violence. An Aboriginal domestic violence educator who runs a support group for Aboriginal victims stated:

My women are in fear because it's a close-knit community. Sometimes they fear repercussions from his family who may live next door. And they don't want to leave their community. It's their land, their home – their community – is their comfort zone and they don't want to be alienated even by just a few community members. But at the same time, she'll have his other relatives who will support her. Especially the women Elders who have been through it themselves. So it's like they're torn between parts of his family who'll blame her and the other who can offer heaps of support.

I would like to talk about an Aboriginal couple, Samantha and Jim, who have experienced family violence. The couple live in an Aboriginal community on the mid-north coast of New South Wales. When I talked to this couple separately in June 2000, I found that the fact of 'close-knit community' was a concern to them, as well as the fear of imprisonment. In brief, Samantha and Jim have been living together for ten years and have three young children. Jim admits to a problem with his anger. He was released from prison in early 2000 after serving a two-month sentence for an assault against a non-Aboriginal man. Jim had been imprisoned twice before, for assaulting Samantha and for breaching an Apprehended Violence Order (AVO). In October 2000 Jim was once again imprisoned for assaulting Samantha. However, when I spoke to Jim he said: 'There hasn't been any domestics lately.' Samantha recalled the last incident as being 'just before he went to gaol, a couple of months ago. He didn't hit me that time, but he did threaten to kill me. It was all over jealousy. He said he'd kill me if I left him, but he also threatened to kill himself if I left him.' When asked 'What triggers the violence?' Jim responded: 'It's just the mood I'm in – I get wild and go into horrors. Mostly I'm drinking and on drugs. Sometimes I'm sober, but I'm just really stressed out. Anything can trigger it.'

Samantha recalled the last physical assault on her by Jim:

[i]t was two years ago. I'd say something and he'd go wild. It's when we're both drinking that we get into bad arguments. And we'll have a punch up – I'd hit him back but he'd knock me down. I'd get up and run next door and ring the police. Sometimes I think the police help – but it really depends on who you get. Some of them are really out to get him – all they wanna do is lock him up. But I just want him moved away – not locked up.

Samantha was concerned about her partner being imprisoned: 'It's not just Aboriginal deaths in custody – it's that I know what the screws [correctional service officers] are like – they hate him – and they bash him because he's a smartarse to them'. She said that the police too hate her partner: 'The pigs they hate his guts. They're racist arseholes. I want to ring the police when he's bashing me but I know they're just gonna lock him up and I'll know he goes psycho and they'll just shoot him.' Samantha also talked about her animosity toward the police: 'The f——— arsehole police – there's more arseholes than there are good ones. They are ignorant. They take fucking ages to come to the mish [the old church mission, where a lot of Aboriginal people live]. You could be dead by the time they get there.'

These concerns of Samantha are common among Aboriginal women. When I interviewed Aboriginal women who had obtained an AVO and who experienced a breach of the order (Kelly, 1999), I also obtained access to the police records and could compare the Aboriginal women's stories to the official police record of incidents. A common story from these Aboriginal women was the racist attitudes of police. One woman stated about a police officer:

He spoke to me like he hated my guts. The only reason I know someone hates my guts without knowing me is about racism. Because racism is an opportunity for a human being to hate another human being without knowing them – just based on physical appearance – and that's all it's based on. (Kelly, 1999: 6)

The majority of Aboriginal women I interviewed believed that having an AVO made no difference to the way the police dealt with their situation. The delay times of police responses, the racist attitudes and concerns about imprisonment of the offenders, were some of the reasons why these women no longer use protection orders (Kelly, 1999: 6). After many talks with Aboriginal women, my own view is that protection orders *should* be used to prevent further violence, but that the way such orders are administered, especially the questionable actions of police, means that justice for Aboriginal victims of family violence is often denied.

Those who have remained in a relationship with their partner emphasized the need for anger management and counseling programs for their partners (Kelly, 1999: 7). However, one Aboriginal domestic violence worker questioned the effectiveness of these programs for perpetrators of violence. She stated that:

Around half of my clients whose men are going to the anger management program say that his behaviour isn't changing, or not significantly. I'm not impressed and I don't think they [the women] are. It doesn't meet their expectations. The violence is either continuing, or it just changes from a physical to an emotional. So any intervention needs to be holistic. A program is needed for families as a whole – it's an issue affecting the whole family, it's not just about him.

Victims of Violence

A major point to make in relation to Aboriginal victims is to dispel the notion that, in Aboriginal communities, a sense of the communal or communitarian overrides the interests of an individual. I believe that in pre-invasion Aboriginal communities communal interests were very important. However, in pre-invasion society communal interests did *not* prevail to the detriment of a victim. Small-scale societies cannot function in disharmony and if there is dissatisfaction with a law process by an individual, this leads inevitably to community disharmony. Hence in pre-invasion Aboriginal communities, restorative justice principles in the context of victim involvement and satisfaction with the dispute management process were not only present but essential to the continued functionality and harmony of the community. However, in contemporary Aboriginal communities, the impact of colonization and dispossession has led to dislocation and the disintegration of traditional cultural values (O'Shane, 1995), so that the dissatisfaction of victims of violence, especially family violence, can be ignored and the community can still continue to function.

Despite the loss of some of our traditional ways, the 'informal' role of women Elders in ensuring the safety and protection of women and children victims of family violence can be enhanced. The importance of women Aboriginal Elders and community leaders in facilitating any process designed to address family violence must be stressed. An Aboriginal women's advocate told me:

For Elders to facilitate or sit-in on the session with the family and help them discuss what's causing the problem, and provide support for women and children, this is far better than the current system. But women's and children's safety must always be a priority. The presence of women Elders is very important to ensure the safety of women and children.

Ann Gummow suggests that one way to ensure that justice is not only done, but seen to be done, would be to include appropriate judicial (or similar) oversight in any restorative justice model together with proper evaluation (Gummow, 1999). The direct role of women Elders may well address such concerns.

Gummow also raises some very important points about the training of restorative justice facilitators. She argues that to ensure that the needs of women generally, and particularly the needs of victims of violence, are met, a great deal of thought and variety of input into training are required. She states that training must include a compulsory component on the dynamics of violence against women in general and domestic violence in particular. Furthermore, the specific needs and concerns of Aboriginal women must be incorporated into such training.

Restorative Justice Theory and Practice in the Indigenous Context: Is it Culturally Appropriate?

The issue of cultural appropriateness of restorative justice theory and practice is quite complex and involves examining whether they reflect the cultural values of the Indigenous peoples, the customary dispute resolution practices of the Indigenous group and Indigenous aspirations for self-determination. Also, it must be understood in the context of the unique status of Indigenous people as First Nations peoples. Without entering into the sovereignty debate for Indigenous Australia, at the very least it must be stated that Indigenous people have a right to self-determination. The relevance of restorative justice must be considered in light of the desire and entitlement of Indigenous peoples to be self-determining. If a restorative justice program does not respect and enhance our right to self-determination, then it is, *prima facie*, culturally inappropriate.

I suggest that five questions must be addressed in deciding whether a restorative justice program is culturally appropriate.

- Do restorative values reflect Indigenous cultural values?
- Are restorative justice processes culturally relevant?
- Is the practice or the implementation of the restorative justice program culturally sensitive?
- Do restorative justice programs empower Indigenous communities?
- Do restorative justice programs meet the desired outcomes for Indigenous communities?

Let us consider the cultural appropriateness of a particular restorative justice process, commonly referred to as conferencing, operating for juvenile offenders in New South Wales. This quote from LaPrairie sums up the rationale for the development of conferencing in Australia:

In Australia, more non-Aboriginal than Aboriginal people have participated in family conferences ... and the approach appears less tied to political or community-based concerns than to providing police with another option for dealing with youth, and meeting public and professional concerns about more effective social control (LaPrairie, 1995a: 79).

Thus, advocates for the introduction of conferencing in Australia did not have Aboriginal people foremost in their minds. Certainly it was a secondary claim, but the primary claim was that it would address the 'youth problem'. But the rhetoric of conferencing is that it will impact positively on Indigenous communities. Cunneen argues that conferencing in Australia:

is couched in 'Indigenous friendly' terms because it is argued that it enables greater Indigenous input into the process of juvenile justice decision-making. Yet the available evidence suggests that negotiation with Aboriginal communities has been poor. In addition Indigenous juvenile incarceration rates have been rising rapidly. (Cunneen, 1997: 296)

Blagg argues that:

too much was taken for granted about the shape and format of conferences as culturally appropriate 'ceremonies': due to an 'essentialising' colonial mind-set which assumed that 'because it works for Maori's' [sic] it must also work for other Indigenous peoples. Too little was said, on the other hand, about the decolonisation of the Indigenous landscape or the regimes and structures which would need to be reformed and redefined before some kind of ceremonial meeting places could be constructed where a range of 'justice' issues could be debated. (Blagg, 1998a: 7)

In relation to the five-point criteria for assessing cultural appropriateness, I suggest that the New South Wales conferencing program fails on all except one criterion (see, for example, Kelly & Oxley, 1999). It does not incorporate 'cultural experts' (Aboriginal Elders); it is administered by an imposed government bureaucracy; it fails to empower grass-roots Aboriginal communities; and in relation to outcomes, it has not so far had an impact on the level of Aboriginal over-representation in the juvenile criminal justice system.

The only criterion that the New South Wales conferencing program may meet is in relation to cultural values. However, analysing the question of cultural values in Aboriginal societies tends to be complicated. Larissa Behrendt describes traditional Aboriginal values as: belief in custodianship of land; equality with all other creatures; oral culture; teaching by example; reluctance to change; communal; egalitarian; co-operative; respect for Elders; and consensus (Behrendt 1995: 18). Behrendt argues too that urban Aboriginal communities also reflect these values and that urban Aboriginal people have stronger connections to traditional cultural values than to non-Aboriginal values (Behrendt, 1995: 76).

There are some similarities between restorative justice values and Aboriginal customary values. Restorative justice is a set of values that guides decisions on policy, programs and practice (Pranis 2000). Restorative justice values are based on the notions that: all parties *involved in* crime should be included in the *response* to crime; offenders become accountable through *understanding* the harm caused by their offence(s), *accepting* the responsibility for that harm and *taking* actions to repair the harm they have caused; and crime is defined as harm to *individuals and community*.

These values are inherent in small-scale societies. In small-scale or 'traditional' societies (for want of a better term), restorative justice values were or are the norm. In small-scale societies, crime impacts on everyone – it disrupts community life. Given the enormous inter-dependency of traditional small-scale societies, a dysfunctional unit within the whole cannot be tolerated. The unit, or the offender, must be either reintegrated or extricated. Ethnographies of traditional Aboriginal societies describe the types of sanctions following an offence – punishment (for example, by way of spearing), an order for reparation (for example, giving over some valuable hunting implements), tempo-rary banishment, and in the most serious offences, permanent exclusion or execution.

It is important not to get 'hung up' on deciding whether a particular sanction is retributive or restorative. Some sanctions can involve ele-ments of both: indeed writers on restorative justice have commented that restorative justice may contain punitive elements. As Sam Garkawe notes, there is a 'false dichotomy between retributive justice, said to be represented by the present adversarial criminal justice system, and restorative justice' (Garkawe, 1999: 9). Similarly, Aboriginal dispute mechanisms may be both restorative and retributive.

What must be emphasized is the commonality of many values between what we call restorative justice today and elements of what my people (Gumbaynggirr) call our *Yuludarra* – our dreaming – which encompasses our customary law. There is a lot in common between restorative justice *values* and traditional Aboriginal customary *values*. I emphasize the term 'values' rather than 'practice' – for it is mostly poor *practice* that makes restorative justice programs culturally inappropriate. Hence restorative justice values may reflect Indigenous cultural values, but this means very little if the practice does not meet the other four criteria mentioned above, and does not enhance self-determination.

Traditional Aboriginal Laws and Spousal Abuse

An Aboriginal women's advocate whom I asked about spousal abuse in traditional Aboriginal society told me that '[w]omen were respected. Spousal abuse was not prevalent. When conflict of any sort arose – direct actions were taken. Sanctions were imposed by the community. If there was violence against women I'm sure action was taken immediately – what action or to what extent I'm not sure.'

I spoke to 60 attendees at a conference held in 2000 in New South Wales on restorative justice and Aboriginal family violence[2] about their understanding of the way in which family violence used to be tackled in traditional Aboriginal society. Thirty respondents stated that they were unable to answer the question; two stated that women were respected and were not abused in traditional society. One respondent stated 'I don't believe it was a great problem as people were taught from childhood the right way to live.' The remainder gave the following responses:

- You broke the traditional law, you paid the consequences – you would be ostracised.
- The punishment would be spearing – this couldn't work today.
- They used to draw a circle and the offender would stand in the middle and the offender would be judged by the Elders.
- An open consultative process with swift and fair outcomes.
- Elders called meetings or gatherings to address the problem and to make the community aware that it is not acceptable.
- Based on respect – so whatever the Elders decided they had to follow.
- Listening to our Elders.
- Discipline.
- Punishment.
- Elders counseling, providing guidance, instructions, directions, support and relevant punishment determined by the degree of violence perpetrated.
- Hard but just.
- Bring both parties and their families together and help them understand that it's not our way.
- Elders dealing with the problem in an holistic way.
- In an holistic view and approach.
- Outcast them and make them ashamed in front of everyone.

This final response leads to the issue of 'shaming'.

Reintegrative Shaming and the Aboriginal Context

Braithwaite (1989) argues for a process he calls 'reintegrative shaming' – a type of social control based upon community condemnation of wrongdoing, with opportunities for reintegration of the offender back into the community. Braithwaite states that 'a communitarian society combines a dense network of individual interdependencies with strong cultural commitments to mutuality of obligation' and that the 'aggregation of individual interdependency is the basis for societal communitarianism'

(p. 85). He maintains that '[i]nterdependencies must be attachments which invoke personal obligation to others within a community of concern' (p. 85).

The 'attachments' in Aboriginal communities where personal obligations are invoked relate to the authority of Elders. In the case study, Samantha said: 'I have a lot of respect for my Elders. My man has a lot of respect for the Elders too. He does a lot for the Elders and they're good to him.' Jim described his respect for, and fear of, the local Elders. When asked whether he would prefer to go to court, or appear before a council of Elders, he preferred court. When asked why, he stated that 'I would be so shamed [to appear before the Elders]. I wouldn't want them knowing how bad I've been.' Following further discussion of who might attend such a council and the support people he might have, he responded: 'I like that'. Jim continued: 'But I haven't been violent for a while, so I don't really need that.' But as I mentioned above, Jim did subsequently reoffend. If a process involving a council of Elders existed, he might now wish to participate in light of his recent offending. Samantha and Jim's community of concern would be the extended family and the relevant family or clan Elders. Braithwaite argues that it is the cohesiveness of a society and the 'social embeddedness' of sanctions that give communitarian shaming its force (Braithwaite, 1989: 54–57).

This notion of social embeddedness is particularly relevant in tradition-oriented Aboriginal settings. The society is relatively cohesive and sanctions are often embedded in the social structure. In pre-invasion Aboriginal society reintegrative shaming occurred for a number of offences – only the most serious offences would be dealt with by extrication – permanent exclusion or execution. Shaming was, and still is for some offences in some traditional communities (for example, religious offences), a highly formalised, ritualized cultural practice.

In traditional Aboriginal society, enormous interdependency will mean that any 'dysfunctional' (for want of a better word) person must be either reintegrated or extricated. However, in non-traditional/urban Aboriginal communities, reintegrative shaming is not a cultural practice. Due to the decimation and dispersal of Aboriginal communities following invasion, the rituals of traditional life have been quashed by oppressive white man's 'rituals'.

Also, in urban and rural Aboriginal communities, the word 'shame' is an entrenched part of Aboriginal English. 'Shame' is often used to connote not just an embarrassing act, but an act that ranges from the uncomfortable to the extremely negative. On the other hand, it is also used in a jocular sense – for example, if my elderly widowed aunt got a new boyfriend, we might say 'Oh, shame, aunt!' Although Braithwaite's shaming theory is set in a positive context, the *word* has such a depth of meaning in most Aboriginal communities that it really cannot be used in restorative justice discourse or practice in Aboriginal communities. Of course, this does not deny the validity of the concept. Nor am I arguing that reintegrative shaming is not relevant in urban and rural Aboriginal communities. Quite the opposite – it is submitted that we need to go back to our traditions and reintegration is an aspect of our customary law.

Potential of Restorative Justice in Dealing with Family Violence

The types of offences that can be referred to a restorative justice conference vary depending on the jurisdiction. For instance, in New South Wales the Youth Justice Conferencing program excludes certain offences from conferencing, including sexual assault offences and offences relating to domestic violence (s.8 Young Offenders Act, NSW, 1997). However, in other jurisdictions these more serious offences are not excluded from restorative justice programs. It has been suggested that it is hard to find good grounds for excluding serious offenders from restorative justice programs (Carbonatto, 1995: 12). The arguments articulated for the inclusion of serious offences include:

- the idea that serious offenders have to incur a really punitive sanction goes back to a purely retributive interpretation of the societal response to crime – a way of dealing with offending which provides little benefit to either the victim or the offender;
- critics contend that the 'public' would not accept a restorative justice approach to serious offenders – but this view is not supported by research which indicates that victims and the public are not as punitive as commonly believed; and
- the assumption that serious offenders would be less receptive to the influence of restorative principles rests upon an unfounded aetiological supposition that the seriousness of an offence reflects the severity and mutability of behaviour (Carbonatto 1995: 12).

Carbonatto argues that:

Current policies concerning spousal abuse in most western countries, including New Zealand, have to a large extent concentrated on the role of law enforcement to stem this violence by the arrest and prosecution of offenders. Despite this noteworthy and important development, criminal justice solutions to spousal abuse have been attacked for not adequately providing solutions for couples who continue to live together after criminal justice intervention has occurred. *Part of this criticism relates to the criminal justice system's inability to adequately contextualise abuse in an on-going and complex relationship.* (Carbonatto, 1995: 2) [emphasis added]

The context of Carbonatto's argument lies in the 'reality' that many women return to their abusive partners: 'We need to face that reality and develop ways to help both partners achieve a relationship based on trust and non-violence' (Carbonatto, 1995: 12). She also acknowledges the diversity of spousal abuse:

The assumption that spousal abuse fits one basic scenario involving a victimised, disempowered woman and her controlling brutal partner is incorrect. The dynamics in spousal abuse are far more complex. There needs to be greater flexibility in the way we deal with different types of offenders and different types of relationships. (Carbonatto, 1995: 12)

Carbonatto, in describing the model suggested by Braithwaite and Daly (1994), sees a restorative justice model differing from traditional mediation because of the engagement with communities of concern. The presence of the community of concern arguably addresses the shortcoming of traditional mediation in matters involving domestic violence. The community of concern is able to support and protect the interests of the victim and act to prevent future violence (Carbonatto, 1995: 10).

In the case of Jim and Samantha, the two had been involved in a complex, ongoing relationship for the past ten years. At the time of the interview, Samantha wanted to remain in the relationship. She said: 'The relationship's real good at this time.' Yet when probed, she describes current incidents of verbal abuse and threats. She said that she did not want anything to do with police and the courts. When asked 'what else do you think can help with stopping the violence?' Samantha replied, 'If the Elders would come and help us, that would be better than the police.' Restorative justice programs may give the appearance of being soft, but having to face up to a victim and other members of the community can be far more demanding than appearing before a court, as illustrated by Jim's comment about feeling shamed in front of a possible council of Elders.

The potential of a restorative justice process is that, whereas in family mediation the conflict is privatized, here the violence is opened up to community scrutiny. It can be a forum to display the community's disapproval of violence. According to another advocate of Aboriginal women victims, 'having someone who the perpetrator respects – has a fearful respect of – will really help. Someone like a male Elder or an older cousin who they really respect and will listen to, speaking out that the violence is not acceptable would be an effective process.' She went on to say that 'any intervention must be holistic. It must address how violence is affecting the whole family. It must give a voice to all of those people hurt by the actions of the abuser.'

According to Judy Atkinson, restorative justice may offer Aboriginal families a further way to heal the post-colonial legacy, which manifests in family violence. She comments that: 'Aboriginal people express the need to heal family relationships ruptured by intergenerational colonial impacts' (Atkinson, 1995: 21), and restorative justice may well offer that.

The potential of restorative justice also lies in its ability to address underlying causes of violence and the effects on all family members. According to an Aboriginal victims' advocate:

We need an Elders council where we can all sit down and talk about the causes and effects of family violence. We need to talk about how the violence is affecting everyone. How it's affecting the women, the children and him. He needs to understand why he is doing this. And if we have Elders and community leaders there they can tell him that his behaviour is unacceptable, and then they can provide ongoing support for him to help him change his behaviour.

This was the same advocate who had some concerns about the perpetrator anger management program. She said that the process of a council of Elders, or an anger management program, must be part of an holistic intervention strategy:

The intervention has to be a holistic plan. You need an action plan to identify the person at risk and remove that person to a safety house where she can be counseled and supported. Then they would attend the Elders council. The presence of victim support workers are essential. Then you can look at the causes of the violence (it may be that he was sexually assaulted as a child, or his dad bashed his mum, of course there's lots of causes). Then after that process the victim, the perpetrator and their children need ongoing counseling (individually, then couple, then family). Then he can go to the anger management program – it will only work if it's part of a holistic strategy. So there has to be a number of interventions to address the problem.

Recommendations

In order for restorative justice to be culturally appropriate, it must invoke Indigenous self-determination. Sarre (1999) refers to the need to redefine Aboriginal community justice within broader criminological and socio-political concepts. He argues that restorative justice and Aboriginal self-determination must go hand-in-hand, binding together a rich spectrum of Aboriginal justice workers, programs and initiatives within this context of Aboriginal community restitution. He goes on to argue that 'diversionary schemes are far more likely to be effective and to avoid the failures of implementation and contradiction that have dogged their forebears if they are framed within the context of Aboriginal community justice rather than imposed by bureaucracies' (Sarre, 1999: 9).

There are four essential elements that must be met in order to implement restorative justice practices for Aboriginal family violence:

Community grass-roots initiative

The potential of restorative justice principles to address family violence in Aboriginal communities lies in their ability to empower local communities. Many writers argue that 'the success of any restorative process relies heavily on community involvement' (Thorsborne, 1999: 3). Kay Pranis states that '[g]reater community involvement in a restorative justice process is a powerful way to break this destructive cycle and increase the connections among community members' (Pranis 2000). Margaret Thorsborne makes the important point that 'community involvement also carries with it responsibilities and accountabilities, but which, if honoured, will assist in the reduction of crime and other wrongdoing and create safer places to live and work' (Thorsborne, 1999: 3). This is where the importance of respected Elders comes in to play. They are the ones who have the wisdom to carry the responsibilities and to be accountable.

Respected Elders control the program and process

Elders and community leaders must be the gatekeepers of the program (not the police and courts). They should be the ones to identify whether the offender is an appropriate person to appear before the council. For example, they would assess whether the perpetrator is a voluntary participant, whether he has the requisite level of respect for Elders in order for their intervention to be successful, and to ensure that he would have support available during and after the process. They are also the ones who would ensure the safety of women and children, and the informed consent of victims.

According to Gumbaynggirr customary law, the Elders were the decision-makers. Despite a loss of many traditional laws, I believe that this value remains among many Aboriginal people. But what sort of characteristics do we want in those who control this process? Elders are not self-appointed, but are those who are widely respected for their fairness, reasonableness, honesty and wisdom. When I asked the attendees at the conference on restorative justice and Aboriginal family violence: 'Do you think Elders should have a role in any justice process for dealing with family violence?', the great majority responded: 'Yes'. When I asked whether Elders should be involved in tackling family violence and, if so, what their role should be, almost all said that the Elders should have some type of role, and the following were suggested:

- Law-makers, law-keepers, counselors, arbitrators, instructors.
- Directors and teachers of the processes.
- For guidance, wisdom and positive role modelling.
- To teach respect and responsibility.
- For guidance, community empowerment and an equitable outcome.
- 'Use their wisdom.'
- 'Helping them understand themselves as Aboriginal people.'
- 'To be mentors.'
- 'Role models, mentors, therapists.'
- 'Getting together and talking.'
- 'Talking to the perpetrator on handling anger.'
- 'To work together as one – young and old.'
- 'To be part of the solution and resolution.'
- 'Talking and support for all the community.'
- 'The Family Elders should be asked.'

The last of these is a particularly important point. There are Elders in each family or clan, so one Elder may not be appropriate to be involved if the perpetrator is from a different family or clan group.

Support from criminal justice agents

Criminal justice agents such as the police and courts must support grass-roots criminal justice initiatives. In line with the principle of self-determination, it must be the decision of the local community members and leaders as to the level of involvement of the local justice agents. For instance, in some communities, Elders may wish the magistrate to sit with them and convey their decision to the offender. The purpose of this may be to prevent the offender taking revenge on any individual Elder.

Part of an holistic strategy

Any such restorative justice program would not be a panacea. An holistic strategy with a number of interventions must be adopted to effectively address the problem of family violence in our communities.

Conclusion

One of the recommendations from the Restorative Justice and Aboriginal Family Violence Conference sums up my suggested path for furthering restorative justice initiatives:

Establish a forum for men and women and Tribal Elders (and other concerned community members) to talk about the problem of family violence – causes and effects – and to find a resolution.

This forum may or may not look like a restorative justice program that theoreticians might envisage. But as long as it is designed and controlled by grass-roots Aboriginal community members, it would be a community justice process, and that is what matters.

Notes

1 Gumbaynggirr word for Aborigine. Gumbaynggirr is the language group that covers the area of the north coast of New South Wales from the south of the Nambucca Valley, to the Clarence River at south Grafton, and inland to the peaks of the Great Dividing Range.
2 I was involved in organizing this conference, held at Yarrawarra Aboriginal Cultural Centre, Corindi Beach. The conference targeted Aboriginal people from the north coast of New South Wales. All Aboriginal people from these regions were invited to attend: invitations were sent to all Aboriginal organizations and all Elders were specifically invited. Sixty Aboriginal people attended this conference. The conference was funded by part of a grant that the School of Law and Justice, Southern Cross University, received from the Law Foundation of New South Wales. All transport, meals and accommodation costs were covered by the grant – even for the young children of some of the women. Thus there were arguably few barriers for people attending.

12 Domestic Violence and Restorative Justice Initiatives: Who Pays if We Get it Wrong?

Ruth Busch

Introduction

Restorative justice has been described as 'a process of bringing together the stakeholders (victims, offenders, communities) in search of a justice that heals the hurt of crime, instead of responding to the hurt with more hurt' (Braithwaite, 1999b: 1728). While to date most restorative justice initiatives have dealt with youth justice offenders, proponents of restorative justice initiatives have argued that the model is also appropriate for dealing with domestic violence cases. John Braithwaite, for example, has asserted that court processing of domestic violence cases 'fosters a culture of denial', while restorative justice 'fosters a culture of apology'. And he comments, 'Apology, when communicated with ritual seriousness, is actually the most powerful cultural device for taking a problem seriously, while denial is a cultural device for dismissing it' (Braithwaite, 2000a: 189).

This discussion is situated in the historic debate surrounding the use of family mediation where one of the participants has been the victim of domestic violence.[1] Battered women's advocates in New Zealand (Robertson & Busch, 1998) and overseas have argued that mediation is inherently unfair and unsafe for their clients (Hart, 1990). They point to disparities of power between perpetrators and victims and question the autonomy of victims in negotiating agreements. They suggest that battered women are better served by using the court system than informal justice processes. Mediation proponents, on the other hand, argue that mediation is more empowering and effective for the victim than the adversarial process in all but the most violent cases (Corcoran & Melamed, 1990).

The recent development of restorative justice initiatives in Australia and New Zealand has expanded the parameters of this debate from family mediation to the criminal justice arena and beyond. It is suggested by some writers (Carbonatto, 1995) that the restorative justice model offers opportunities for both victims[2] and perpetrators[3] to effectively address cases of domestic violence that come to the attention of the police, the community and the courts. The purpose of this chapter is to critically evaluate arguments about the use of a restorative justice model for domestic violence cases. I presume that the primary goals of any intervention in domestic violence situations – including restorative justice programmes – must entail the prioritization of the safety and autonomy of victims over any other outcomes, including the re/conciliation of the parties. Safety and autonomy are the measures by which practitioners and researchers can monitor and evaluate the appropriateness and efficacy of domestic violence-related interventions (Pence, 1996).

From the work of Pennell and Burford (Pennell & Burford, 2000a) it may be possible to envision a hybrid system appropriately incorporating restorative justice processes as a final step in a limited number of domestic violence cases, but I stress that such processes should only be utilized after safety mechanisms are first set in place that can be enforced through court sanctions. I also believe that for the incidence of domestic violence to be curtailed, clear and unambiguous messages must be given by our legal system that such violence is wrong.

Until the late 1980s in New Zealand, there were few consequences for acts of domestic violence (Busch et al, 1992). Rather than arresting and charging perpetrators of domestic violence, police saw themselves as mediating disputes. It is only in the past 15 years that there has been more than lip service on the part of the New Zealand criminal justice and Family Court systems to taking domestic violence seriously and since then, the public too has become more sensitized to issues of violence. New legislation in effect since 1995 allows a wide range of adult victims and children exposed to domestic violence to be protected from the coercive tactics of their abusers (Busch & Robertson, 2000).

I contend that if restorative justice processes are to be used to deal with domestic violence cases, it is imperative that facilitators are well trained in the power and control dynamics of domestic violence (Pence & Paymar, 1986), knowledgeable about risk-assessment issues and understand the intersectionality of race and gender in the lived realities of battered victims' lives (Crenshaw, 1994). I agree with Braithwaite's recent statement that:

> it is unlikely that restorative justice processes in themselves are likely to have a major impact on the crime rate. The reason for the latter is that it is implausible that what happens during a one- or two-hour encounter will often turn around all the other variables operating during all the other hours of a person's life. (Braithwaite, 1999b: 1747)

It is a wise caution; one which we ignore in the area of domestic violence at the peril of others' lives.

The Court System: Inadequacies and Recent Ameliorations

Debates between those who support the utilization of restorative justice processes for domestic violence situations and those who support handling these cases through the court system (possibly through proceedings in both the criminal and Family courts) sometimes take on a Zoroastrian spin, seeming to pit optimists against pessimists, healers against punishers, communitarians against adversaries. One aim of this chapter is to break down some of these binaries and attempt to bridge dichotomies while not forgetting that disagreements about perspective, practice and vision are real and need to be addressed.

I begin from a position against the use of restorative justice models for the vast majority of domestic violence cases. This does not mean I am blind to problems in the New Zealand legal system's handling of domestic violence cases. One does not have to search too far to discover the inadequacies of the court process for domestic violence victims. For example, the existing criminal justice system excludes victims from an active role in determining the outcomes of crimes committed against them or their property. Indeed in some American jurisdictions, mandatory arrest policies and no-drop prosecutions result in outcomes which can be destructive to victims' autonomy: all too often in states and cities with mandatory arrest and no-drop prosecution policies, the result of police attendance will be the dual arrest and prosecution of both perpetrators and victims. Alternatively, victim participation in criminal processes can be coerced, with the threat of imprisonment for refusal to testify against a perpetrator (Hanna, 1996)

Some writers have commented that under these mandated policies battered women are re-victimized by the very system that purports to act on their behalf.

As well, research demonstrates that mandated participation of victims falls most heavily on women of colour and immigrant women (Mills, 1999). Issues involving the intersectionality of race and gender are a root problem:

Afro-American women may often view cooperation with state officials against Afro-American men as a breach of loyalty. Also Afro-American women may be very suspicious of the criminal justice system because it has historically ignored violence against black women and perpetrated violence against black men. (Hanna, 1996: 1880)

In other jurisdictions, the trend to trivialize domestic violence incidents, to blame the victim for the violence against her, to decontextualize the violence by failing to take account of the disparity of power between the victim and the perpetrator, to minimize the victim's perception of the possibility of her imminent danger, to see the violence as a 'symptom of a real problem in the relationship' but not a real problem of itself (Busch, 1994) – these commonplace responses of police and courts all too often send messages to both the victim and her offender that domestic violence is not really criminal activity, that such violence may be an understandable (if regrettable) response to provocative actions by the victim, and that the legal system will not afford effective protection to 'unworthy' victims, i.e. those who fight back, those who break racial and gender role norms, those who cannot forgive or look away or at least keep silent about the impact of abuse on their lives and/or the system's failure to address it.

In addition to failing victims, the court system also often fails to hold offenders accountable for their violence. By focussing on offender actions in isolation, it neither acknowledges the context within which offending has occurred nor the social legitimization for the sexist, classist and/or racist attitudes that philosophically underpin an offender's use of violence against his victim (Pence & Paymar, 1990).

But there are risks in discarding the court system without first establishing whether proposed alternatives are capable of providing as much protection as it presently does. As mentioned, in New Zealand, it has only been in the last six years that domestic violence cases have been dealt with in any numbers by either the criminal justice system or the Family Court. Not until 1987 was the unsuccessful police approach of trying to defuse the conflict by supposedly mediating the dispute officially jettisoned (although continued in practice at the local and regional level long after that) (Police Commissioner Policy Circular, 1992). Prior to that, the police as well as District Court judges and other practitioners saw domestic violence as relationship-based, not involving real police work and not deserving criminal censure (Busch et al, 1992).

The New Zealand police now have a pro-arrest policy and attempt to shield the victim from testifying at court through better investigative procedures and their own laying of charges against the perpetrator (Busch & Robertson, 1994). As many victims are afraid of retributive violence if they pursue prosecutions against their abusers, the current police policies can provide for successful prosecutions, sometimes without the necessity for victims to be involved as witnesses at trial. One outcome of this policy is that in many cases offenders have less control than previously over the criminal justice process; their intimidatory tactics are no longer as effective in controlling whether an arrest or prosecution will occur. Coupled with these new police approaches, breaches of protection orders are now dealt with. Protection orders for victims are no longer simply pieces of paper as they had been at the end of the 1980s; they can at times be effective in stopping ongoing harassment and threats, and have an impact on contact arrangements, a primary site of ongoing abuse of both women and children once the abuser and his victim have separated (Busch, 1995).

Major initiatives in New Zealand since the early 1990s have led to the development of coordinated community responses to domestic violence and the broadening of public awareness about its negative developmental effects on child witnesses. In 1995, the statutory definition of violence under the New Zealand Domestic Violence Act was expanded to include psychological as well as physical and sexual violence. That Act specifically names as child abuse a perpetrator's action that causes a child to be exposed to violence against anyone with whom s/he has a domestic relationship, including members of the child's extended family. (Section 3(3) DVA 1995). Amendments to the New Zealand Guardianship Act now allow courts to make orders to protect victims who have custody of children from being harassed or abused on access visits and mandates a risk assessment on the safety of the child to be carried out prior to unsupervised access being awarded to perpetrators. (Sections 16A-16C Guardianship Act 1968). Given what is now known about the deleterious effects on children of being the direct and intentional targets of violence or being exposed to witnessing it, a major category of invisible victims of domestic violence has (finally) been 'outed' (Busch, 1995 and Busch & Robertson, 2000).

Rehabilitation of offenders, not punishment, is the major outcome of criminal court and/or Family Court involvement in domestic violence cases, unless serious or repetitive violence has been used (Robertson, 2000) Perpetrators' programs are court mandated; perpetrators are required to attend programs or risk prosecution, though only a very limited number of prosecutions have in fact been pursued for failure to attend such programs. The content of the programs allows perpetrators to look at the belief systems which underpin their use of violence and learn about the effects of domestic violence on children, including the ways violence has impacted on their own lives. There are regulation-mandated Maori principles which must be included in all programs which are designed for or in which a majority of participants is Maori.[4] For adult and child victims of domestic violence, culturally appropriate, court-funded programs provide safety planning, support and healing. Adult and child protected persons programs can be accessed within three years of the protection order having been made, are voluntary and cost-free to participants.

One conclusion that emerges is that the criminal justice/Family Court system which deals with domestic violence situations in New Zealand is a far cry from notions of the traditional adversary system with its myopic concentration on punishment and rules of evidence, and its lack of focus on victim's needs or victim's safety. Rehabilitation of perpetrators and protection for victims are primary focuses of the legal system's intervention in domestic violence cases. Solutions are seen to lie not only in changes by individual perpetrators or victims but also in developing culturally appropriate coordinated community interventions which consistently challenge societal attitudes which construct and legitimize the power disparities within which domestic violence occurs.

Victim–Offender Mediation and Domestic Violence: The Myth of Consensus Decision-Making

For the past decade or so, ideas about mediation and Alternative Dispute Resolution have permeated a range of areas in New Zealand from family and workplace conflict to environmental and international disputes. Hailed by many as a superior option for resolving conflict where there is an ongoing relationship, many proponents point to the benefits of informal processes over adversarial processes. It is claimed that because mediation is able to address underlying issues and break down problematic patterns of communication that hold the conflict in place, it offers a superior process to that found in the traditional courtroom.

While this claim may be justified in some family and workplace conflicts, great care must be taken not to globalize these gains into a general acceptance that these techniques are invariably superior to the court system. There are grave risks in assuming that all relationship conflicts can be patched by consensus. Since the consensual resolution of conflict requires an attitude of 'give a little, take a little' to reach an agreement, there are risks in translating these principles unthinkingly into relationships affected by violence, especially if that approach sees a victim taking responsibility for her perpetrator's abuse.

In the area of domestic violence, it is claimed (Carbonatto, 1995) that mediation enables the parties to focus on relationship issues in a way that is not possible during court proceedings. Because many women reconcile with their abusers or continue some form of relationship with them long after the court case has finished, it is said that mediation can help both parties to develop ways of achieving a relationship based on trust and non-violence (Carbonatto, 1995). This claim highlights a number of important issues about mediation processes for domestic violence cases. For instance, to reach a consensus, the parties must have the capacity to negotiate with each other. There must be some capacity for accord, a willingness to be honest, a desire to settle the dispute and some capacity for compromise (Astor, 1994). But the relationships between perpetrators and victims in domestic violence settings are typically not characterized by consensus, honesty, mutuality and compromise.

This carries with it two further implications in terms of the appropriateness of mediation in dealing with domestic violence cases. The first is that the assumption that the prior relationship will assist the mediation process may not apply. This is particularly so where one of the parties does not wish to continue the relationship because of previous violence. It also means that the facilitators must be highly skilled in the dynamics of domestic violence, lethality risk assessment, and domestic violence screening techniques in order to recognize the warning signs for further violence and address the high levels of emotion and duress which might be involved.

In New Zealand, one philosophical problem has been the claim that any member of the community can act as a facilitator (Mansill, 2000). This claim is dangerous in a domestic violence context where the risk of further violence is high and the need for expertise in handling issues of violence, relationships and victimization is essential. There must be initial training and annual up-skilling requirements in the area of domestic violence for anyone who acts as a facilitator in mediation or restorative justice conferences dealing with domestic violence, either as a primary or backdrop issue.

Violence often escalates at the time of separation. Indeed, domestic homicides are most likely to occur when a woman attempts to separate or during the first year after separation (Hart, 1993). Mediations occurring during this period take place when the perpetrator is often using particularly aggressive efforts to control his estranged partner (Liss & Stahly, 1993). These mediations may have the consequence of suggesting that domestic violence is inherently a 'couple problem' which can be addressed by offering conciliation to the parties. As a chilling example, in one case that ended in a murder/suicide at a counseling centre in New Zealand (Busch et al, 1992) it became clear that the perpetrator's hopes of reconciliation had been raised by the fact that he and his wife had been ordered to attend Family Court ordered conciliation sessions. Although the wife had specifically stated in her court affidavits that she 'feared for her life' and there had been several violent incidents at her workplace and at her parents' home, the counseling centre inadvertently advised the perpetrator of the time of his wife's separate appointment. The discourse of 'conciliation counseling' had led the centre to fail to prioritize precautions about divulging such information despite the fact that the wife had adamantly refused to engage in joint sessions with her husband. Interestingly in this case, the husband was being treated as a potential suicide risk and was known to be purchasing guns but none of the mental health professionals involved seemed to have been alert to obvious lethality risk assessment factors in dealing with this case.

The primary goal of any dispute resolution process must be the protection and prevention of further harm to both the victim and the offender during – and after – the session. Clearly, however, some perpetrators use mediation as an opportunity for further contact with the victim. This tendency, referred to as 'negative intimacy', is a recognized basis for refusing to continue a family mediation (National Working Party on Mediation, 1996). Of particular concern in relation to cases of domestic violence is the reality that there is often insufficient safety planning and a lack of available resources to guarantee the protection of the victim during the mediation itself, let alone after the session is completed or after she has returned home (National Committee on Violence Against Women, 1991).

There are, obviously, significant differences in the type, severity and frequency of violence used in domestic violence cases. As well, there are important differences in the forms and quality of resources available to victims of such violence. However, due to the power imbalances and dynamics of control that characterize many domestic violence relationships, in most instances, the victims of violence do not have the capacity to negotiate freely and on an equal footing with their abusers (Astor, 1994). Frequently the perpetrator's pattern of dispute resolution is characterized by coercion and intimidation. In an attempt to avoid further violence, the victim's responses often involve compliance with and placation of his wishes.

The mediation process requires victims to assert and negotiate for their own needs and interests. Mediation carried out against the backdrop of domestic violence, therefore, requires the victim to negotiate effectively on her own behalf although her experiences may have in all likelihood led her to renounce or adapt her needs in an attempt to avoid repetitions of past violence. There is a strong likelihood, therefore, that a battered woman will negotiate for what she thinks she can get, rather than for what she actually wants (Astor, 1994).

In 1994, Newmark, Harrell and Salem carried out a research study in the Family Courts of two centres in the United States: Portland, Oregon and Minneapolis, Minnesota. The purpose of the study was to assess the perceptions of men and women involved in custody and access cases where there had been a history of domestic violence. The study found that there were significant differences in the perceptions of women who had been the victims of violence as opposed to those who had not been abused during their relationships. Women who had been abused were more likely than women who had not to feel that they could be 'out-talked' by their partners (Newmark et al, 1994). They also felt that their partners were more likely to retaliate against them if they held out for what they wanted. Newmark et al reported that abused women were 'afraid of openly disagreeing with [their partner] because he might hurt [her] or the children if [she did]' (pp. 14–15).

These findings accord with comments made by some New Zealand women interviewed following their involvement in Family Court mediation and counselling (Busch et al, 1992). They also are congruent with the findings of a very recent Australian report on the effects of the 1995 Family Law Reform Act (Rhoades et al, 1999). In that latter study, the authors conclude that many women agree to consent to contact arrangements that do not provide them with the level of protection they had wanted (e.g., they agree during mediation conferences to unsupervised contact with neutral hand-over arrangements although they had wanted supervised contact) either because of the intransigence of their estranged violent partners during the conferences or because of pressure by their own lawyers to agree to orders that the lawyers advise are the 'usual' ones for the court to make at the interim contact stage.

The traditional mediation process relies heavily on the judicial model of neutrality and impartiality. Like judges, however, mediators are not exempt from the politics of gender, class, race and culture. Moreover, it is naïve to suggest that mediators are immune to the minimizing, trivialising and victim-blaming attitudes toward battered women that are so commonly found in legal and psychological discourses about domestic violence. This is especially true if the mediator is untrained in domestic violence issues and perceives the problem as being relationship-based, with each party contributing in different ways to the perpetrator's use of violence.

It is claimed that the issue of power balancing can be addressed by process changes, such as dictating who goes first or ensuring that the less dominant party has access to adequate legal advice (Moore, 1991). While these interventions may compensate for minor differences in power, they are not capable of re-establishing equality where violence has occurred. In these cases, the power imbalances may be extreme, depending on the type, severity and frequency of the tactics of violence used.

Several final issues about mediation need to be mentioned. First, the labelling of 'crime' as 'conflict' is an integral part of the mediation process. In situations of domestic violence, it can be misleading to define violent acts as simply an escalation in the conflict level. This labeling tends to have the effect of masking the perpetrator's responsibility for the behaviour. In fact, rather than an escalation in conflict, the use of violence by a party often suppresses the conflict.[5] Most importantly, until recently there had been tacit or overt acceptance of spousal violence by the legal system and society at large. Rather than having seen such violence as criminal behaviour, the focus had instead been on marital privacy and the desire to preserve the family as an intact unit (Rowe, 1985). All of these factors have contributed to the trivialization of domestic violence and the creation of a veil of secrecy which is only now being lifted. There is a danger that outdated paradigms of secrecy and marital privacy may be legitimized by the confidentiality of the mediation process at a time when such secrecy seems to be losing its hold.

Some argue that power imbalances can be addressed through the use of 'shuttle' mediation (Carbonatto, 1995) It is suggested that this will contribute to the protection of the victim by ensuring that the parties do not come face-to-face with one another. Although the use of the shuttle process is not uncommon in mediation, research has shown that it is time consuming and ultimately less effective than a direct meeting between the parties (Marshall & Merry, 1990). This is because a key purpose of the process is to enable the victim and the offender to become directly involved in discussing what response is necessary to 'put things right'. The use of shuttle mediation, moreover, fails to address an even more significant issue. If the parties are unable to negotiate face-to-face because of one party's fears about confronting the other, does the use of shuttle mediation merely mask power disparities and provide an illusion of safety? For instance, if the perpetrator makes it clear that he desires a specific outcome to result from the mediation, how can a mediator ensure that a victim's fear of post-mediation retaliation has not coerced her into agreeing to the provisions of the apparently consensual outcome?

At its worst, shuttle mediation places the mediator in the invidious position of having to decide whether to pass on a threat by the perpetrator to the victim. If the mediator passes the threat on 'word for word', he or she colludes in the possible re-victimization of the victim. What can one think of an agreement reached as a result of the mediator communicating the perpetrator's threats verbatim to the victim? If the mediator refuses to pass on the threats, however, the real danger to the victim should she refuse to reach the agreement desired by the offender may be invisibilized. No matter which option is selected, victim safety and the integrity of the process are compromised.

Family Group Conferences: Limitations of this Process in the Youth Justice Area

On each occasion when restorative justice programs are being established, a detailed discussion ensues over the process options that are available. Of course any program will ultimately be a hybrid of the most successful features of other national and international projects. The difficulty is that success in some areas may be seen as a licence to expand perceived gains into other arenas without fully exploring the consequences and the unique context within which particular crimes or acts of violence occur. Not all offending or offenders or violence are alike. It cannot be assumed that instances of successful resolution of property offences or of one-off stranger assaults by juveniles necessarily signify that utilization of the same dispute resolution processes can safely and effectively resolve domestic violence cases. The conclusion becomes even less persuasive unless there have been long-term, methodologically sound evaluations of the 'successes'.

In the main, where restorative justice processes have been utilised in Australasia, the New Zealand conferencing model has been used as a base. The Family Group Conference ('FGC') approach was adopted in New Zealand in 1989 as the centrepiece of youth justice initiatives codified in the Children, Young Persons and Their Families Act (CYP&F Act). It was adopted because of frustrations encountered with the existing criminal justice model in addressing the problems of juvenile offending, especially for Maori young people. The conferencing process applies to children and young offenders and children in need of care and protection under 17 years of age. The format of and the procedures followed during FGCs are described in detail earlier in this volume (Morris) and I shall not repeat what has been said there. What I wish to concentrate on instead is the research about the effectiveness of FGCs in the youth justice area which it was designed for and then to look at the appropriateness of repackaging this approach to deal with adult perpetrators of domestic violence and their victims.

A satisfactory FGC comprises at least the young offender, a family member, a coordinator, the victim, a youth worker and a member of the Department of Social Welfare. Despite this, some FGCs surprisingly continue in the absence of a number of these key stakeholders, including the offender. In those conferences where the offender and his family are present, there appears to be a common perception by the offenders and their families that they have not been participants in the decision-making process. For instance, only 67 percent of the families and 34 percent of the young offenders reported feeling that they were actively involved in the process. Participants' assessments of who had decided the outcome of the conference were similarly disappointing. Young offenders and their family members felt that the young person had only a limited input into the decision-making process, 11 percent of offenders felt they were only partly involved while 45 percent of offenders believed that they were not involved in the process at all (Maxwell & Morris, 1993).

FGC advocates have expressed the view that the victim's presence is to be encouraged and is indeed the key to the conferencing process (McElrea, 1993). Although it is clear that the victim's presence is important as part of healing, reconciliation and accountability, only 46 percent of the Family Group Conferences in the Maxwell and Morris (1993) sample included the victim or a representative of the victim. This clearly runs contrary to the ideal position with little possibility of the offender understanding the victim's perspective on the violence and/or its impact.

The most disturbing part of the research findings about FGCs is that over one-third of the victims who attended conferences felt worse than before participating. Victims reported feelings of depression, fear, distress and unresolved anger. The researchers linked this to dissatisfaction with the outcomes in terms of the victim's reasons for participating in the process. The most common reason for dissatisfaction was that the victim did not feel that the offender or his or her family were truly sorry (Maxwell & Morris, 1993). Other victims felt that they had not been heard, were unhappy that the offender was not able to pay compensation or felt that the participants were uninterested in them or unsympathetic to them. Some felt that they were viewed as the 'problem' (Maxwell & Morris, 1994).

Low victim participation figures and satisfaction rates may reflect the focus of the Children, Young Persons and their Families Act, which is the young offender within the context of his family. They also may be a reflection on the processes used. Clearly more preparation work needs to be done to ensure that the offender is prepared to accept responsibility for his actions at the conference.

One would surmise that there is a direct relationship between an offender's acceptance of accountability and the victim's satisfaction with the outcome of the conference. As Hooper has noted from his experiences in running conferences in New Zealand and Australia, if the offender enters the process attempting to justify his behaviour, the victim will respond by moving quickly toward a punishment focus, demanding higher levels of penalty, whether by way of compensation or community work. In turn, the offender becomes either more withdrawn from the process or more aggressive in the defence of his position. However, if the offender is encouraged before the meeting to accept responsibility for his actions without blaming someone or something else, this elicits a more empathetic response from victims who tend then to talk about times that they themselves have made mistakes. The victims' perspectives seem to shift from punishment to restitution for the *harm done (Hooper, 2000).*

Maxwell and Morris's 1993 evaluation of FGCs found that difficulties arose when the offenders and the victims were from different ethnic groups. Pakeha victims in the Family Group Conference process on occasions commented that they felt intimidated by the presence of large numbers of Maori whanau. These victims also stated that they resented the discussions in Maori and felt alienated in a Maori environment.

Research indicates that victim involvement in the Family Group Conference decision-making process is very minor. Only two percent of participants felt that the victim had decided the outcome (Maxwell & Morris, 1994). As a restorative justice program can operate only if the victim is actively involved in the decision-making process, this is a major drawback. The problem may arise at the point when the young person's family withdraws from the wider conference to determine a resolution plan. The victim has no role/input into the development of the plan and only a limited right of veto of it.

Social workers, police, lawyers and the conference coordinators were viewed by FGC participants as having a major effect on the process and its outcomes (Hudson et al, 1996). It was almost always the professionals who provided the information for the decisions made by the participants and sometimes they were perceived as arguing strongly against the proposed preferences of the family. As well, monitoring of the outcomes of FGCs was viewed as poor. Little attention was paid to whether the plan was carried out and few victims were informed of the eventual outcome. This is a source of considerable anger for the victims (Maxwell & Morris, 1993).

Since the inception of Family Group Conferencing in New Zealand, a large percentage of young offenders dealt with by this process have been Maori. One of the concerns about FGCs is that, although at times the process used has been able to transcend tokenism and embody a Maori process, the process has often failed to reach outcomes in accordance with Maori philosophies and values. The FGC process has been labeled by both Maori and Pacific Island conference participants to be a pakeha one and Maxwell and Morris (1993) conclude that the FGC model has remained largely unresponsive to cultural differences. Indeed, rather than conferencing being seen as a successful incorporation of Maori values into the legal system, to some Maori legal researchers the process represents an illusion of biculturalism, with Pakeha social workers and police holding the power despite lip service being paid to the importance of whanau decision-making (Te Piringa, 2000). What is advocated for in the name of social justice is the development of parallel legal systems for Maori and non-Maori, with Maori control over who, what, and how offences will be dealt with (Jackson, 1988).

Limitations of the FGC Approach in Relation to Domestic Violence Offences

There are several aspects of the FGC model which make its use problematic for domestic violence offences. Some concerns have already been raised in terms of the discussion about mediation and its inappropriateness for domestic violence cases. Other problems are specific to the conferencing model itself. Clearly the FGC emphasis on consensus decision-making with the conference facilitator fulfilling the role of the mediator who negotiates between participants with widely differing perspectives on the offending (Maxwell & Morris, 1993) is highly problematic. Other concerns involve the issue of community support for victims in domestic violence situations, safety of participants at conferences, and participation by and empowerment of victims to express themselves freely. These concerns are heightened where the victim is not a stranger to the perpetrator but his partner or a family member and has been the repeated target of his violent behaviour and/or intimidation. The risks of getting the process wrong are far more serious than in cases of one-off, non-violent property offences involving young offenders and strangers.

Two-thirds of Family Group Conference facilitators describe hostility being directed either at family members or at Department of Social Welfare staff during the conferences (Robertson, 1996). This hostility has included shouting, verbal abuse, threats and even physical violence. Over half of the facilitators reported that the safety of at least one party had been threatened during Family Group Conferences. Anecdotal evidence also exists to support these views. A facilitator reported to the author that she had had to hurriedly abort an FGC about the care and protection of a child when a husband told his battered wife: 'One more f—— word from you and I'll throw you out this bloody window.'[6] Another facilitator described how at a conference held to deal with the effects on the children of witnessing their mother's repeated beatings, the perpetrator was able to force his partner to forgo the support of her family by simply snapping his fingers and pointing to the empty chair next to him. The wife, who had initially sat down with her family, moved 'automaton-like to his side' immediately after his gesture. A year later, the woman was killed and her partner was found guilty of her murder.

Clearly the safety of participants may be compromised during FGCs. This is of particular concern in cases of domestic violence where there is a history of threats and intimidation and where the perpetrator has already used violence as a means of getting his way. This risk may extend beyond the perpetrator's typical targets of violence (e.g., his spouse and/or his children) and influence the participation of all family and community members at the conference.

Facilitators themselves may be fearful of challenging an abuser's behaviours and belief systems because of worries about their own safety. As an example, an experienced facilitator conducted a conference involving an assault. After openly confronting the offender about his use of violence, the mediator immediately began to feel nervous about pressing on with that line of questioning. The offender had a history of explosive episodes of violence and the mediator was concerned about putting himself at risk (Hooper, 2000). The most recent evaluation of New Zealand's Children, Youth and Family Service indicates that social worker fear of violent clients/family members is widespread which sometimes undermines the efficacy of the service's interventions (Brown, 2000).

What is the message to a perpetrator and his victim if the conference facilitator and participating family members refuse to challenge his use of power and control tactics? If threats are made or violence is used, what should the facilitator do to ensure the safety of the victim and other conference participants? If an appropriate approach is for the facilitator to abort the conference, what additional steps are put into place to ensure the safety of the victim after the conference is terminated? All too often, the perpetrator's violence appears neither to be confronted nor dealt with at conferences precisely because of the fear factor (Hooper, 2000). Alternatively, barring known batterers from a conference calls into question the utility of holding a conference at all.

Craig Manukau: A Cautionary Note About a Little Boy

A final caution about Family Group Conferences can be found in the Report of the Commissioner of Children on the Death of Craig Manukau (Hassall, 1993). Craig was kicked to death by his father on the 18th of November 1992. He had attended a dance despite his father having told him he wasn't allowed to go. In his videotaped confession, Craig's father asserted that he hadn't intended to kill the boy, but 'he was never going to dance again'. During this incident Craig's mother testified that she sat in the kitchen with the radio turned up, banging her head against the wall. A jury acquitted her of manslaughter on the basis of Battered Women's Syndrome.

Over the two years since Craig had come to the attention of the then named Children Young Persons Service (now CYFS) issues involving his safety had been seen as secondary to the primary focus, 'relationship problems' between his parents (Hassall, 1993: 5). Even after Craig was known to be afraid of his father and it was reported that he had recently been 'given a hiding', no medical reports were called for, no formal investigations were initiated. It was felt that Craig and his siblings would be at greater risk of violence from their father if anything but informal processes were used. There had been a whanau hui (a meeting of Craig's extended family) but there was no record of what was discussed or decided at it. The Child Protection Coordinator on Craig's case was committed to the principle of 'the least intrusive action' (Hassall, 1993: 7).

In the two years prior to his death, Craig had been the subject of at least two Family Group Conferences. But Craig's safety and his father's violence were never the central issues of those conferences. Despite worries that Craig was being abused and knowledge that he was afraid of his father, the first notification about Craig was about his behavioural problems, i.e. his stealing, his swearing, refusal to work at school, poor achievement, and his relationship with his mother. Relationship issues between the parents, the whanau history of drug and alcohol abuse, unemployment and criminal behaviour, the desire to develop/maintain trust between the public health nurse and Craig's mother were also focuses of the conference. As the Commissioner for Children commented:

It is not that other considerations should be ignored but bitter experience shows that over time these considerations tend to take over. The whole purpose of the intervention which is the safety of the child is lost sight of unless the social worker or some other competent person with the power to return proceedings to this focus does not deliberately and repeatedly bring forward the slogan, 'The child must be made safe now'. (Hassall, 1993: 16)

In the end, the Commissioner concluded that Craig's death was 'foreseeable and possibly preventable' (Hassall, 1993: 12). These words echo the conclusions of at least two more recent New Zealand inquiries into the deaths of children at the hands of their caregivers, the Bristol children (Davison, 1994)[7] and James Whakaruru (McLay, 2000). It behoves us to learn from these cases to 'get it right, right away'. Not to be captured by 'the rule of optimism', the expectation held by Craig's social worker and others that things would work out well, despite all the evidence of abuse to the contrary (Hassall, 1993: 20).

There was no monitoring by CYPS in the eight months from the second Family Group Conference until Craig's death. Lack of statutorily mandated monitoring of conference plans is an all too common CYFS resourcing problem, among a myriad of others (Brown, 2000). And it came out in trial testimony that whanau conference participants had themselves witnessed and/or experienced Craig's father's abuse and were very reluctant to challenge him. But perhaps the most significant comment for the purposes of this chapter is found in the Commissioner's discussion of the results of Craig's first Family Group Conference which was held on the 20th of December 1991. He concluded:

Through lack of preparation, lack of an understanding of its purpose and a lack of awareness of the options available, the first Family Group Conference may have achieved nothing except to warn those members of the whanau with a mind to, to better conceal their activities and to convince them of the New Zealand Children and Young Persons Service's ineffectiveness. It may also have discouraged the social worker and whanau members from taking this route again ... A failed Family Group Conference may not simply be ineffective but by demonstrating its failure may discourage future efforts to protect the children. (Hassall, 1993: 9–10)

The Community Group Conferencing Process in Australia

In Queensland and in other states of Australia, the New Zealand Family Group Conferencing process has been adapted into a process known as the Community Group Conference. The Australian community group conference posits a communitarian approach to offender accountability. Relative to its New Zealand counterpart, the results have been nothing short of spectacular, with high levels of participant satisfaction and very low reoffending rates (Palk et al, 1998).

The Australian community conference relies on the notion of a family, or community of people with shared values, who are capable of exercising surveillance and control over the offender's future behaviour (Stubbs, 1995). The conferencing process is a reflection of reintegrative shaming proposed by Braithwaite who purports to approach the issue of what causes offending from a different direction. Rather than examining why people offend, Braithwaite argues that we must explore what factors prevent the majority of people from offending (Braithwaite, 1989).

Braithwaite argues that there are two components which stop most people offending. The first is that people in the community do not offend because of their private sense of right or wrong. As a result of their 'conscience' they would be personally ashamed if they offended or victimized others. The second reason people do not offend is because they would experience embarrassment or shame in the eyes of those they care about. According to Braithwaite the key ingredient in preventing offending is 'shaming' and he argues that those countries which have low reoffending rates utilize shaming in a positive way to bring about change.

A crucial distinction is drawn between reintegrative and disintegrative or stigmatizing shaming. Reintegration requires expressions of community disapproval of the behaviour followed by gestures of reacceptance of the offenders back into the community. The aim is to reaffirm that the offender is part of a community that cares for him or her despite the community's disapproval of his or her behaviour. This can occur only if the shaming takes place in a context of close community attachment, interdependency and respect (Braithwaite, 1989).

It is claimed by Braithwaite that the existing retributive system stigmatizes offenders. The use of prisons is seen as the ultimate form of disintegration of families and communities. Separating the offender from his or her support erects barriers against those people who could assist the offender to change and this carries with it the risk that the offender will seek approval from those who are also outcasts. This leads to gang activity and entering of criminal 'subcultures'.

Braithwaite and Pettit (1994) also reaffirm that crime is ultimately an attack on the rights of the victim. They emphasize that the criminal justice process must recognize this aspect of offending and place a greater emphasis on reparation for the damage done.

An important aspect of Braithwaite's work lies in its emphasis on the restoration of the victim and role of the community as a means of ensuring that offenders leave offending behind. The theory acts as a reminder of the importance of involving the community of the offender in determining what should happen as a result of the offending. This reflects something of the purpose of reintegrative shaming: to allow offenders to fully understand that although they have made mistakes they remain an integral part of their community. They are accepted even though their behaviour is not acceptable. The process allows families and communities to be involved in the process in a positive way.

However, as with all attempts to develop theories which aim to capture the diversity of human beings, it is difficult to establish an all-encompassing theory of why some people commit offences and others do not. As well, there is a vast array of offences and communities clearly vary in their responses to these offences, depending on social concepts about gender issues, family autonomy, and the use of violence to maintain those values.

A first difficulty lies in the definition of who is the offender's community. The usual definition relates to the offender's community of concern: those people who have a belief in the offender as a person and a willingness to support the offender during any meeting with the victim. Usually this is limited to family members and occasionally includes teachers or counselors working with the offender. However it may be that when working with teenage offenders, the most powerful influence is their peer group. This group does not 'cause' the crime but their influence acts as a life support system for the offending. The peer group supports the 'habit' by encouraging the offending.

This was graphically demonstrated in a colleague's dealings with a 17-year-old offender who identified his peer group as one factor contributing to his offending. At the end of a joint family session, the boy stated that he felt capable of standing up to peer pressure, this would not be a problem. Within two weeks of this joint meeting he was enticed by one of his colleagues to steal a car (Hooper, 2000). It is clear that a wider definition of community than those previously adopted needs to be explored.

The second difficulty is that these concepts of shaming require an integrated community. As we increasingly move about within our respective countries and overseas the concept of a close-knit community has become more problematic. The absence of a clearly defined community makes it more difficult to generate a clear community of concern. This is even more apparent when dealing with adult offenders. No longer do they necessarily have the support of parents or siblings as part of their network. In a Hamilton restorative justice pilot project the author was involved in, it was common for adult offenders to attend conferences with few support people. In the absence of support people, reintegration becomes a difficult task.

Most importantly in terms of domestic violence conferencing, the concept of reintegrative shaming requires a uniform community view of right and wrong. It operates on the assumption that there is a 'core consensus ... that compliance with the criminal law is an important social goal' (Braithwaite, 1989: 38). It therefore relies on an assumption that those offences which are criminalized are universally accepted to be wrong. This can create problems where there is no universal condemnation of a particular offence. One case in the Hamilton pilot project involved an assault by a father on his son. In this case the father struggled to acknowledge any form of embarrassment or shame for his actions. He did not appreciate that the assault on his son was wrong and neither did several of the other conference participants. Without community condemnation, a process relying on reintegrative shaming cannot operate effectively.

Community Group Conferencing and Domestic Violence

One concern about the conferencing process is the assumption that the offender in a domestic violence situation will be shamed into changing his behaviour. In domestic violence cases, the concept of reintegrative shaming posits the view that each member of the offender's community will accept that domestic violence is unacceptable (Stubbs, 1995). It needs to be acknowledged, however, that in New Zealand at present there is no such societal consensus about domestic violence. Instead, as already discussed, researchers have found that an offender's abusive behaviour takes place within a social context which often legitimizes, condones and even supports his use of violence. There is no reason to believe that violent men will readily be shamed into accepting that their violent acts are wrong. As well, the parties' families or communities may not be supportive of a victim's attempts to hold the perpetrator accountable for his actions.

In order to see the use of the conferencing model as appropriate in domestic violence cases, it is necessary to understand how a family or community seeks to 'explain' the occurrence or causes of abuse. Some of these explanations may attribute the responsibility for violence wholly, or in part, to the victim. She may be seen as provoking him by not living up to his expectations of her as a mother or a partner. Others may assume that the use of violence may, in certain circumstances, be an acceptable response to a conflict situation. To others, the violence may seem 'understandable' because of the perpetrator's jealousy or hurt pride or even because of his own apparent victimization as a result of racism, unemployment etc. In a recent worrying comment, Braithwaite himself posits that:

> With an incident of [stranger] violence at a pub, there may be a girlfriend who can commit to sorting out a relationship problem that was engendering jealousy. (Braithwaite, 1999b: 1748)

The perpetrator is solely responsible for his violence and his jealousy is not necessarily a symptom of a relationship problem which he and his girlfriend need to work on. His jealousy and his subsequent violence are the problems. They are power and control tactics which in all likelihood keep his girlfriend 'in her place' as well as serving as a convenient and societally condoned excuse for his pub violence.

Given that the conferencing model relies heavily on the participation of the victim's and offender's communities for solutions to the offending, the discourses of the community about gender roles and violence will influence the discussion of causes of the violence and proposals to resolve the abuse. The definition of causality clearly determines the options perceived as solutions.

The same issue arises in terms of the conference facilitators' discourses. For instance, if the facilitator is a social worker in New Zealand, s/he will be trained to assess risk of further violence against children in terms of the Manitoba Risk Estimation Instrument. That tool describes battered women who will not/cannot leave their abusers as 'co-perpetrators' of violence against their children in that they 'cause', or at least cannot prevent, their children witnessing their own abuse (Reid et al, 1996). The author, who has done extensive training of social workers about domestic violence, has often heard a battered woman described as both a 'hostage' and a 'co-perpetrator' in respect of the violence meted out against her. Similar results have been seen when the conference facilitators' analyses of violence involve the use of the conflict tactics scale, an instrument which counts 'slap for slap' but does not distinguish between violence used in a premeditated attack versus violence used in self-defence and does not count injury or fear of further violence as relevant factors in assessing who the more violent partner is (Busch & Robertson, 1997).[8] Even the Minnesota Multi-Phasic Instrument which is often used by custody evaluators to determine mental health issues of parents vying for custody has been critiqued for labeling women who are actually being stalked by their perpetrator partners as 'paranoid' (Walker, 2000).

If the community discourse about domestic violence sites the cause of abuse in the relationship between the partners, the conference outcomes will, in all likelihood, reflect commonly held justifications and excuses for violence, e.g. 'she provoked him', 'it takes two to tango', 'what can you expect from that family?' A focus on the relationship as the cause of violence fails to identify the ways in which social attitudes legitimize the use of power and control tactics, including male privilege and may fail to hold the perpetrator accountable for his violence.

Conciliation or reconciliation may be prioritized over the victim's need (and legal right) to safety. Given the high incidence of continuing abuse by perpetrators after separation, a focus on the relationship as the cause of the violence may lead to a minimization of the well-documented risks of separation violence once the relationship has broken down. In New Zealand, for example, approximately 40 percent of female homicide victims are killed by their estranged partners, typically during access changeover times (Davison, 1994). If the community believes that the violence will stop when she leaves, what safety mechanisms will be put into place to protect the victim from ongoing abuse during visitation arrangements? To illustrate, about five years ago the author was advocating for the New Zealand Government to fund professional supervised access sessions in situations where one of the parents had been violent to the other parent or to a child. The response of the then Minister of Justice to a question concerning this elicited the following response: 'Why would you need that? The couple's separated, aren't they?'

Finally, from my experiences in dealing with domestic violence cases, it may be that sometimes shaming will produce further alienation and more violence than integration. It may be dangerously naïve to believe that shaming and a process of apology and forgiveness will result in the perpetrator abandoning his use of violence. Can we believe that empowering the victim to describe the impacts of the violence on her and the children will engender a life-changing epiphany in the perpetrator? This assumption posits that the perpetrator does not already know the power of his violence, that he will be surprised and moved by the consequences of his actions.

From my experience in dealing with perpetrators' stopping violence groups, while this may occur, it is more likely that a perpetrator knows the power of his violence. He knows violence works, that it controls his victim's behaviour and typically results in her doing what he wants her to do. Or, that it punishes her for doing what he'd told her she couldn't do. It 'teaches her a lesson' for the future. One facilitator of an anti-violence program has commented to me that it can take six to eight weeks for perpetrators to move from feeling that they are the victims of their partners' 'nagging' or 'disobedience' or 'uncooperativeness' to accepting even partial blame or responsibility for their actions. A typical statement in groups is, 'I'm not a violent person/I'm not an abuser. But she made me so angry ...'.

There are repeated examples of the conferencing process producing greater risk of violence. For example, a Family Group Conference was held concerning whether a couple's children were in need of care and protection. The background to the conference was severe and repetitive physical and psychological violence against the then estranged female partner, often in the presence of the children. Many of the participants at the conference had witnessed the perpetrator's violence and also had direct experiences of his intimidatory behaviour. The central issue of the conference, however, was about whether the couple's children should be placed with other family members because the mother 'wasn't coping' with them.

In the initial stages of the conference, the male partner talked at length about how 'hopeless' the woman was as a wife, mother, and sexual partner. The conference facilitator then introduced the issue of his violence. Because of her fear, the woman's response was to state that the social worker had exaggerated the violence, that it was mutual, and when it wasn't, she provoked it by her actions. Interviewed later, the social worker advised the writer that this often happened at Family Group Conferences. Women recanted what they'd said during the conference preparation time after issues of violence were raised in the conference in the presence of their abusers.

This conference took a different turn, however, because the perpetrator's sister then stated that she had witnessed the violence against her sister-in-law and had herself been the target of her brother's physical and sexual violence. After the conference, the brother threatened the sister. He related that he had been very ashamed by what she'd said in front of their family and other respected community members. That it had been much worse for him than any of his previous appearances in court; in fact, it had been one of the worst experiences of his life. He clearly had gone through the shaming process in front of respected community members. But rather than being contrite, his statement to his sister was 'So I'm really going to get you now.' The outcome of that conference was that his estranged wife and children were no safer and his sister left town and went into hiding.

The Pennell and Burford Conferencing Model and Domestic Violence

Joan Pennell and Gale Burford have trialled the use of a family group conference model for child abuse and family violence cases in Newfoundland and Labrador. The results from 37 conferences are promising. They found that in the main the conferences enhanced family units, increased safety for families within the project, and reduced abuse for project children and women. Two important points emerged from the study. First, though the project primarily received referrals concerning child abuse and neglect, there was a backdrop of violence against women and cross-generational violence within the subject families. Second, a great deal of time and preparation went into planning the conferences to ensure the safety of participants. As Pennell and Burford state:

Given the extent of violence against child and adult family members, careful negotiations were crucial for ensuring that the right people were invited to the conferences, that family group and professional participants were adequately prepared for their roles at the conference, that necessary measures were put into place to protect participants, and that practical arrangements were made such as plans for travel to the conferences or a neutral place in which to hold the conferences. (Pennell & Burford, 2000a: 139)

Because of this careful planning, no violence occurred during the conferences and no violence was reported as a result of the conferences. Pre-conference meetings with the parties' support people ensured that the victim's supporters would be prepared to stand up for her against the perpetrator, if need be. Those meetings also revealed what gaps in safety might arise and allowed for the development of strategies to ensure safety. In addition, monitoring of the implementation of the plans reached by families and follow-up monitoring after a year were carried out. Unexpectedly but worthy of note, in those families where the conference plans had been carried out completely or at least partially implemented, families reported that the conferencing had made them 'better off'. In the few cases where the plans were not carried out at all, half the interviewees stated that the family was 'left the same or worse off'.

Under the Pennell and Burford model, the conferencing was one stage of a process of providing safety for women and children and enhancing their abilities to live without violence. Many of the victims already had protection orders in place and there was resort to the criminal justice system and Child Protection Services when the need arose, even after the conference had occurred. Indeed, the family case referrals were made by Child Protection Services and there was collaboration between government agencies and community groups throughout.

Conclusion

Sadly, the Canadian Government has ceased its commitment to the Pennell/Burford project. Reinforcing the fears of many who worry that restorative justice models provide 'cheap justice', the Canadian Government saw the project as too expensive and it was terminated. The approach, however, is an important contribution to bridging the hiatus between restorative justice proponents and battered women's advocates. Its emphasis on protection of victims through extensive pre-conference preparation, through ensuring that victims will not be isolated or silenced during conference, the researchers' willingness to use the criminal justice system's protections when necessary, their commitment to ongoing monitoring and evaluation of families who have been through the conferencing process – these demonstrate that restorative justice processes may be useful in some domestic violence cases, at a late stage, after safety issues have been dealt with, in conjunction with other measures also aimed at providing safety and autonomy for victims. The model demonstrates again the necessity for integrated, coordinated government and community responses to domestic violence.

One of the strengths of the Pennell and Burford model is its commitment to culturally appropriate processes to deal with violence. I support this commitment. While domestic violence may sometimes manifest itself in similar ways across ethnic lines, violence is often expressed in culturally specific ways and the meaning of and/or risks entailed in certain behaviours can only be fully understood by someone from within that cultural group. Because violence is socially constructed, moreover, the solutions to such violence must be found in the stories and values of the participants' cultures. Processes used by one cultural group are not necessarily appropriate in resolving issues which arise in other groups. Successes cannot be 'taken on the road' and tried out on totally disparate cultures. What works for Navajo or Maori is not necessarily exportable to resolve conflicts among Kosovarians or East Timorese. The processes are a reflection of cultural understandings and values. They cannot be separated from their cultural contexts without loss and disrespect to those cultures.

A Maori legal activist recently gave a lecture where he was asked about 'post-colonialism'. He raised his eyebrows and asked, 'Oh, have they gone then?' We need to watch out for manifestations of neo-colonialism even in this supposedly post-modernist, post-gendered, post-identity politics age.

In domestic violence literature, a cycle of assault, apology and forgiveness has long defined the 'cycle of violence'. It's time to envision new dance steps to the now discredited 'tango' of violence. John Braithwaite states that we need 'a culture of apology, rather than a culture of denial' (Braithwaite, 2000a:188) to effectively address domestic violence issues. I suggest that what is needed is the creation of a culture of safety.

Notes

1   The 1993 New Zealand Review of the Family Court recognized domestic violence as 'a reflection of power' and recommended that wherever it exists, 'mediation should be avoided by the judicial process as a legitimate means of dispute resolution'. This perspective has been carried forward into the most recently implemented criminal court-referred restorative justice pilot program announced in July 2000. Domestic violence offences have been

specifically excluded from the category of offences which the program will deal with.

2 In this chapter, I refer to the abused spouse as a 'victim'. I am aware that the term 'victim' does not encapsulate the entirety of this person's identity; s/he is clearly more than just a victim. Within the criminal justice context, however, I seek to differentiate between the violent offender and the target of his abuse. 'Target of abuse' seems inappropriate because it depersonalizes the recipient of the abuse. The use of the word 'complainant' is not always an accurate description as police often lay charges in domestic violence-related offences. So, reluctantly and with full awareness of the live debates about this issue, I employ the concept of 'victim'.

3 I use the words 'offender,' 'abuser', and 'perpetrator' interchangeably in this article. As well, I adopt the convention of referring to offenders as male and to adult victims as female. I recognize that there are male victims of domestic violence but as Gelles has stated: 'It is categorically false to imply that there are the same number of battered men as there are battered women. Although men and women may hit one another with about the same frequency, women inevitably suffer the greatest physical consequences of such violence. Women victims of intimate violence also suffer more emotional and psychological consequences than do men' (Gelles, 1994).

4 Regulation 27 Domestic Violence (Programmes) Regulations. The regulation states that 'Every programme that is designed for Maori or that will be provided in circumstances where the persons attending the programme are primarily Maori, must take into account Tikanga Maori, including (without limitation) the following Maori values and concepts:
   * Mana wahine (the prestige attributed to women)
   * Mana tane (the prestige attributed to men)
   * Tiaki tamariki (the importance of the safeguarding and rearing of children)
   * Whanaungatanga (family relationships and their importance)
   * Taha wairua (the spiritual dimension of a healthy person)
   * Taha hinengaro (the psychological dimension of a healthy person)
   * Taha Tinana (the physical dimension of a healthy person).

5 This comment was made by Heather McPherson, an experienced facilitator of Men's Stopping Violence groups at the Hamilton Abuse Intervention Project. In addition to sharing her experiences of such groups with me, I would like to thank Heather for reading and commenting on this chapter as it progressed through its various drafts.

6 Personal interview between Ruth Busch and a Care and Protection conference facilitator, February 1996.

7 For a fuller discussion of the events leading up to the deaths of the Bristol children, see R Busch and N Robertson, (1994) 'I Didn't Know Just How Far You Could Fight: Contextualising the Bristol Inquiry', 2 *Waikato Law Review*, 41.

8 Quoting from footnote 157 therein: 'The Conflict Tactics Scale asks how often in the past 6 months the respondent has used specific violent acts. Ellen Pence has illustrated the absurdity of this decontextualized approach by the hypothetical example of a man who had "grabbed his partner around the neck and is trying to throttle her". She "bites his arm in an attempt to make him loosen his grip". Under the Conflict Tactics Scale, the partners will be scored as equally violent.'

References

Aboriginal Family and Children's Services Legislative Review (1992) *Liberating Our Children, Liberating Our Nations* (report), Victoria, BC, Ministry of Social Services.

Aboriginal Justice Council (1999) *Our Mob Our Justice: Keeping the Vision Alive. The 1998 Monitoring Report of the Aboriginal Justice Council on the Recommendations of the Royal Commission into Aboriginal Deaths in Custody*, Perth, Aboriginal Justice Council Secretariat.

Aboriginal Women's Task Force and the Aboriginal Justice Council (1995) *A Whole Healing Approach to Family Violence*, Perth, Aboriginal Justice Council.

Abrams, K (1999) 'From autonomy to agency: feminist perspectives on self-direction', *William and Mary Law Review*, 40: 805–846.

Achilles, M & Zehr, H (2000) 'Restorative justice for crime victims: the promise, the challenge', in G Bazemore & M Schiff (eds) *Restorative and Community Justice: Cultivating Common Ground for Victims, Communities and Offenders*, Cincinnati, OH, Anderson Publishing.

Adams, D (1988) 'Treatment models of men who batter: a profeminist analysis', in K Yllö & M Bograd (eds) *Feminist Perspectives on Wife Abuse*, Newbury Park, CA; London, UK; New Delhi, India, Sage.

Adler, M, Hax, H, Stanley, J & Zhou, W (2000) *Coordinated Community Response to Domestic Violence in Three Maryland Communities*, Baltimore, MD, Southern Sociological Society.

Almeida, R V & Dolan-Delvecchio, K (1999) 'Addressing culture in batterers intervention: the Asian Indian community as an illustrative example', *Violence Against Women*, 5 (6): 65–83.

Ammons, Linda L (1995) 'Mules, madonnas, babies, bathwater, racial imagery and stereotypes: the African-American woman and the battered woman syndrome', *Wisconsin Law Review*, Sept–Oct (5): 1003–1080.

Anderson, V (1997) *A Woman Like You: The Face of Domestic Violence*, Seattle, WA, Seal Press.

Andrews, D A & Bonta, J (1994) *The Psychology of Criminal Conduct*, Cincinnati, OH, Anderson Publishing.

Andy Rowe Consultants Inc. (1997) 'Comparative cost and cost-effectiveness of family group decision making project: technical report', St. John's, NF, Andy Rowe Consultants Inc.

Arrigo, B & Scher, R (1998) 'Restoring justice for juveniles: a critical analysis of victim–offender mediation', *Justice Quarterly*, 14 (4): 629–666.

Asbury, J (1993) 'Violence in families of colour in the United States', in T P Hampton (ed) *Family Violence: Prevention and Treatment*, Newbury Park, CA, Sage.

Ashworth, Andrew (2000) 'Victims' rights, defendants' rights and criminal procedure', in A Crawford & J Goodey (eds) *Integrating a Victim Perspective Within Criminal Justice: International Debates*, Aldershot, Ashgate.

Astor, H (1991) 'Mediation and violence against women', paper prepared for the National Committee on Violence Against Women, Barton, ACT, Office of the Status of Women, Department of the Prime Minister and Cabinet.

—— (1994) 'Swimming against the tide: keeping violent men out of mediation', in J Stubbs (ed) *Women, Male Violence and the Law*, Sydney, Institute of Criminology.

Atkinson, J (1990) 'Violence against Aboriginal women: reconstitution of Aboriginal law', *Aboriginal Law Bulletin*, 2 (46): 69.

—— (1991) 'Stinkin' thinkin' – alcohol, violence and government responses', *Aboriginal Law Bulletin*, 3 (51): 811.

—— (1993) *The Political And the Personal: Racial Violence Against Aboriginal and Torres Strait Islander Women and Women of Non-English-Speaking-Backgrounds*, Canberra, National Committee on Violence and the Office of the Status of Women.

—— (1995a) 'Aboriginal people, domestic violence and the law: indigenous, alternative justice strategies', in D Lawrence (ed) *Future Directions: Proceedings of the Queensland Domestic Violence Conference*, Brisbane, Central Queensland University.

—— (1995b) 'Review – *Restorative Justice: Healing the Effects of Crime*', *Aboriginal Law Bulletin*, 3 (77): 21–22.

—— (1996) 'A nation is not conquered', *Aboriginal Law Bulletin*, 3 (80): 4–9.

Attwood, B & Markus, A, in collaboration with D Edwards & K Schilling (1997) *The 1967 Referendum, or, When Aborigines Didn't Get the Vote*, Canberra, Aboriginal Studies Press.

Australian Bureau of Statistics (1996) *Australia's Indigenous Youth: 1994 National Aboriginal and Torres Strait Islander Survey*, Canberra, Australian Bureau of Statistics.

Australian Law Reform Commission (1994) *Equality Before the Law: Justice for Women*, Sydney, Australian Law Reform Commission.

Bachman, R & Coker, A (1995) 'Police involvement in domestic violence: the interactive effects of victim injury, offender's history of violence and race', *Violence and Victims*, 10 (2): 91–106.

Baines, C T, Evans, P M & Neysmith, S M (1991) *Women's Caring: Feminist Perspectives on Social Welfare*, Toronto, McClelland & Stewart.

Bargen, J (1996), 'Kids, cops, courts, conferencing and children's rights: a note on perspectives', *Australian Journal of Human Rights*, 2 (2): 209–228.

—— (1998) (update for 1996–98), unpublished, on file with the author.

Barnett, Ola W & LaViolette, Alyce D (1993) *It Could Happen to Anyone: Why Battered Women Stay*, Newbury Park, CA, Sage Publications.

Bartlett, K T (1999) 'Feminism and family law', *Family Law Quarterly*, 33: 475–500.

Basher, Gill (1999) 'Children who talk on tape: the facts behind the pictures', *Social Work Now*, 12: 4–12.

Bazemore, G (1998) 'Restorative justice and earned redemption: communities, victims and offender reintegration', *American Behavioral Scientist*, 41 (6): 768–813.

(2000a) 'Community justice and a vision of collective efficacy: The case of restorative conferencing', in National Institute of Justice (ed) *Criminal Justice 2000*, 3, Washington DC, US Department of Justice.

(2000b) 'Rock and roll, restorative justice, and the continuum of the real world: a response to "purism" in operationalizing restorative justice', *Journal of Contemporary Criminal Justice*.

Bazemore, G & Dooley, M (2000) 'Social relationships, offenders and reintegration', in G Bazemore & M Schiff (eds) *Restorative and Community Justice: Cultivating Common Ground for Victims, Communities and Offenders*, Cincinnati, OH, Anderson Publishing.

Bazemore, G & Schiff, M (2000) *Restorative and Community Justice: Cultivating Common Ground for Victims, Communities and Offenders*, Cincinnati, OH, Anderson Publishing.

Bazemore, G & Terry, C (1997) 'Developing delinquent youth: a reintegrative model for rehabilitation and a new role for the juvenile justice system', *Child Welfare*, 74 (5): 665–716.

Bazemore, G & Umbreit, M (1995) 'Rethinking the sanctioning function in juvenile court: retributive or restorative responses to youth crime', *Crime and Delinquency*, 41 (3): 296–316.

(2001) 'A comparison of four restorative conferencing models', *Office of Juvenile Justice and Delinquency Prevention Bulletin*, February, Washington, US Department of Justice.

Bazemore, G & Walgrave, L (1999) *Restorative Juvenile Justice: Repairing the Harm of Youth Crime*, Monsey, NY, Criminal Justice Press.

Beaudry, M (1985) *Battered Women*, L Huston & M Heap trans., Montreal, Black Rose.

Behrendt, L (1995) *Aboriginal Dispute Resolution*, Sydney, The Federation Press.

Berndt, R M & Berndt, C H (1981) *The World of the First Australians*, Sydney, Lansdowne Press.

Blackbear, T (1991) 'Beyond the shelter doors: making the connections', in conference proceedings, *Alternatives: Directions in the Nineties to End the Abuse of Women*, Winnipeg, Manitoba, Educational Committee Against the Abuse of Women (Manitoba) Inc.

Blagg, H (1997) 'A just measure of shame? Aboriginal youth and conferencing in Australia', *British Journal of Criminology*, 37 (4): 481–506.

(1998a) 'Restorative visions and restorative justice practices: conferencing, ceremony and reconciliation in Australia', *Current Issues in Criminal Justice*, 10 (1): 5.

(1998b) *Working With Adolescents To Prevent Domestic Violence: Phase 2 the Indigenous Rural Model*, Canberra, Attorney General's Department, National Crime Prevention.

(1999) *'It Breaks All Law': Crisis Intervention in Aboriginal Family Violence. Report*, Perth, Domestic Violence Prevention Unit.

(2000a) *Models Of Intervention at the Point of Crisis in Aboriginal Family Violence: Summary Report*, Canberra, Partnerships Against Domestic Violence/Office of the Status of Women.

(2000b) *Models Of Intervention at the Point of Crisis in Aboriginal Family Violence: Strategies and Models for Western Australia*, Canberra, Partnerships Against Domestic Violence/Office of the Status of Women.

(2001) 'Aboriginal youth and restorative justice: critical notes from the frontier', in A Morris & G Maxwell (eds) *Conferencing, Mediation and Circles*, Oxford, Hart Publishing.

Bolger, Audrey (1991) *Aboriginal Women and Violence*, Darwin, Australian National University, North Australia Research Unit.

Bonvillain, N (1989) 'Gender relations in Native North America', *American Indian Culture Research Journal*, 13: 1–28.

Bopp, J & Bopp, M (1997) *At the Time of Disclosure*, Ontario, Solicitor General of Canada.

Bowen, Helen & Consedine, Jim (1999) *Restorative Justice: Contemporary Themes and Practices*, Lyttleton, Ploughshares Publications.

Bowker, Lee (1983) *Beating Wife-beating*, Lexington, MA; Toronto, Canada, Lexington Books.

(1998) 'On the difficulty of eradicating masculine violence', in L H Bowker (ed) *Masculinities and Violence*, Newbury Park, CA; London, UK; New Delhi, India, Sage.

Bowman, C G (1992) 'The arrest experiments: a feminist critique', *Journal of Criminal Law and Criminology*, 83: 201–208.

(1994) 'The arrest experiments: a feminist critique', in R Monk (ed) *Taking Sides: Clashing Views on Controversial Issues in Crime and Criminology*, Gilford, CT, Dushkin Publishing Group.

Braithwaite, John (1989) *Crime, Shame and Reintegration*, Cambridge, Cambridge University Press.

(1995) 'Inequality and republican criminology', in J Hagan & R Peterson (eds) *Crime and Equality*, Palo Alto, Stanford University Press.

(1999a) 'Restorative justice: assessing optimistic and pessimistic accounts', in M Tonry (ed) *Crime and Justice, A Review of Research*, 25, Chicago, University of Chicago Press.

(1999b) 'A future where punishment is marginalised: realistic or utopian?', *UCLA Law Review*, 46: 1727–1750.

(2000a) 'Restorative justice and social change', *Saskatchewan Law Review*, 63: 185–194.

(2000b) 'The new regulatory state and the transformation of criminology', *British Journal of Criminology*, 40 (2): 222–238.

(2001) *Restorative Justice and Responsive Regulation*, New York, Oxford University Press.

Braithwaite, John & Daly, Kathleen (1994) 'Masculinities, violence and communitarian control', in T Newburn & E A Stanko (eds) *Just Boys Doing Business? Men, Masculinities, and Crime*, London, Routledge.

Braithwaite, John & Parker, Christine (1999) 'Restorative justice is republican justice', in Lode Walgrave & Gordon Bazemore (eds) *Restoring Juvenile Justice: An Exploration of the Restorative Justice Paradigm for Reforming Juvenile Justice*, Monsey, NY, Criminal Justice Press.

Braithwaite, John & Pettit, Phillip (1994) 'Republican criminology and victim advocacy', *Law and Society Review*, 28 (4): 764–776.

(1990) *Not Just Deserts: A Republican Theory of Criminal Justice*, Oxford, Clarendon Press.

Braithwaite, John & Roche, D (2000) 'Responsibility and restorative justice', in G Bazemore & M Schiff (eds) *Restorative and Community Justice: Cultivating Common Ground for Victims, Communities and Offenders*, Cincinatti, OH, Anderson Publishing.

Brewster, S (1997) *To Be an Anchor in the Storm: A Guide for Families and Friends of Abused Women*, New York, Ballantine.

Broadhurst, R (1987) 'The imprisonment of Aboriginal people in Western Australia', in K Hazlehurst (ed) *Ivory Scales: Black Australians and the Law*, Sydney, University of New South Wales Press.

Brooks, Lyn (undated) 'The impact on Inuit women of gender bias in the justice system', Canada, The Status of Women Council of the North West Territories, on file with the author.

Brown, J (1994) 'The use of mediation to resolve criminal cases: A procedural critique', *Emory Law Journal*, 43: 1247–1309.

Brown, M (2000) *Care and Protection is About Adult Behaviour: The Ministerial Review of the Department of Child, Youth and Family Services*, Wellington, Ministry of Social Policy.

Brown, W (1991) 'Feminist hesitations, postmodern exposures', *Differences: A Journal of Feminist Cultural Studies*, 3 (1): 63–84.

Browne, A (1995) 'Reshaping the rhetoric: the nexus of violence, poverty, and minority status in the lives of women and children in the United States', *Georgetown Journal on Fighting Poverty*, 3 (1): 17–23.

Bumiller, Kristin (1990) 'Fallen angels: the representation of violence against women in legal culture', *International Journal of the Sociology of Law*, 18: 125–142.

Burbank, V (1988) *Aboriginal Adolescence: Maidenhood in an Australian Community*, New Brunswick, Rutgers University Press.

(1994) *Fighting Women: Anger and Aggression in Aboriginal Australia*, Berkeley, CA, University of California Press.

Burford, G (1990) *Assessing teamwork: A comparative study of group home teams in Newfoundland and Labrador*, unpublished PhD dissertation, University of Stirling, Scotland.

Burford, G & Casson, S (1989) 'Including families in residential work: educational and agency tasks', *British Journal of Social Work*, 19 (1): 19–37.

Burford, G & Pennell, J (1995) 'The family group decision making project: an innovation in child and family welfare', in Burt Galaway & Joe Hudson (eds) *Canadian Child Welfare: Research and Policy Implications*, Toronto, ON, Thompson Educational Publications.

Burford, G & Pennell, J (1998a) 'Family group decision making project: outcome report volume I', St. John's, NF, Memorial University of Newfoundland.

(1998b) 'Family group decision making project: outcome report volume II', St. John's, NF, Memorial University of Newfoundland.

Burford, G, Pennell, J & MacLeod, S (1999) 'Family group decision making', in B R Compton & Burt Galaway (eds) *Social Work Processes* (6th ed), Pacific Grove, CA, Brooks/Cole.

Busch, R (1994) 'An analysis of New Zealand judges' attitudes towards domestic violence', in J Stubbs (ed) *Women, Male Violence and the Law*, Sydney, Institute of Criminology.

(1995) 'Safeguarding the welfare of children', *Butterworths Mental Health and the Law Bulletin*, 4: 47–52.

Busch, R & Robertson, N (1994) 'Ain't no mountain high enough to keep me from getting to you: an analysis of the Hamilton Abuse Intervention Project', in J Stubbs (ed) *Women, Male Violence and the Law*, Sydney, Institute of Criminology.

(1997) 'The gap goes on: an analysis of issues under the Domestic Violence Act', *NZ Universities Law Review*, 17: 337–378.

(2000) 'Innovative approaches to child custody and domestic violence in New Zealand: the effects of law reform on the discourses of battering', in R Geffner, P Jaffe & M Sudermann (eds) *Children Exposed to Domestic Violence: Current Issues in Research, Intervention, Prevention and Policy Development*, New York, The Haworth Press.

Busch, R, Robertson, N & Lapsley, H (1992) *Protection From Family Violence: A Study of Protection Orders under the Domestic Protection Act*, Wellington, Victims Task Force.

Bush, Diana & O'Reilly, Barbara (1998) 'Creating magic moments for children and families', *Social Work Now*, 11: 15–19.

Bush-Baskette, S R (1998) 'The war on drugs as a war against black women', in S L Miller (ed) *Crime Control and Women*, Thousand Oaks, CA, Sage.

Bushie, Berma (1997) 'A personal journey', in *The Four Circles of Hollow Water*, Aboriginal Peoples Collection, Aboriginal Corrections Policy Unit, Hull, Quebec, Supply and Services Canada (JS5-1/15-1997E).

(1999) 'Community holistic circle healing: a community approach', proceedings of the Building Strong Partnerships for Restorative Practices Conference, Vermont Department of Corrections and Real Justice, Burlington, Vermont.

Butler, S (1978) *Conspiracy of Silence: the Trauma of Incest*, San Francisco, New Glide.

Buzawa, Eva & Buzawa, Carl (1996a) *Do Arrests and Restraining Orders Work?*, Thousand Oaks, CA, Sage.

Buzawa, Eva & Buzawa, Carl (eds) (1996b) *Domestic Violence: The Criminal Justice Response*, Newbury Park, CA, Sage.

Buzawa, Eva, Hotaling, G T, Klein, A, & Byrne, J (1999) 'Response to Domestic Violence in a Pro-Active Court Setting: Final Report', *The NIJ Research Review*, 1 (3), Rockville, US Department. of Justice, #95-IJ-CX-0027.

Callahan, M (1993) 'Feminist approaches: women recreate child welfare', in B Wharf (ed) *Rethinking Child Welfare in Canada*, Toronto, McClelland & Stewart.

Cameron, G (1990) 'The potential of informal social support strategies in child welfare', in G Cameron & M Rothery (eds) *Child Maltreatment: Expanding Our Concept of Helping*, Hillsdale, NJ, Lawrence Erlbaum.

Campbell, Beatrix (1993) *Goliath: Britain's Dangerous Places*, London, Methuen.

Campbell, Jacquelyn C (1995) 'Homicide of and by battered women', in Jacquelyn C Campbell (ed) *Assessing Dangerousness: Violence by Sexual Offenders, Batterers and Child Abusers*, Thousand Oaks, CA, Sage.

Caplow, T & Simon, J (1999) 'Understanding prison policy and population trends', in M Tonry & J Petersilia (eds) *Prisons: crime and justice*, Chicago, Ill., University of Chicago Press.

Carbonatto, Helene (1994) 'Dilemmas in the criminalization of spousal abuse', *Social Policy Journal of New Zealand*, 2, 21–31.

(1995) 'Expanding intervention options for spousal abuse: the use of restorative justice', *Occasional Papers in Criminology New Series No. 4*, Wellington, New Zealand, Institute of Criminology, Victoria University of Wellington.

(1998) 'The criminal justice response to domestic violence in New Zealand', *Criminology Aotearoa/New Zealand: A Newsletter from the Institute of Criminology, Victoria University of Wellington, No. 10*, 7–8.

Carrillo, R & Goubaud-Reyna, R (1998) 'Clinical treatment of Latino domestic violence offenders', in R Carrillo & J Tello (eds) *Family Violence and Men of Color: Healing the Wounded Male Spirit*, New York, Springer.

CERD/C/56/Misc.42/rev.3, 2000 (United Nations Document).

Chantrill, P (1997) 'The Kowanyama Justice Group: a study of the achievements and constraints on local justice administration in a remote Aboriginal community', paper presented to the Australian Institute of Criminology's occasional seminar series.

Chaudhuri, M & Daly, Kathleen (1992) 'Do restraining orders help? Battered women's experience with male violence and legal process', in Eva Buzawa & Carl Buzawa (eds) *Domestic Violence: The Changing Criminal Justice Response*, Westport, CT, Auburn House.

Chesney-Lind, M (1998) 'Foreword', in S L Miller (ed) *Crime Control and Women*, Thousand Oaks, CA, Sage.

Chilton, R & Datesman, S K (1987) 'Gender, race, and crime: an analysis of urban trends, 1960–1980', *Gender and Society*, 1: 152–171.

Christie, Nils (1977) 'Conflicts as Property', *British Journal of Criminology*, 17: 1–26.

Clarke, S & Varos, G (1995) *Kimberley Regional Domestic Violence Plan*, Perth, Domestic Violence Prevention Unit.

Clear, T & Karp, D (1999) *The Community Justice Ideal: Preventing Crime and Achieving Justice*, Boulder, CO, Westview Press.

Cobb, S (1997) 'The domestication of violence in mediation', *Law and Society Review*, 31 (3): 397–440.

Cohen, Stan (1985) *Visions of Social Control*, Cambridge, UK, Polity Press.

(1992) 'Heat of passion and wife killing: men who batter/men who kill', *Southern California Review of Law and Women's Studies*, 2: 71–130.

Coker, D (1999) 'Enhancing autonomy for battered women: lessons from Navajo peacemaking', *UCLA Law Review*, 47 (1): 1–111.

(2000) 'Shifting power for battered women: law, material resources, and poor women of color', *U.C. Davis Law Review*, 33: 1009–1055.

(2001) 'Crime control and feminist law reform in domestic violence law: a critical review', *Buffalo Criminal Law Review*, 4 (2): 801–860.

Connolly, Marie (1994) 'An act of empowerment: The Children, Young Persons and Their Families Act (1989)', *British Journal of Social Work*, 24: 87–100.

Connolly, M & McKenzie, M (1999) *Effective Participatory Practice: Family Group Conferencing in Child Protection*, Hawthorne, NY, Walter de Gruyter Inc.

Corcoran, L & Melamed, J (1990) 'From coercion to empowerment: spousal abuse and mediation', *Mediation Quarterly*, 7: 303.

Cornell, D (1996) *The Imaginary Domain*, New York, Routledge.

Coumarelos, Christine & Allen, Jacqui (1998) 'Predicting violence against women: the 1996 Women's Safety Survey', *Crime and Justice Bulletin*, 42, NSW Bureau of Crime Statistics and Research.

(1999) 'Predicting women's response to violence: the 1996 Women's Safety Survey', *Crime and Justice Bulletin*, 47, NSW Bureau of Crime Statistics and Research.

Crawford, A (1997) *The Local Governance of Crime: Appeals to Community and Partnerships*, Oxford, Clarendon Press.

(2000a) 'Introduction', in A Crawford & J Goodey (eds) *Integrating a Victim Perspective into the Criminal Justice System: International Debates*, Aldershot, Ashgate.

(2000b) 'Salient themes towards a victim perspective and the limitations of restorative justice: some concluding comments', in A Crawford & J Goodey (eds) *Integrating a Victim Perspective into the Criminal Justice System International Debates*, Aldershot, Ashgate.

Crenshaw, K (1991) 'Mapping the margins: intersectionality, identity politics, and violence against women of color', *Stanford Law Review*, 43: 1241–1299.

Crenshaw, K (1994) 'Mapping the margins: intersectionality, identity politics, and violence against women of color', in M Fineman & R Mykitiuk (eds) *The Public Nature of Private Violence*, New York, Routledge.

Crime Research Centre & Donovan Research (2000) *A National Survey Of Young People's Attitudes To Violence*, Canberra, Attorney General's Department, National Crime Prevention.

Crime Research Centre (1995) *Aboriginal Youth and the Juvenile Justice System of Western Australia*, Perth, Department of Aboriginal Affairs.

Cunneen, C (1997) 'Community conferencing and the fiction of indigenous control', *Australian and New Zealand Journal of Criminology*, 30 (3): 292–311.

(1999) 'Diversion and best practice for indigenous people: a non-indigenous view', paper presented to the Best Practice in Corrections for Indigenous People Conference, Adelaide, Australian Institute of Criminology and Department for Corrections, South Australia.

(2001) 'Reparations and restorative justice: responding to the gross violations of human rights', in Heather Strang & John Braithwaite (eds) *Restorative Justice and Civil Society*, Cambridge, Cambridge University Press.

Cunneen, C & Kerley, K (1995) 'Indigenous women and criminal justice: some comments on the Australian situation', in K Hazlehurst (ed) *Perceptions of Justice*, Aldershot, Avebury.

Cunneen, C & Macdonald, D (1996) *Keeping Aboriginal and Torres Strait Islander People Out of Custody: An Evaluation of the Implementation of the Royal Commission into Aboriginal Deaths in Custody*, Canberra, Aboriginal and Torres Strait Islander Commission.

Currie, D H (1993) 'Battered women and the state: from the failure of theory to a theory of failure', in K Faith & D Currie (eds) *Seeking Shelter: A State of Battered Women*, Vancouver, Collective Press.

Dalai Lama (1999) *Ethics for the New Millennium*, New York, Riverhead Books.

Daly, Kathleen (1989) 'Criminal justice ideologies and practices in different voices: Some feminist questions about justice', *International Journal of the Sociology of Law*, 17 (1): 1–18.

(1994a) *Gender, Crime, and Punishment*, New Haven, CT, Yale University Press.

(1994b) 'Men's violence, victim advocacy, and feminist redress', *Law and Society Review*, 28(4): 777–786.

(1997) 'Different ways of conceptualising sex/gender in feminist theory and their implications for criminology', *Theoretical Criminology*, 1 (1): 25–51.

(2000a) 'Restorative justice in diverse and unequal societies', *Law in Context*, 17 (1): 167–190. (http://www.gu.edu.au/school/ccj/kdaly.html)

(2000b) 'Revisiting the relationship between retributive and restorative justice', in Heather Strang & John Braithwaite (eds) *Restorative Justice: From Philosophy to Practice*, Aldershot, Dartmouth. (http://www.gu.edu.au/school/ccj/kdaly.html)

(2002) 'Restorative justice: the real story', *Punishment and Society*, 4 (1) (in press). (http://www.gu.edu.au/school/ccj/kdaly.html)

Daly, Kathleen & Chesney-Lind, M (1988) 'Feminism and criminology', *Justice Quarterly*, 5 (4): 497–538.

Daly, Kathleen & Hayes, H (2001) 'Restorative justice and conferencing in Australia', *Trends and Issues in Crime and Criminal Justice*, 186: 1–6, Canberra, Australian Institute of Criminology. (http://www.aic.gov.au/publications/tandi/tandi186.html)

(2002) 'Restorative justice and conferencing' (forthcoming), in A Graycar & P Grabosky (eds) *The Cambridge handbook of Australian criminology*, Cambridge, Cambridge University Press. (http://www.gu.edu.au/school/ccj/kdaly.html)

Daly, Kathleen & Immarigeon, R (1998) 'The past, present, and future of restorative justice: some critical reflections', *Contemporary Justice Review*, 1 (1): 21–45.

Daly, Kathleen & Maher, L (1998) 'Crossroads and intersections: building from feminist critique', in Kathleen Daly & L Maher (eds) *Criminology at the Crossroads: Feminist Readings in Crime and Justice*, New York, Oxford University Press.

Daly, Kathleen & Stephens, Deborah (1995) 'The "dark" figure of criminology: towards a black and multi-ethnic feminist agenda for theory and research', in Nicole Rafter & Frances Heidensohn (eds) *International Feminist Perspectives in Criminology: Engendering a Discipline*, Buckingham, Open University Press.

Davies, Jill, Lyon, Eleanor & Monti-Catania, Dianne (1998) *Safety Planning with Battered Women: Complex Lives/Difficult Choices*, Thousand Oaks, CA, Sage.

Davies, M. (1997) 'Taking the inside out: sex and gender in the legal subject', in N Naffine & R J Owens (eds) *Sexing the Subject of Law*, Sydney, LBC Information Services, Sweet & Maxwell.

Davison, R (1994) *Report of Inquiry into Family Court Proceedings Involving Christine Madeleine Bristol and Alan Robert Bristol*, Wellington, Department of Justice.

DeKeseredy, W S (1990) 'Male peer support and woman abuse: the current state of knowledge', *Sociological Focus*, 23 (2): 129–139.

Delgado, R (2000) 'Goodbye to Hammerabi: concerns about restorative justice', *Stanford Law Review*, 52 (4), 751.

Department of Aboriginal and Torres Strait Islander Policy and Development (2000) *Aboriginal and Torres Strait Islander Women's Task Force on Violence Report*, 2nd printing, Brisbane.

Dignan, Jim (1999) 'The Crime and Disorder Act and the prospects for restorative justice', *Criminal Law Review* (January), 48–60.

Dobash, R E & Dobash, R P (1979) *Violence Against Women: A Case Against the Patriarchy*, New York, Free Press.

(1992) *Women, Violence and Social Change*, New York, Routledge.

(1998) 'Violent men and violent contexts', in R E Dobash & R P Dobash (eds) *Rethinking Violence Against Women*, Newbury Park, CA, Sage.

(1999a) 'Criminal justice for men who assault their partners', in C Hollin (ed) *Handbook of Offender Assessment and Treatment*, Chichester, John Wiley & Sons.

(1999b) 'A research evaluation of British programmes for violent men', *Journal of Social Policy*, 28 (2): 205–233.

Dobash, R E, Dobash R P, Cavanagh, K & Lewis R (1998) 'Separate and intersecting realities: a comparison of men's and women's accounts of violence against women', *Violence Against Women*, 4 (4): 382–414.

(2000) *Changing violent men*, Thousand Oaks, CA, Sage.

Dodson, P (1991) *Regional Report of Inquiry into Underlying Issues in Western Australia*, Vol. 1, Canberra, Australian Government Printing Service.

Drummond, S G (1999) *Incorporating the Familiar: An Investigation into Legal Sensibilities in Nunavik*, Montreal & Kingston, McGill-Queen's University Press.

Duff, R A (1992) 'Alternatives to punishment – or alternative punishments?', in W Cragg (ed) *Retributivism and Its Critics*, Stuttgart, Franz Steiner.

(1996) 'Penal communications: Recent work in the philosophy of punishment', in M Tonry (ed) *Crime and Justice: A Review of Research*, 20, Chicago, University of Chicago Press, 1–97

(2001) 'Restoration and retribution', paper presented to Cambridge Seminar on Restorative Justice, 12–13 May, Toronto.

Duran, E & Duran, B (1995) *Native American Postcolonial Psychology*, Albany, NY, SUNY Press.

Duran, E, Duran, B, Woodis, W & Woodis, P (1998) 'A postcolonial perspective on domestic violence in Indian country', in R Carrillo & J Tello (eds) *Family Violence and Men of Color: Healing the Wounded Male Spirit*, New York, Springer.

Dutton, D G (1995) *The Domestic Assault of Women: Psychological and Criminal Perspectives*, Vancouver, Canada, UBC Press.

Dutton, D & Golant, S (1995) *The Batterer: A Psychological Profile*, New York, Basic Books.

Earle, T H (1998) 'Through a whole new looking glass: questions of liberty and justice and all', paper presented at Executive Sessions on Sentencing and Corrections, National Institute of Justice, Washington DC, US Department of Justice.

Edleson, J L (1999) 'The overlap between child maltreatment and woman battering', *Violence Against Women*, 5 (2): 134–154.

Edleson, J L & Tolman, R M (1992) *Intervention for Men Who Batter: An Ecological Approach*, Newbury Park, CA, Sage.

Eisenstein, H (1983) *Contemporary Feminist Thought*, Boston, G K Hall.

Elam, D (1994) *Feminism and Deconstruction*, New York, Routledge.

Erez, E & Belknap, J (1998) 'In their own words: battered women's assessment of the criminal processing system's responses', *Violence and Victims*, 13 (3): 251–268.

Espenoza, C M (1999) 'No relief for the weary: VAWA relief denied for battered immigrants lost in the intersections', *Marquette Law Review*, 83: 163–220.

Estrich, S (1986) 'Rape', *Yale Law Journal*, 95 (6): 1087–1184.

Fagan, J (1993) 'Social structure and spouse assault', in B Frost (ed) *The Socio-Economics of Crime and Justice*, Toronto, M E Sharpe.

Fedders, Barbara (1997) 'Lobbying for mandatory-arrest policies: race, class and the politics of the battered women's movement', *New York University Review of Law and Social Change*, 33: 281–300.

Feld, B (1999) 'Rehabilitation, retribution and restorative justice: alternative conceptions of juvenile justice', in G Bazemore & L Walgrave (eds), *Restorative Juvenile Justice: Repairing the Harm of Youth Crime*, Monsey, NY, Criminal Justice Press.

Fellows, M L and Razack, S (1998) 'The race to innocence: confronting hierarchical relations among women', *Journal of Gender, Race and Justice*, 1: 335–352.

Fenton, Z E (1999) 'Mirrored silence: reflections on judicial complicity in private violence', *Oregon Law Review*, 78: 995–1060.

Fergusson, Dave (1998) 'The Christchurch Health and Development Study: an overview and some key findings', *Social Policy Journal of New Zealand*, 10: 154–176.

Ferrante, A, Morgan, F, Indermaur, D & Harding, H (1996) *Measuring the Extent of Domestic Violence*, Sydney, Hawkins Press.

Ferraro, K J (1989) 'The legal response to woman battering in the United States', in J Hanmer, J Radford & E Stanko (eds) *Women, Policing, and Male Violence: International Perspectives*, London, UK; New York, NY, Routledge.

Fields, M D (1994) 'Criminal justice responses to violence against women', in A Duff, S Marshall, R E Dobash & R P Dobash (eds) *Penal Theory and Practice: Tradition and Innovation in Criminal Justice*, Manchester, UK, Manchester University Press.

Finckenauer, J & Gavin, P (1999) *Scared Straight: The Panacea Phenomenon Revisited*, Prospect Heights, IL, Waveland Press.

Fineman, M A (1995) *The Neutered Mother, the Sexual Family and Other Twentieth Century Tragedies*, London, UK; New York, NY, Routledge.

Fischer, K, Vidmar, N & Ellis, R (1993) 'The culture of battering and the role of mediation in domestic violence cases', *Southern Methodist University Law Review*, 46: 2117–2174.

Fontana, V & Besharov, D (1996) *The Maltreated Child: The Maltreatment Syndrome in Children*, Springfield, IL, Charles C. Thomas Publishing.

Fontes, Lisa Aronson (1997) 'Conducting ethical cross-cultural research on family violence', in Glenda Kaufman Kantor and Jana Jasinski (eds) *Out of the Darkness: Contemporary Perspectives on Family Violence*, Thousand Oaks, Sage Publications.

Ford, David (1991) 'Prosecution as a victim power resource: a note on empowering women in violent conjugal relationships', *Law and Society Review*, 25: 313–334.

Fraser, Sarah & Norton, Jenni (1996) 'Family group conferencing in New Zealand child protection work', in Joe Hudson, A Morris, G Maxwell & Burt Galaway (eds) *Family Group Conferences: Perspectives on Policy and Practice*, Sydney, The Federation Press.

Freire, P (1989/1968) *Pedagogy of the Oppressed*, trans. M B Ramos, New York, Continuum.

Freshman, C (1997) 'Privatizing same-sex "marriage" through alternative dispute resolution: community-enhancing versus community-enabling mediation', *UCLA Law Review*, 44: 1687–1770.

Friedmann, J (1987) *Planning in the Public Domain: From Knowledge to Action*, Princeton, NJ, Princeton University Press.

Frohmann, L (1991) 'Discrediting victims' allegations of sexual assault: prosecutorial accounts of case rejections', *Social Problems*, 38 (2): 213–226.

Gale, F (1986) 'Introduction', in F Gale (ed) *Women's Role in Aboriginal Society*, Canberra, Australian Institute of Aboriginal Studies.

Gamache, D & Asmus, M (1999) 'Enhancing networking among service providers: elements of successful coordination strategies', in M F Shepard & E Pence (eds) *Coordinating Community Responses to Domestic Violence: Lessons from Duluth and Beyond*, Newbury Park, CA, Sage.

Garbarino, J (1977) 'The human ecology of child maltreatment', *Journal of Marriage and the Family*, 39: 721–735.

Garkawe, S (1999) 'Restorative justice from the perspectives of victims', paper presented at the conference Restoring the Balance Between Victims, Offenders and the Community, Brisbane, 22–23 July (also appeared in *Queensland University of Technology Law Journal*, 15).

Garland, David (1996) 'The limits of the sovereign state: strategies of crime control in contemporary society', *British Journal of Criminology*, 36 (4): 445–471.

Gatens, M. (1996) *Imaginary Bodies: Ethics, power, and corporeality*, New York, Routledge.

Gayford, J J (1983) 'Battered wives', in R J Gelles & C P Cornell (eds) *International Perspectives on Family Violence*, Lexington, MA; Toronto, Canada, Lexington Books.

Geddes, David (1993) 'A critical analysis of the family group conference', *Family Law Bulletin*, 3: 141–144.

Gelles, R (1994) 'Violence toward men: fact or fiction', paper delivered to the American Medical Association Council on Scientific Affairs, Chicago.

(1997) *Intimate Violence in Families*, Thousand Oaks, CA, Sage.

Gilman, S T (1988) 'A history of the sheltering movement for battered women in Canada', *Canadian Journal of Community Mental Health*, 7 (2): 9–21.

Goel, R (2000) 'No women at the center: the use of Canadian sentencing circles in domestic violence cases', *Wisconsin Women's Law Journal*, 15: 293–334.

Goldfarb, S F (2000) 'Violence against women and the persistence of privacy', *Ohio State Law Journal*, 61 (1): 1–87.

Gondolf, E (1990) *Psychiatric Response to Family Violence*, Massachusetts & Toronto, Lexington Books.

(1997) 'Expanding batterer program evaluation', in G K Kantor & J Jasinski (eds) *Out of Darkness: Contemporary Research Perspectives on Family Violence*, Thousand Oaks, CA, Sage.

Gondolf E & Fisher, E (1988) *Battered Women as Survivors: Alternatives to Treating Learned Helplessness*, Lexington, MA, Lexington Books.

(1997) 'Batterer programs: what we know and need to know', *Journal of Interpersonal Violence*, 12 (1): 83–99.

Gordon, L (1988) *Heroes of Their Own Lives: The Politics and History of Family Violence, Boston 1880–1960*, New York, Viking/Penguin.

Greer, Pam (1994) 'Aboriginal women and domestic violence in New South Wales', in J Stubbs (ed) *Women, Male Violence and the Law*, Sydney, Institute of Criminology.

Griffiths C & Hamilton, R (1996) 'Sanctioning and healing: restorative justice in Canadian Aboriginal communities', in Burt Galaway & Joe Hudson (eds) *Restorative Justice: International Perspectives*, Monsey, NY, Criminal Justice Press.

Gummow, A (1999) 'Women's issues with restorative justice – how can the balance be restored?', paper presented at the conference Restoring the Balance Between Victims, Offenders and the Community, Brisbane, 22–23 July, 1999.

Hamberger, L K & Potente, T (1994) 'Counseling heterosexual women arrested for domestic violence: implications for theory and practice', *Violence and Victims*, 9: 125–137.

Hampton, J (1998) 'Punishment, feminism, and political identity: a case study in the expressive meaning of the law', *Canadian Journal of Law and Jurisprudence*, 11 (1): 23–45.

Hampton, R L (1987) *Violence in the Black Family*, Lexington, MA, Lexington Books.

Hanna, C (1996) 'No right to choose: mandated victim participation in domestic violence prosecutions', *Harvard Law Review*, 109 (3): 1850–1910.

Harrell, A & Smith, B E (1996) 'Effects of restraining orders on domestic violence victims', in E S Buzawa & C G Buzawa (eds) *Do Arrests and Restraining Orders Work?*, Thousand Oaks, CA, Sage.

Harris, A (1990) 'Race and essentialism in feminist legal theory', *Stanford Law Review*, 42: 581–616.

(1997) 'Criminal justice as environmental justice', *Journal of Gender, Race and Justice*, 1: 1–45.

(2000) 'Gender, violence, race, and criminal justice', *Stanford Law Review*, 52: 777–806.

Harris, M K (1987) 'Moving into the new millennium: toward a feminist vision of justice', *The Prison Journal*, 67 (2): 27–38.

(1989) 'Alternative visions in the context of contemporary realities', in Joe Hudson, Burt Galaway, A Morris & G Maxwell (eds), *Justice: The Restorative Vision*, Mennonite Central Committee, U.S. Office of Criminal Justice, Washington DC.

(1990) 'Moving into the new millennium: toward a feminist vision of justice' in H Pepinsky & R Quinney (eds) *Criminology as Peacemaking*, Bloomington, Indiana University Press.

Harris, Nathan (2001) 'Part II – Shaming and Shame: Regulating Drink-Driving', in Eliza Ahmed, Nathan Harris, John Braithwaite & Valerie Braithwaite, *Shame Management Through Reintegration*, Cambridge, Cambridge University Press.

Harrison, A, Wilson, M, Pine, C, Chank S & Buriel, R (1990) 'Family ecologies of ethnic minority children', *Child Development*, 61: 347–362.

Hart, Barbara (1988) 'Beyond the "duty to warn": a therapist's "duty to protect" battered women and children', in K Yllö & M Bograd (eds) *Feminist Perspectives on Wife Abuse*, Newbury Park, CA; London, UK; New Delhi, India, Sage.

(1990) 'Gentle jeopardy: the further endangerment of battered women and children in custody mediation', *Mediation Quarterly*, 7: 317. (www.mincava.umn.edu/hartindx.asp)

(1993) 'The legal road to freedom', in M Hansen & M Harway (eds) *Battering and Family Therapy*, Newbury Park, Sage. (www.mincava.umn.edu/hartindx.asp)

Hassall, I (1993) *Report to the Minister of Social Welfare on the New Zealand Children and Young Persons Service's Review of Practice in Relation to Craig Manukau and His Family*, Wellington, Commissioner for Children.

(1996) 'Origin and development of family group conferences', in Joe Hudson, A Morris, G Maxwell & Burt Galaway (eds) *Family Group Conferences: Perspectives on Policy and Practice*, Sydney, The Federation Press.

Hazel, S & Rodriguez, L (1997) *Understanding and responding to Aboriginal family Violence*, Hedland, Hedland College Social Research Centre.

Healey, K H & Smith, C (1998) 'Batterer programs: what criminal justice agencies need to know', *NIJ Issues and Practices*, NCJ 168638.

Hearn, J (1998a) *The Violences of Men: How Men Talk About and How Agencies Respond to Men's Violence to Women*, Newbury Park, CA, Sage.

(1998b) 'Men will be men: the ambiguity of men's support for men who have been violent to known women', in J Popay, J Hearn & J Edwards (eds) *Men, Gender Divisions and Welfare*, London & New York, Routledge, 147–180.

Herman, Susan (1999) 'The search for parallel justice', paper presented to the Restoration for Victims of Crime Conference, AIC, Melbourne, September 1999, copy on file with the author.

Holder, R (1999) 'Pick 'n mix or replication: the politics and process of adaptation', in M F Shepard & E L Pence (eds) *Coordinating Community Responses to Domestic Violence: Lessons from Duluth and Beyond*, Newbury Park, CA, Sage.

Homel, R, Lincoln, R & Herd, B (1999) 'Risk and resilience: crime and violence prevention in Aboriginal communities', *Australian and New Zealand Journal of Criminology*, 32 (2): 111–122.

Hoop, P G (1986) *The Sacred Hoop: Recovering the Feminine in American Indian Traditions*, Boston, Beacon Press.

Hooper, Stephen (2000) 'Domestic violence and the criminal justice process', unpublished paper.

Hooper, Stephen & Busch, Ruth (1996) 'Domestic violence and restorative justice initiatives: the risks of a new panacea', *Waikato Law Review* 4 (1): 101–130.

Hudson, Barbara (1993) *Penal Policy and Social Justice*, London, Macmillan Press.

(1998) 'Restorative justice: the challenge of sexual and racial violence', *Journal of Law and Society*, 25 (2): 237–256.

Hudson, Joe & Galaway, Burt (1996) 'Introduction', in Burt Galaway & Joe Hudson (eds) *Restorative Justice: International Perspectives*, Monsey, NY, Criminal Justice Press.

Hudson, Joe, Galaway, Burt, Morris, A & Maxwell, G (1996) 'Introduction', in Joe Hudson, A Morris, G Maxwell & Burt Galaway, *Family Group Conferences: Perspectives on Policy and Practice*, Sydney, The Federation Press.

Human Rights and Equal Opportunity Commission (1991) *Racist Violence: Report of the National Inquiry into Racist Violence in Australia*, Canberra, Australian Government Publishing Service.

(1997) *Face the Facts*, Sydney, Human Rights and Equal Opportunity Commission.

(1997) *Bringing Them Home: Report of the National Inquiry into the Separation of Aboriginal and Torres Strait Islander Children from Their Families*, Sydney, Human Rights and Equal Opportunity Commission.

(1999) *Social Justice Report 1999*, Sydney, Human Rights and Equal Opportunity Commission.

Hutchinson, I & Hirschel J (1998) 'Abused women, help-seeking strategies and police utilization', *Violence Against Women*, 4 (4): 436–455.

Immarigeon, R (1999) 'Implementing the balanced and restorative justice model: a critical appraisal', *Community Corrections Report*, 6 (2): 35–47.

Indermaur, D, Atkinson, L & Blagg, H (1997) *Working With Adolescents To Prevent Domestic Violence: Phase 1 the Indigenous Rural Model*, Canberra, Attorney General's Department, National Crime Prevention.

Indian Child Welfare Act of 1978, 25 U.S.C.A. sec. 1911 *et seq.*

Jackson, M (1988) *The Maori and the Criminal Justice System: A New Perspective*, Wellington, Policy Research Division, Ministry of Justice.

(1999) 'Canadian Aboriginal women and their "criminality": the cycle of violence in the context of difference', *Australian and New Zealand Journal of Criminology*, 32 (2): 197–209.

Jacobson, N S & Gottman, J M (1998) *When Men Batter Women*, New York, Simon & Schuster.

Jaffe, P G, Wolfe, D A & Wilson, S K (1990) *Children of Battered Women*, Newbury Park, CA, Sage.

Jenkins, Alan (1990) *Invitations to responsibility: the therapeutic engagement of men who are violent and abusive*, Adelaide, Dulwich Centre Publications.

Joseph, L (1997) 'Comparative analysis of black and white women', in G Kaufman Kantor & J Jasinski (eds) *Out of the Darkness: Contemporary Perspectives on Family Violence*, Thousand Oaks, CA, Sage.

Kahan, D M (1999) 'Privatizing criminal law: strategies for private norm enforcement in the inner city', *UCLA Law Review*, 46: 1859–1872.

Kamerman, S B & Kahn, A J (1997) *Children and Their Families in Big Cities: Strategies for Service Reform*, New York, Columbia University.

Karan, J A (1999) 'Domestic violence courts: what are they and how should we manage them?', *Juvenile and Family Court Journal*, Spring: 71–84.

Karp, D & Walther, L (2000) 'Community Reparative Boards: theory and practice', in G Bazemore & M Schiff (eds) *Restorative and Community Justice: Cultivating Common Ground for Victims, Communities and Offenders*, Cincinnati, OH, Anderson Publishing.

Kartinyeri v. Commonwealth (1998) 195 CLR 337.

Katz, J (1988) *Seductions of Crime: Moral and Sensual Attractions in Doing Evil*, New York, Basic Books.

Kaufman, J & Zigler, E (1996) 'Child abuse and social policy', in E F Zigler, S L Kagan & N W Hall (eds) *Children, Families and Government: Preparing for the Twenty-first Century*, New York & Melbourne, Cambridge University Press.

Keilitz, Susan, Hannaford, Paula & Efkeman, Hillery (1998) 'Civil protection orders: the benefits and limitations for victims of domestic violence', extracted in US Department of Justice and American Bar Association *Legal Interventions in Family Violence: Research Findings and Policy Implications*, NIJ Research Report 47.

Kelly, Liz (1988) *Surviving Sexual Violence*, Minneapolis, University of Minnesota Press.

(1996) 'Tensions and possibilities: enhancing informal responses to domestic violence', in J Edleson & Z Eisikovits (eds) *Future Interventions With Battered Women and Their Families*, Thousand Oaks, CA, Sage.

(1999) 'Indigenous women's stories speak for themselves: the policing of apprehended violence orders', *Indigenous Law Bulletin*, 4 (25): 4–7.

Kelly, Loretta & Oxley, E (1999) 'A dingo in sheep's clothing? The rhetoric of youth justice conferencing and the indigenous reality', *Indigenous Law Bulletin*, 4 (18): 4.

Kendrick, K (1998) 'Producing the battered woman: shelter politics and the power of the feminist voice', in N A Naples (ed) *Community Activism and Feminist Politics: Organizing Across Race, Class, and Gender*, London, UK; New York, NY, Routledge.

Keys Young (1998) *Against the Odds: How Women Survive Domestic Violence*, Canberra, Office of the Status of Women.

Klein, E, Campbell, J, Soler, E & Ghez, M (1997) *Ending Domestic Violence: Changing Public Perceptions/Halting the Epidemic*, Newbury Park, CA, Sage.

Kline, M. (1992) 'Child welfare law, "best interests of the child" ideology, and First Nations', *Osgoode Hall Law Journal*, 30 (2): 375–425.

Lacey, B (1993) *Police Response to Wife Assault: An Examination of the Charge Laying Policies in Newfoundland and Labrador*, St. John's, NF, Women's Policy Office, Government of Newfoundland and Labrador.

Lacey, Nicola (1998) 'Unspeakable subjects, impossible rights: sexuality, integrity and criminal law', *Canadian Journal of Law and Jurisprudence*, 11 (1): 47–68.

Lackey, C & Williams, K (1995) 'Social bonding and the cessation of partner violence across generations', *Journal of Marriage and the Family*, 57: 295–305.

Lajeunesse, T (1993) *Community Holistic Circle Healing: Hollow Water First Nation*, Aboriginal Peoples Collection, Canada, Supply and Services.

Langton, M (1992) 'The Wentworth Lecture: Aborigines and policing: Aboriginal solutions from Northern Territory communities', *Australian Aboriginal Studies*, 2 (14): 17–24.

LaPrairie, Carol (1989) 'Some issues in Aboriginal justice research: the case of Aboriginal women in Canada', *Women in Criminal Justice*, 1 (1): 54–67.

(1995a) 'Community justice or just communities? Aboriginal communities in search of justice', *Canadian Journal of Criminology*, October, 521–545.

(1995b) 'Conferencing in aboriginal communities in Canada: finding middle ground in criminal justice?', *Criminal Law Forum*, 6: 576–598.

(1995c) 'Altering course: new directions in criminal justice – sentencing circles and family group conferences', *Australian and New Zealand Journal of Criminology*, 28: 78.

(1999) 'Some reflections on new criminal justice policies in Canada: restorative justice, alternative measures and conditional sentences', *Australian and New Zealand Journal of Criminology*, 32 (2): 139–152.

Lather, P (1991) *Getting Smart: Feminist Research and Pedagogy Within the Postmodern*, New York, Routledge.

Leeder, E (1994) *Treating Abuse in Families: A Feminist and Community Approach*, New York, Springer Publishing.

Levine, Marlene, Eagle, Aaron, Tuiavii, Simi & Roseveare, Christine (1998) *Creative Youth Justice Practice*, Wellington, Social Policy Agency.

Levrant, S, Cullen, F, Fulton, B & Wozniak, J (1999) 'Reconsidering restorative justice: the corruption of benevolence revisited?', *Crime and Delinquency*, 45 (1): 3–27.

Lewis, Ruth, Dobash, Russell, Dobash, Rebecca & Cavanagh, Kate (2000) 'Protection, prevention, rehabilitation or justice? Women's use of law to challenge domestic violence', *International Review of Victimology*, 7 (1/2/3): 179–207.

Liberating our Children, Liberating our Nations (1992), Report of the Aboriginal Family and Children's Services Legislative Review in British Columbia, Victoria, BC, Ministry of Social Services.

Lipsey, M (1992) 'Juvenile delinquency treatment: a meta-analytic inquiry into the variability of effects', in D Thomas, T Cook, H Cooper, D Cordray, H Hartmann, L Ledges, R Light, T Louis & F Mosteller (eds) *Meta-Analysis for Explanation: A Casebook*, New York, Sage.

Liss, M & Stahly, G (1993) 'Domestic violence and child custody', in M Hansen & M Harway (eds) *Battering and Family Therapy*, Newbury Park, CA, Sage.

Lloyd, J & Rogers, N (1992) *Without Consent: Confronting Adult Sexual Violence*, Canberra, Australian Institute of Criminology.

Lyon, T D (1999) 'Are battered women bad mothers? Rethinking the termination of abused women's parental rights for failure to protect', in H Dubowitz (ed) *Neglected Children: Research, Practice, and Policy*, Thousand Oaks, CA, Sage.

MacLeod, L (1990) 'Sharing the responsibility for justice', speech presented at the Provincial Symposium on Woman Abuse and the Criminal Justice System, Moncton, New Brunswick.

(1995) 'Policy decisions and persecutory dilemmas: the unanticipated consequences of good intentions', in L Valverde, M Macleod & K Johnson (eds) *Wife Assault and the Canadian Criminal Justice System*, Toronto, Centre for Criminology.

Madriz, Esther (1997) *Nothing Bad Happens to Good Girls: Fear of Crime in Women's Lives*, Berkeley, University of California Press.

Maguigan, H (1991) 'Battered women and self defense: myths and misconceptions in current reform proposals', *University of Pennsylvania Law Review*, 140: 379.

Mahoney, Martha (1991) 'Legal images of battered women: redefining the issue of separation', *Michigan Law Review*, 90: 1–94.

(1994) 'Victimization or oppression? women's lives, violence, and agency', in M A Fineman & R Mykitiuk (eds) *The Public Nature of Private Violence: The Discovery of Domestic Abuse*, London, UK; New York, NY, Routledge.

Malcolm, D K, Hon Mr Justice (1994) *Report of the Chief Justice's Task Force on Gender Bias*, Perth, Supreme Court of Western Australia.

Males, M (1996) *The Scapegoat Generation*, Monroe, ME, Common Courage Press.

Mansill, D (2000) 'Restorative justice', paper presented at the Just Peace? Peace Making and Peace Building for the New Millennium Conference, 24–28 April 2000, Auckland, New Zealand.

Marciniak, E M (1994) *Community Policing of Domestic Violence: Neighborhood Differences in the Effect of Arrest*, unpublished PhD dissertation, University of Maryland.

Marshall T & Merry S (1990) *Crime and Accountability: Victim Offender Mediation in Practice*, London, Home Office.

Martin, D L (1998) 'Retribution revisited: a reconsideration of feminist criminal law reform strategies', *Osgoode Hall Law Journal*, 36 (1): 151–188.

Martin, M. E. (1997) 'Policy promise: community policing and domestic violence victims satisfaction', *Policing: An International Journal of Police Strategies and Management*, 20 (3): 519–531.

(1999) 'From criminal justice to transformative justice: the challenges of social control for battered women', *Contemporary Justice Review*, 2 (4): 415–436.

Martin, Paula (1996) 'Restorative justice: a family violence perspective', *Social Policy Journal of New Zealand*, 6: 56–68.

Maxwell, Gabrielle & Morris, Allison (1993) *Families, Victims and Culture: Youth Justice in New Zealand*, Wellington, Social Policy Agency and Institute of Criminology.

(1994) 'The New Zealand models of family group conferences', in C Alder & J Wundersitz (eds) *Family Conferencing and Juvenile Justice: The Way Forward or Misplaced Optimism?*, Canberra, Australian Institute of Criminology.

(1996) 'Research on family group conferences with young offenders in New Zealand', in Joe Hudson, A Morris, G Maxwell & Burt Galaway (eds) *Family Group Conferences: Perspectives on Policy and Practice*, Sydney, The Federation Press.

(1999) *Understanding Re-offending*, Wellington, Institute of Criminology.

Maxwell, Gabrielle, Morris, Allison & Anderson, T (1999) 'Community panel adult pre-trial diversion: supplementary evaluation', Research Report, Crime Prevention Unit, Department of Prime Minister and Cabinet and Institute of Criminology, Victoria University of Wellington, New Zealand.

Maxwell, Gabrielle & Robertson, Jeremy (1996) 'Responding to child offenders', *Social Policy Journal of New Zealand*, 6: 123–133.

McCallion, P & Toseland, R (1995) 'Supportive group interventions with caregivers of frail older adults', in M Galinsky & J Schopler (eds) *Support Groups: Current Perspectives on Theory and Practice*, New York & London, Haworth Press.

McCold, P (2000) 'Toward a holistic vision of restorative juvenile justice: a reply to the maximalist model', *Contemporary Justice Review*, 3 (4): 357–372.

McElrea, F (1993) *The Youth Court in New Zealand: A New Model of Justice*, Wellington, New Zealand Legal Research Foundation.

McGarrell, Edmund E, Olivares, Kathleen, Crawford, Kay & Kroovand, Natalie (2000) 'Returning justice to the community: the Indianapolis juvenile restorative justice experiment', Indianapolis, Crime Control Policy Center, Hudson Institute.

McGillivray, A (1987) 'Battered women: definition, models and prosecutorial policy', *Canadian Journal of Family Law*, 6: 16–45.

McGillivray, A & Comaskey, B (1999) *Black eyes all of the time: intimate violence, Aboriginal women, and the justice system*, Toronto, University of Toronto Press.

McLay, R (2000) *Final Report on the Investigation into the Death of Riri-O-Te Rangi (James) Whakaruru, 1994–1999*, Wellington, Office of the Commissioner for Children.

McMaster, Ken, Maxwell, Gabrielle & Anderson, Tracy (2000) *Evaluation of Community Based Violent Prevention Programmes*, Wellington, Institute of Criminology, unpublished report.

McMullen, S & Jayerwardene, C (1995) 'Systemic discrimination, Aboriginal people, and the miscarriage of justice in Canada', in K Hazlehurst (ed) *Perceptions of Justice: Issues in Indigenous and Community Empowerment*, Aldershot, Avebury.

McNamara, K & Kinnaird, C (2000) *Have We Stopped the Violence? Recommendations for Evaluating Domestic Violence Intervention Programs*, Greenville, SC, Southern Sociological Society.

McTimoney, D (1993) *A Resource Guide on Family Violence Issues for Aboriginal Communities*, Ontario, Health Canada and Department of Indian Affairs.

Meares, T (1997) 'It's a question of connections', *Valparaiso University Law Review*, 31: 579–596.

Melton, A (1995) 'Indigenous justice systems and tribal society', *Judicature*, 70: 126–133.

Merry, Sally Engle (1995) 'Gender violence and legally engendered selves', *Identities*, 2 (1–2): 49–73.

Miccio, G K (2000) 'Notes from the underground: battered women, the state, and conceptions of accountability', *Harvard Women's Law Journal*, 23: 133–172.

Miller, J L & Krull, A C (1997) 'Domestic violence: victim resources and police intervention', in G K Kantor & J L Jasinski (eds) *Out of the Darkness: Contemporary Perspectives on Family Violence*, Thousand Oaks, CA, Sage.

Mills, Linda G (1999) 'Killing her softly: intimate abuse and the violence of state intervention', *Harvard Law Review* 113 (2): 550–613.

Ministry of Justice (1995) *Report of the Review of Restraining Orders*, Perth, Ministry of Justice.

(1995) *Restorative Justice – A Discussion Paper*, Wellington, Ministry of Justice.

(1998) *Restorative Justice – The Public Submissions*, Wellington, Ministry of Justice.

Ministry of Social Policy (2001) *The Social Report 2001*, Wellington, Ministry of Social Policy.

Minow, M. (1990) 'Words and the door to the land of change: law, language, and family violence', *Vanderbilt Law Review*, 43: 1665–1699.

(1998) *Between Vengeance and Forgiveness: Facing History After Genocide and Mass Violence*, Boston, MA, Beacon Press.

(2000) 'Between intimates and between nations: can law stop the violence?', *Case Western Law Review*, 50: 851–868.

Moore, C (1991) *The Mediation Process: Practical Strategies for Resolving Conflict*, San Francisco, Jossey-Bass.

Moore, David (1995) *A New Approach to Juvenile Justice: An Evaluation of Family Conferencing in Wagga Wagga*, Wagga Wagga, New South Wales, Centre for Rural Social Research, Charles Sturt University.

Moore, D & McDonald, J (1995) 'Achieving the "Good Community": a local police initiative and its wider ramifications', in K Hazlehurst (ed) *Perceptions of Justice: Issues in Indigenous and Community Empowerment*, Avebury, Aldershot.

(2000) *Transforming Conflict*, Sydney, Transformative Justice Australia.

Morley, R & Mullender, A (1994) *Preventing Domestic Violence to Women*, Home Office Police Research Group Paper 48, London, HMSO.

Morris, Allison (1998) *The Women's Safety Survey*, Wellington, Ministry of Justice.

Morris, Allison & Gelsthorpe, Loraine (2000) 'Re-visioning men's violence against their female partners', *Howard Journal of Criminal Justice*, 412–428.

Morris, Allison & Maxwell, Gabrielle (2000) 'The practice of family group conferences in New Zealand: assessing the place, potential and pitfalls of restorative justice', in A Crawford & J Goodey (eds) *Integrating a Victim Perspective Within Criminal Justice: International Debates*, Aldershot, Ashgate.

Morris, Allison & Young, Warren (2000) 'Reforming criminal justice: the potential of restorative justice', in Heather Strang & John Braithwaite (eds) *Restorative Justice: From Philosophy to Practice*, Aldershot, Dartmouth.

Morris, R (1994) 'Not enough!', *Mediation Quarterly*, 12 (3): 284–291.

(1995) *Penal Abolition: the Practical Choice*, Toronto, Canada, Canadian Scholars' Press Inc.

Mosey, A (1994) *Remote Community Aboriginal Night Patrols*, Alice Springs, DASA.

Mouzos, J (1999) 'Stirrings: new statistics highlight high homicide rate for indigenous women', *Indigenous Law Bulletin*, 4 (25): 16.

Mow, K E (1992) *Tjunparni: family violence in indigenous Australia: a report and literature review for the Aboriginal and Torres Strait Islander Commission*, Canberra, Aboriginal and Torres Strait Islander Commission.

Myers, K (1996) *An Overview of Corrections Research and Development Projects on Family Violence*, Canada, Solicitor General of Canada. (www.scg.gc.ca)

Myers, S & Filner, B (1993) *Mediation Across Cultures: A Handbook About Conflict and Culture*, San Diego, Intercultural Development Inc.

NACRO (1997) *A New Three Rs for Young Offenders*, London, NACRO.

Naffine, N & Owens, R J (eds) (1997) *Sexing the Subject of Law*, Sydney, LBC Information Services, Sweet & Maxwell.

Nahanee, T (1992) 'Dancing with a gorilla: Aboriginal women, justice and the charter', paper prepared for the Royal Commission on Aboriginal Peoples, Canada, on file with the author.

National Committee on Violence Against Women (1991) 'Position Paper on Mediation'.

National Research Council (1998) *Violence in Families: Assessing Prevention and Treatment Programs*, Washington DC, National Academy Press.

National Working Party on Mediation (1996) *Guidelines for Family Mediation: Developing Services in Aotearoa-New Zealand*, Wellington, Butterworths.

Nedelsky, J (1989) 'Reconceiving autonomy', *Yale Journal of Law and Feminism*, 1: 7-36.

(1995) 'Meditations on embodied autonomy', *Graven Images*, 2: 159–170.

New South Wales Department for Women (1996) *Heroines of fortitude: the experiences of women in court as victims of sexual assault*, Woolloomooloo, NSW, NSW Department for Women.

New Zealand Police Commissioner (1992) *Policy Circular, 1992/07*, Wellington, New Zealand Police.

Newburn, T & Stanko, E A (1994) 'Men, masculinity and crime', in T Newburn & E A Stanko (eds), *Just Boys Doing Business? Men, Masculinities and Crime*, London, UK; New York, NY, Routledge.

Newmark, L, Harrell, A & Salem, P (1994) 'Domestic violence and empowerment in custody and visitation Cases: an empirical study on the impact of domestic abuse', paper published by the Association of Family and Conciliation Courts, Thousand Oaks, CA, Sage.

Nichols, A (1991) 'Whose rights are wronged? The N.W.T. faces a change in the way its legal system treats women', *Northerner: North America's First Circumpolar Women's Magazine*, 1 (1): 7–9.

Nicholson v. Nat Williams, 00-CV-2229 (E.D. N.Y. 2000).

Nightingale, Margo (1994) *Just-us and Aboriginal Women*, report prepared for the Aboriginal Justice Directorate, Department of Justice, Canada, copy on file with the author.

O'Malley P (1996) 'Indigenous governance', *Economy and Society*, 25 (1): 310–326.

(1997) 'The politics of crime prevention', in P O'Malley & A Sutton (eds) *Crime Prevention in Australia: Issues in Policy and Research*, Leichhardt, NSW, The Federation Press.

O'Reilly, Barbara & Bush, Diana (1999) 'Making a difference: advocacy and care and protection coordinators', *Social Work Now*, 12: 29–35.

O'Shane, P (1995) 'The psychological impact of white settlement on Aboriginal people', *Aboriginal and Islander Health Worker Journal*, 19 (3): 24.

Office of Aboriginal and Torres Strait Islander Affairs (1998) *Community Justice Initiatives*, Brisbane, Office of Aboriginal and Torres Strait Islander Affairs.

Office of Women's Policy (1996) *Aboriginal Family Violence*, Occasional Paper No. 12, Darwin, Northern Territory Government.

Okun, L (1986) *Woman Abuse: Facts Replacing Myths*, Albany, NY, State University of New York.

Osland v. The Queen (1998) 159 *Australian Law Reports* 170, Justice Kirby, at pp. 209–218.

Pagelow, M (1981) *Woman Battering: Victims and Their Experiences*, Newbury Park, CA, Sage.

Palk, G, Pollard G & Johnson L (1998) 'Community conferencing in Queensland', paper presented to the Conference of the Australian and New Zealand Society of Criminology, 8–10 July 1998.

Parker, Christine (1999) *Just Lawyers*, Oxford, Oxford University Press.

Pateman, C (1989) *The Disorder of Women: Democracy, Feminism and Political Theory*, Cambridge, Polity Press.

Paterson, Karen & Harvey, Michael (1991) *An Evaluation of the Organisation and Operation of Care and Protection Family Group Conferences*, Wellington, Department of Social Welfare.

Pavlich, G (1996) 'The power of community mediation: government and formation of self-identity', *Law and Society Review*, 30 (4): 707–733.

(1998) 'Justice in fragmentation: The political logic of mediation in "new times"', *Critical Criminologist Newsletter* 8 (2): 20–23.

Pence, E (1996) 'Safety for battered women in a textually mediated legal system', unpublished PhD dissertation, University of Toronto.

(1999) 'Some thoughts on philosophy', in M F Shepard & E L Pence (eds) *Coordinating Community Responses to Domestic Violence: Lessons from Duluth and Beyond*, Thousand Oaks, CA, Sage.

Pence, E & McDonnell, C (1999) 'Developing policies and protocols', in M F Shepard & E L Pence (eds) *Coordinating Community Responses to Domestic Violence: Lessons from Duluth and Beyond*, Thousand Oaks, CA, Sage.

Pence, E & Paymar, M (1986) *Power and Control: Tactics of Men who Batter*, Duluth, Minn., Domestic Abuse Intervention Project.

(1993) *Education Groups for Men who Batter: The Duluth Model*, New York, Springer.

Pence, E & Shepard, M (1988) 'Integrating feminist theory and practice: the challenge of the battered women's movement', in Yllö & M Bograd (eds) *Feminist Perspectives on Wife Abuse*, Newbury Park, CA.

Pennell, J (1990) 'Democratic hierarchy in feminist organizations', *Dissertation Abstracts International*, 50/12-A, 4118 (University Microfilms No. AAD90-15034).

Pennell, J & Burford, G (1994) 'Widening the circle: the family group decision making project', *Journal of Child and Youth Care*, 9 (1): 1–12.

(1995) 'Family group decision making: new roles for "old" partners in resolving family violence: implementation report', (Vol. I–II), St. John's, NF, Memorial University of Newfoundland.

(1997) 'Family group decision making: after the conference – progress in resolving violence and promoting well-being', St. John's, NF, Memorial University of Newfoundland.

(2000a) 'Family group decision making: protecting children and women', *Child Welfare*, 79, 2: 131–158.

(2000b) 'Family group decision making and family violence,' in G Burford & J Hudson (eds) *Family Group Conferences: New Directions in Community-Centered Child and Family Practice*, Hawthorne, NY, Aldine de Gruyter.

Pennell, J & Weil, M (2000) 'Initiating conferencing: community practice issues', in G Burford & J Hudson (eds) *Family Group Conferences: New Directions in Community-Centered Child and Family Practice*, Hawthorne, NY, Aldine de Gruyter.

Perilla, J L (1999) 'Domestic violence as a human rights issue: the case of immigrant Latinos', *Hispanic Journal of Behavioral Science*, 21: 107–33.

Peterson-Lewis, S, Turner, C W & Adams, A M (1998) 'Attributional processes in repeatedly abused women', in G W Russell (ed) *Violence in Intimate Relationships*, New York, PMA.

Phelan, S (1993) '(Be)Coming out: lesbian identity and politics', *Signs: Journal of Women in Culture and Society*, 18 (4): 765–790.

Phillips, J (1992) 'Comment: re-victimized battered women: termination of parental rights for failure to protect children from child abuse', *The Wayne Law Review*, 38: 1549–1578.

Polk, K (2001) 'The crisis of abandoned youth', in G Bazemore & M Schiff (eds) *Restorative and Community Justice: Cultivating Common Ground for Victims, Communities and Offenders*, Cincinnati, OH, Anderson Publishing.

Porter, T W (1999) 'The spirit and the law', *Fordham Urban Law Journal*, 26: 1155–1165.

Pranis, K (1996) 'Communities and the justice System – turning the relationship upside down', Washington DC, U.S. Department of Justice.

(1997) 'From vision to action', *Presbyterian Church Journal of Just Thoughts, on Church and Society*, 87: 32–42.

(2000) 'Building community support for restorative justice principles and strategies'. (http://www.realjustice.org/Pages/building.html)

(2001) 'Restorative justice, social justice, and the empowerment of marginalized populations', in G Bazemore & M Schiff (eds) *Restorative and Community Justice: Cultivating Common Ground for Victims, Communities and Offenders*, Cincinnati, OH, Anderson Publishing.

Pranis, K & Bazemore, G (2000) *Engaging the Community in the Response to Youth Crime: A Restorative Justice Approach*, monograph, Washington DC, U.S. Department of Justice, Office of Juvenile Delinquency Prevention.

Presser, L & Lowenkamp, C (1999) 'Restorative justice and offender screening', *Journal of Criminal Justice*, 27 (4): 333–343.

Presser, L & Gaarder, E (2000) 'Can restorative justice reduce battering? Some preliminary considerations', *Social Justice*, Spring 2000, 27 (1): 175–195.

Pressman, B (1989) 'Treatment of wife abuse: the case for feminist therapy', in B Pressman, G Cameron & M Rothery (eds) *Intervening with Assaulted Women: Current Theory, Research and Practice*, Hillsdale, NJ, Lawrence Erlbaum.

Ptacek, J (1999) *Battered Women in the Courtroom: The Power of Judicial Responses*, Boston, Northeastern University Press.

Rangihau, J (1986) *Pau-te-Ata-tu (Daybreak): Report of the Ministerial Advisory Committee on a Maori Perspective for the Department of Social Welfare*, Wellington, Department of Social Welfare, Government Printing Office.

Raphael, J (1995) 'Domestic violence and welfare receipt: the unexplored barrier to employment', *Georgetown Journal on Fighting Poverty*, 3: 29–34.

——— (1996) 'Domestic violence and welfare receipt: toward a new feminist theory of welfare dependency', *Harvard Women's Law Journal*, 19: 201–227.

Razack, Sherene (1994) 'What is to be gained by looking white people in the eye? Culture, race and gender in cases of sexual violence', *Signs: Journal of Women in Culture and Society*, 19 (4): 894–923.

——— (1998) *Looking White People in the Eye: Gender, Race, and Culture in Courtrooms and Classrooms*, Toronto, University of Toronto Press.

Regional Domestic Violence Coordinating Committee (1997) *Kimberley Domestic Violence Resource Directory*, Broome, Regional Domestic Violence Coordinating Committee.

Reid, G, Sugurdson, E, Christianson-Wood, J & Wright, A (1996) *Basic Issues Concerning the Assessment of Risk in Child Welfare Work*, Winnipeg, University of Manitoba.

Reistenberg, N (1996) *Restorative Measures in the Schools*, Roseville, MN, Minnesota Department of Children, Families and Learning.

Renzetti, C (1998) 'Connecting the dots: women, public policy, and social control', in S L Miller (ed) *Crime Control and Women*, Thousand Oaks, CA, Sage.

Retzinger, S M & Scheff, T J (1996) 'Strategy for community conferences: emotions and social bonds', in Burt Galaway & Joe Hudson (eds) *Restorative Justice: International Perspectives*, Monsey, NY, Criminal Justice Press.

Rhoades, H, Graycar, R & Harrison, M (1999*) Family Law Reform Act: Can Changing Legislation Change Legal Culture, Legal Practice and Community Expectations? Interim Report*, The University of Sydney and the Family Court of Australia, April 1999, i–xi; 1–67.
(http://www.law.usyd.edu.au/Research_Family_Court.html)

Richie, Beth (1996) *Compelled to Crime: The Gender Entrapment of Battered Black Women*, New York, Routledge.

Ristock, J L & Pennell, J (1996) *Community Research as Empowerment: Feminist Links, Postmodern Interruptions*, Toronto, ON, Oxford University Press.

Ritzer, G (1992) *Sociological Theory* (3rd ed), New York, McGraw-Hill.

Rivera, J (1994) 'Domestic violence against Latinas by Latino males: an analysis of race, national origin, and gender differentials', *B.C. Third World Law Journal*, 14: 231–257.

Roberts, D (1995) 'The only good woman: unconstitutional conditions and welfare', *Denver University Law Review*, 72: 931–948.

——— (1997) *Killing the Black Body: Race, Reproduction, and the Meaning of Liberty*, New York, Pantheon Books.

——— (1999) 'Is there justice in children's rights?: the critique of federal family preservation policy', *University of Pennsylvania Journal of Constitutional Law*, 2: 112–140.

Robertson, B (chairperson) (2000) Aboriginal and Torres Strait Islander Women's Task Force on Violence report (2nd printing). Brisbane, Queensland, Department of Aboriginal and Torres Strait Islander Policy and Development.

Robertson, Jeremy (1996) 'Research on family group conferences in child welfare in New Zealand', in Joe Hudson, A Morris, G Maxwell & Burt Galaway (eds) Family Group Conferences: Perspectives on Policy and Practice, Sydney, The Federation Press.

Robertson, N (2000) 'Reforming institutional responses to violence against women', unpublished PhD dissertation, University of Waikato, Hamilton, New Zealand.

Robertson, N & Busch, R (1998) 'The dynamics of spousal violence: paradigms and priorities', in M Pipe & F Seymour (eds) Psychology and Family Law: A New Zealand Perspective, Dunedin, University of Otago Press.

Roche, D (1999) 'Mandatory sentencing', Trends and Issues in Crime and Criminal Justice, 138: 1–6, Canberra, Australian Institute of Criminology.

Ross, Rupert (1996) Returning to the Teachings: Exploring Aboriginal Justice, London, Penguin Books.

Ross, S M (1996) 'Risk of physical abuse to children of spouse-abusing parents', Child Abuse and Neglect, 20: 589–598.

Rowe, J (1985) 'Comment: the limits of the Neighbourhood Justice Center: why domestic violence cases should not be mediated', Emory Law Journal, 34: 855–910.

Royal Commission into Aboriginal Deaths in Custody (1991) National Report, Canberra, Australian Government Publishing Service.

Ruttenberg, M (1994) 'A feminist critique of mandatory arrest: an analysis of race and gender in domestic violence policy', Journal of Gender and the Law, 2: 171–199.

Salzman, E (1994) 'The Quincy District Court domestic violence prevention program: a model legal framework for domestic violence intervention', Boston University Law Review, 74: 329–364.

Sampson, R, Roedenbush, S & Earls, F (1997) 'Neighborhoods and violent crime: a multilevel study of collective efficacy', Science Magazine, 277.

Sarre, R (1999) 'An overview of the theory of diversion: notes for correctional policy makers', paper presented at the Best Practice Interventions in Corrections for Indigenous People Conference, Adelaide, 13–15 October 1999.

Saunders, Daniel (1995) 'Prediction of wife assault', in Jacquelyn C Campbell (ed) Assessing Dangerousness: Violence by Sexual Offenders, Batterers and Child Abusers, Thousand Oaks, CA, Sage.

Schechter, S (1982) Women and Male Violence: The Visions and Struggles of the Battered Women's Movement, Boston, MA, South End Press.

Scheingold, S, Olson, T & Pershing, J (1994) 'Sexual violence, victim advocacy and Republican criminology: Washington State's Community Protection Act', Law and Society Review, 28 (4): 729–763.

Schneider, Elizabeth (1991) 'The violence of privacy', Connecticut Law Review, 23: 973–998.

(1992) 'Particularity and generality: challenges of feminist theory and practice in work on woman-abuse', *New York University Law Review*, 67: 520–568.

Sengupta, S (2000) 'Tough justice: taking a child when one parent is battered', *New York Times*, July 8: A1, B2.

Shapland, J (2000) 'Victims and criminal justice: creating responsible criminal justice agencies', in Adam Crawford & Jo Goodey (eds) *Integrating a Victim Perspective Within Criminal Justice: International Debates*, Aldershot, Ashgate.

Sherman, L, Strang, Heather, Barnes, G, Braithwaite, John & Inkpen, N (1998) *Experiments in Restorative Policing: A Progress Report to the National Police Research Unit on the Canberra Reintegrative Shaming Experiment (RISE)*, Australian Federal Police, Australian National University. (www.aic.gov.au/rjustice/rise/index.html)

Siegel, R B (1996) ' "The rule of love": wife-beating as prerogative and privacy', *Yale Law Journal*, 105: 2117–2207.

Smallwoood, M (1996) 'Violence is not our way', in R Thorpe & J Irwin (eds) *Women and Violence: Working for Change*, Sydney, Hale & Iremonger.

Smart, C (1989) *Feminism and the power of law*, New York, Routledge.

Snider, Laureen (1994) 'Feminism, punishment and the potential of empowerment', *Canadian Journal of Law and Society*, 9 (1): 75–104.

(1998) 'Towards safer societies: punishment, masculinities and violence against women', *British Journal of Criminology*, 38 (1): 1–39.

Solicitor General of Canada (1994) *Understanding the Role of Healing in Aboriginal Communities*, Toronto, Solicitor General of Canada.

Sorenson, S A (1996) 'Violence against women: Examining ethnic differences and commonalities', *Evaluation Research* 20: 123–145.

South Australian Attorney-General's Department (1999) *Crime and Justice in South Australia, 1998, Juvenile Justice*. Adelaide, Office of Crime Statistics.

(2000) *Crime and Justice in South Australia, 1999, Juvenile Justice*. Adelaide, Office of Crime Statistics.

Sparks, A (1997) 'Feminists negotiate the executive branch: the policing of male violence', in C Daniels with R Brooks, P DeSoto, E Felter, S Marshall, L Naranch & A Sparks (eds) *Feminists Negotiate the State: The Politics of Domestic Violence*, Lanham, University Press of America.

Spivak, G C (1996) *The Spivak reader* Edited by D Landry & G Maclean, London, RKP.

Spohn, C & Horney, J (1992) *Rape Law Reform*, New York, Plenum.

Stanko, Elizabeth (1999) 'Identities and criminal violence: observations on law's recognition of vulnerable victims in England and Wales', in A Sarat & P Ewick (eds) *Studies in Law, Politics, and Society*, Connecticut, JAI Press.

Stark, E (1996) 'Mandatory arrest of batterers: a reply to its critics', in E S Buzawa & C G Buzawa (eds) *Do Arrests and Restraining Orders Work?*, Thousand Oaks, CA, Sage.

Stets, J E (1988) *Domestic Violence and Control*, New York, Springer.

Strang, Heather (1992) *Homicides in Australia 1990–91*, Canberra, Australian Institute of Criminology.

(1999) 'Restoring victims: an international view', paper presented to the Restoration for Victims of Crime Conference, AIC, Melbourne, Sept 1999.

(forthcoming) *Repair or Revenge: Victims and Restorative Justice*, Oxford, Oxford University Press.

Straus, M A & Gelles, R J (1990) *Physical Violence in American Families: Risk Factors and Adaptions to Violence in 8,145 families*, New Brunswick, NJ, Transaction.

Stuart, B (1996) 'Circle sentencing: turning swords into ploughshares', in Burt Galaway & Joe Hudson (eds) *Restorative Justice: International Perspectives*, Monsey, NY, Criminal Justice Press.

(2001) 'Guiding principles: for designing peacemaking circles', in G Bazemore & M Schiff (eds) *Restorative and Community Justice: Cultivating Common Ground for Victims, Communities and Offenders*, Cincinnati, OH, Anderson Publishing.

Stubbs J (1995) 'Communitarian conferencing and violence against women: a cautionary note', in M Valverde, L MacLeod & K Johnson (eds) *Wife assault and the Canadian criminal justice system: issues and policies*, Toronto, Centre of Criminology, University of Toronto.

(1997) 'Shame, defiance and violence against women: a critical analysis of "communitarian" conferencing', in S Cook & J Bessant (eds) *Women's Encounters with Violence: Australian Experiences*, Thousand Oaks, CA, Sage.

Stubbs, J & Powell, D (1989) *Domestic Violence: Impact of Legal Reform in NSW*, NSW Bureau of Crime Statistics and Research, Sydney.

Stubbs, J & Tolmie, J (1995) 'Race, gender and the Battered Woman Syndrome: an Australian case study', *Canadian Journal of Women and Law*, 8 (1): 122–158.

Sullivan, C M & Bybee, D I (1999) 'Reducing violence using community-based advocacy for women with abusive partners', *Journal of Consulting and Clinical Psychology*, 67: 43–53.

Sullivan, Dennis & Tifft, Larry (2001) *Restorative Justice: Healing the Foundations of Our Everyday Lives*, New York, Willow Tree Press.

Taub, N & Schneider, E M (1990) 'Women's subordination and the role of law', in D Kairys (ed) *The Politics of Law: A Progressive Critique*, New York, Pantheon Books.

Tauri, J (1999) 'Explaining recent innovations in New Zealand's criminal justice system: empowering Maori or biculturalising the state', *Australian and New Zealand Journal of Criminology*, 32 (2): 153–167.

Te Piringa (2000) unpublished interviews conducted by the author with the Maori staff, University of Waikato, School of Law.

Tello, J (1998) 'El hombre noble buscando balance: the noble man searching for balance', in R Carrillo & J Tello (eds) *Family Violence and Men of Color: Healing the Wounded Male Spirit*, New York, Springer.

Thorne, B with Yalom, M (1982) *Rethinking the Family: Some Feminist Questions*, New York, Longman.

Thorsborne, M (1999) 'Building community support for restorative justice: the local context', paper presented at the conference Restoring the Balance Between Victims, Offenders and the Community, Brisbane, 22–23 July.

Tifft, L (1993) *Battering of Women: The Failure of Intervention and the Case for Prevention*, Boulder & Oxford, Westview Press.

Toews-Shenk, B & Zehr, H (2001) 'Restorative justice and substance abuse: the path ahead', *Youth and Society*, 33 (2): 314–328.

Togni, S (1997) *Liquor, Law and Community: An Evaluation of Local Responses to Alcohol Abuse and Related Offending in a Remote Kimberley Town*, unpublished Masters dissertation, University of Melbourne Department of Criminology,

Tolman, R (1996) 'Expanding sanctions for batterers: what can we do besides jailing and counseling them?', in J Edleson & Z Eisikovits (eds) *Future Interventions with Battered Women and Their Families*, Thousand Oaks, CA, Sage.

Trimboli, Lily & Bonney, Roseanne (1997) *An Evaluation of the NSW Apprehended Violence Order Scheme*, NSW Bureau of Crime Statistics and Research, Sydney.

Umbreit, M (1996) 'Responding to important questions related to restorative justice', St. Paul, MN, Centre for Restorative Justice and Mediation, University of Minnesota.

(1999) 'Avoiding the marginalization and Mcdonaldization of victim offender mediation: a case study in moving toward the mainstream', in G Bazemore & L Walgrave (eds) *Restoring Juvenile Justice: Repairing the Harm of Youth Crime*, Monsey, NY, Criminal Justice Press.

Umbreit, M & Zehr, H (1996) 'Restorative family group conferences: differing models and guidelines for practice', *Federal Probation*, 60: 24–29.

Ursel, J (1992) *Private Lives, Public Policy: 100 Years of State Intervention into the Family*, Toronto, Women's Press.

Van Ness, D (1993) 'New wine in old wineskins', *Criminal Law*, 4 (2): 251–276.

Van Ness, D & Strong, K (1997) *Restorative Justice Practice*, monograph, Washington DC, Justice Fellowship.

von Hirsch, A (1985) *Past or future crimes: deservedness and dangerousness in the sentencing of criminals*, New Brunswick, NJ, Rutgers University Press.

(2001) 'Proportionate sentences for juveniles: how different than for adults?', *Punishment and Society*, 3 (2): 221–236.

Waits, K (1998) 'Battered women and their children: lessons from one woman's story', *Houston Law Review*, 35: 29–108.

Walgrave, L (2000a) 'Extending the victim perspective towards a systemic restorative justice alternative', in Adam Crawford & Jo Goodey (eds) *Integrating a Victim Perspective Within Criminal Justice: International Debates*, Aldershot, Ashgate.

(2000b) 'Restorative justice and the republican theory of criminal justice: an exercise in normative theorizing on restorative justice', in John Braithwaite & Heather Strang (eds) *Restorative Justice: from Philosophy to Practice*, London, Ashgate.

Walker, L (1989) *Terrifying Love: Why Battered Women Kill and How Society Responds*, New York, Harper Collins.

(1999) 'Psychology and domestic violence around the world', *American Psychologist*, 54 (1): 21–29.

(2000) 'Custody evaluations and domestic violence', paper delivered to the 5th International Conference on Family Violence, San Diego, CA, 22 September 2000.

Wallace, B & Doig, M (1999) 'Sexual offending and restorative justice: the challenge for family conferencing practice in South Australia', paper presented at the Victimology Conference 1999, Melbourne, Adelaide, Family Conference Team, Courts Administration Authority.

Warhaft, E, Palys T & Boyce W (1999) '"This is how we did it": one Canadian First Nation community's efforts to achieve Aboriginal justice', *Australian and New Zealand Journal of Criminology*, 32 (2): 168–181.

Welfare, Anne & Miller, Robyn (1999) 'A confrontational interview for victims of intrafamilial sexual abuse: an alternative to an apology that reverses power differentials in a therapeutic way', paper presented to the Restoration for Victims of Crime Conference, AIC, Melbourne, Sept 1999.

West, T C (1999) *Wounds of the Spirit: Black Women, Violence, and Resistance Ethics*, New York, NYU Press.

Western Australian Government Task Force (1986) *Break the Cycle: Report of the Task Force on Domestic Violence*, Perth, Office of Women's Policy.

Wharf, B (1995) 'Organizing and delivering child welfare services: the contributions of research', in Joe Hudson & Burt Galaway (eds) *Child Welfare in Canada: Research and Policy Implications*, Toronto, Thompson.

Wiehe, V (1998) *Understanding Family Violence: Treating and Preventing Partner, Child, Sibling and Elder Abuse*, Thousand Oaks, CA; London, UK; New Delhi, India, Sage.

Wilkinson, R (1997) 'Back to basics: modern restorative justice principles have their roots in ancient cultures', *Corrections Today* (December), 6.

Williams, F (1989) *Social Policy: A Critical Introduction: Issues of Race, Gender, and Class*, Cambridge, Polity Press.

Williams, G (1999) *Human Rights under the Australian Constitution*, Melbourne, Oxford University Press.

Williams, O J (1998) 'Healing and confronting the African American male who batters', in R Carrillo & J Tello (eds) *Family Violence and Men of Color: Healing the Wounded Male Spirit*, New York, Springer.

Wilson, K (1997) *When Violence Begins at Home: A Comprehensive Guide to Understanding and Ending Domestic Abuse*, Alameda, CA, Hunter House Inc.

Wilson, M & Daly, M (1994) 'Spousal homicide', *Juristat Service Bulletin*, 14 (8), Statistics Canada Cat. No. 85-002.

Winters, K C, Latimere, W L & Stinchfield, R D (1999) 'Adolescent treatment in public schools', in R E Tarter & R T Ammonman (eds) *Source Book on Substance Abuse*, Boston, MA, Allyn & Bacon.

Wittner, J (1998) 'Reconceptualizing agency in domestic violence courts', in N A Naples (ed) *Community Activism and Feminist Politics: Organizing Across Race, Class, and Gender*, London, UK; New York, NY, Routledge.

Wolf, D (1995) 'Strategies to address violence in the lives of high-risk youth', in E Peled, P Jaffe & J Edleson (eds) *Ending the Cycle of Violence: Community Responses to Children of Battered Women*, Thousand Oaks, CA, London & New Delhi, Sage.

Wundersitz, J (1996) *The South Australian Juvenile Justice System: a review of its operation*, Adelaide, Office of Crime Statistics, South Australian Attorney-General's Department.

Wundersitz, J & Hetzel, S (1996) 'Family conferencing for young offenders: the South Australian experience', in Joe Hudson, A Morris, G Maxwell & Burt Galaway (eds) *Family Group Conferences: Perspectives on Policy and Practice*, Sydney, The Federation Press.

Yamamoto, E K (1999) *Interracial Justice: Conflict and Reconciliation in Post-Civil Rights America*, New York, NYU Press.

Yantzi, M (1998) *Sexual offending and restoration*, Waterloo, Ontario, Herald Press.

Yazzie, R & Zion, J W (1996) 'Navajo restorative justice: the law of equality and justice', in Burt Galaway & Joe Hudson (eds) *Restorative Justice: International Perspectives*, Monsey, NY, Criminal Justice Press.

Yllö, K & Bograd, M (1988) *Feminist Perspectives on Wife Abuse*, Newbury Park, CA.

Young, Margrette, Byles, Julie & Dobson, Annette (2000) 'The effectiveness of legal protection in the prevention of domestic violence in the lives of young Australian women', *Trends and Issues in Crime and Criminal Justice*, 148: 1–6, Canberra, Australian Institute of Criminology.

Zauberman, R (2000) 'Victims as consumers of the criminal justice system?', in Adam Crawford & Jo Goodey (eds) *Integrating a Victim Perspective Within Criminal Justice: International Debates*, Aldershot, Ashgate.

Zehr, Howard (1990) *Changing Lenses: A New Focus for Crime and Justice*, Scottsdale, PA, Herald Press.

Zehr, H & Mika, H (1998) 'Fundamental concepts of restorative justice', *Contemporary Justice Review*, 1 (1): 47–55.

Zellerer, E (1996) *Violence Against Inuit Women in the Canadian Eastern Arctic*, unpublished PhD dissertation, Simon Fraser University, Burnaby, British Columbia.

Zellerer, E & Cunneen, C (2000) 'Restorative justice, indigenous justice and human rights', in G Bazemore & M Schiff (eds) *Restorative and Community Justice: Cultivating Common Ground for Victims, Communities and Offenders*, Cincinnati, OH, Anderson Publishing.

Zion, J W & Zion, E B (1993) 'Hozho' Sokee' – stay together nicely: domestic violence under Navajo common law', *Arizona State Law Journal*, 25: 407–426.

Zorza, J (1991) 'Woman battering: a major cause of homelessness', *National Clearinghouse Review, Special Issue*, 25 (4): 421–430.

(1994) 'Women battering: high costs and the state of the law', *National Clearinghouse Review, Special Issue*, 28 (4): 383–395.

Zorza, J & Woods, L (1994) *Mandatory Arrest: Problems and Possibilities*, New York, NY, National Center on Women and Family Law.

Index

Lightning Source UK Ltd.
Milton Keynes UK
UKOW051216010312

188152UK00003B/14/P